C000108972

Edexcel GCSE
Poetry Anthology
Teacher Guide

Written by:

Lis Green, Kath Howard and Pat West

Consultants:

Peter Thomas and Pam Taylor

naldic EAL guidance

A PEARSON COMPANY

Published by Pearson Education Limited, a company incorporated in England and Wales, having its registered office at Edinburgh Gate, Harlow, Essex, CM20 2JE. Registered company number: 872828

Edexcel is a registered trademark of Edexcel Limited

Text © Pearson Education Limited 2010
EAL guidance for teaching poetry © NALDIC 2010

The rights of Lis Green, Kath Howard and Pat West to be identified as the authors of this work have been asserted by them in accordance with the Copyright, Designs and Patent Act 1988

First published 2010

12 11 10
10 9 8 7 6 5 4 3 2 1

British Library Cataloguing in Publication Data
A catalogue record for this book is available from the British Library

ISBN 978 1 846906 43 5

Copyright notice
All rights reserved. No part of this publication may be reproduced in any form or by any means (including photocopying or storing it in any medium by electronic means and whether or not transiently or incidentally to some other use of this publication) without the written permission of the copyright owner, except in accordance with the provisions of the Copyright, Designs and Patents Act 1988 or under the terms of a licence issued by the Copyright Licensing Agency, Saffron House, 6–10 Kirby Street, London EC1N 8TS (www.cla.co.uk). Applications for the copyright owner's written permission should be addressed to the publisher.

Typeset by Juice Creative Limited, Hertfordshire
Printed and bound in Great Britain by Ashford Colour Press Ltd, Gosport, Hants

Acknowledgements
We would like to thank Peter Thomas, Pam Taylor and NALDIC, the professional association for English as an Additional Language for their invaluable help in the development of this material.

Cover images: Alamy Images: Colin Crisford; **Getty Images:** Jason Hosking; **iStockphoto:** Simon Alvinge, Huseyin Tuncer.

All thumbnail images within this printed book appear within the accompanying Edexcel Poetry Anthology ActiveTeach (ISBN 978 1 846906 42 8) and are acknowledged there.

Every effort has been made to contact copyright holders of material reproduced in this book. Any omissions will be rectified in subsequent printings if notice is given to the publishers.

Websites
The websites used in this book were correct and up to date at the time of publication. It is essential for tutors to preview each website before using it in class so as to ensure that the URL is still accurate, relevant and appropriate. We suggest that tutors bookmark useful websites and consider enabling students to access them through the school/ college intranet.

Disclaimer
This material has been published on behalf of Edexcel and offers high-quality support for the delivery of Edexcel qualifications.
This does not mean that the material is essential to achieve any Edexcel qualification, nor does it mean that it is the only suitable material available to support any Edexcel qualification. Edexcel material will not be used verbatim in setting any Edexcel examination or assessment. Any resource lists produced by Edexcel shall include this and other appropriate resources.

Copies of official specifications for all Edexcel qualifications may be found on the Edexcel website: www.edexcel.com

Contents

Introduction

The Edexcel Poetry Anthology is common to both GCSE English and GCSE English Literature. It consists of four themed collections, each containing 15 poems:

- Collection A: Relationships
- Collection B: Clashes and collisions
- Collection C: Somewhere, anywhere
- Collection D: Taking a stand

The selection of poems in each collection is largely contemporary, with a focus on poems that students will be able to relate to.

Edexcel will provide a copy of the Poetry Anthology for every candidate, as well as clean copies to be used in the English Literature examination or English controlled assessment task-taking sessions.

How is poetry assessed?
English – Unit 3: Creative English
This unit is internally assessed under controlled conditions, and externally moderated by Edexcel. This unit has three parts: Speaking and Listening; Poetry; and Creative Writing. Students will need to complete one Poetry Reading task, with up to two hours of task-taking time. This task is worth 10% of the GCSE.

In the Poetry Reading task, students will respond to a literary heritage poem set by Edexcel from outside the anthology, drawing on at least two additional poems from the anthology collection they have studied. There is no requirement to compare the poems. An appropriate literary heritage poem and task will be set for each of the four themed collections. Each task will be available for one year.

You have the opportunity to choose a form of response that will most engage your students in poetry and allow them to achieve their potential. Students can produce a traditional written response of up to 1000 words or a multi-modal response (such as a PowerPoint presentation) or a digital media response (such as a podcast or short film).

English Literature – Unit 2: Understanding Poetry
Students are assessed through a 1 hour and 45 minute examination, available at both Foundation Tier and Higher Tier. There are two sections in the examination paper:

- Section A: Unseen poetry – students answer one question on an unseen poem, worth 20 marks. The unseen poems will be different for Foundation and Higher Tier. At Foundation Tier students will be given bullets to support their response. At Higher Tier students will be directed towards the main focus of the poem to guide them in their response.
- Section B: Anthology poems – students answer one question on the collection they have studied from the anthology, worth 30 marks. The question is divided into two parts. Students must answer part a) on a named poem. They will then be asked to compare this poem with another named poem in part b) i) OR a poem of their own choice from the collection they have studied in part b) ii).

Clean copies of the Edexcel Poetry Anthology may be used in the examination. The first examination will be in June 2011 – subsequently the paper will be available in both the January and June examination series.

About this Teacher Guide
This Teacher Guide provides a scheme of work for each of the four poetry collections, with lesson plans that contain a range of suggested activities for each poem that will help you to start teaching the new collections quickly and easily. In addition, there is a scheme of work on unseen poetry, which will help you to prepare students for this element of the English Literature examination. At the end of this introduction you will also find guidance on teaching poetry to students with English as an Additional Language, contributed by NALDIC, the subject association for EAL teachers.

To help you prepare your students for the assessment, each lesson contains peer assessment opportunities and plenaries written by the senior examining team to help you demonstrate to students what they need to do to succeed. The final lesson in each collection draws together the learning and focuses on preparing students for the assessment.

Each lesson plan is presented in a highly visual, easy-to-use format, which makes it easy for you to see how to make full use of all the resources available on the Digital Anthology ActiveTeach. Throughout, there are also activities which are designated as 'Access' or 'Extend' to help you cater for a range of abilities within your group of students. You can pick and choose from these activities to suit your own needs.

The length of lessons also varies, due largely to the length and complexity of the poem covered, and it will not necessarily be possible to complete all activities within the lesson time. Editable Word versions of the lesson plans are available within the Teacher Guide section of the Digital Anthology, allowing you to tailor the material to the needs of your students.

Each lesson plan contains the following elements:

Plenaries help to focus students on the requirements of the assessment

At-a-glance guide to what students will learn in this lesson and what resources you will require

Thumbnails of digital resources available on the Poetry Anthology ActiveTeach show how you can integrate these materials into your teaching

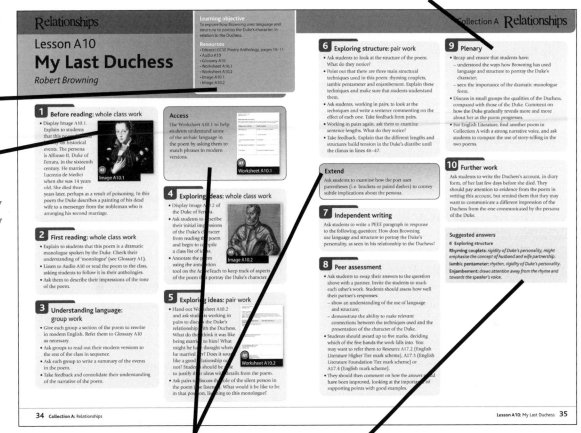

Alternative Access and Extend activities are suggested to support differentiation

Suggested answers to activities support you in helping students to understand the poems; suggested answers for worksheets can be found in the editable Word versions of the lesson plans

The Digital Anthology

Accompanying this Teacher Guide is a **Digital Anthology ActiveTeach** – an easy-to-use, on-screen version of the Poetry Anthology with added digital resources to enhance your teaching. You can install the digital anthology onto your centre's network or VLE for easy access in lessons without needing to be online.

The Digital Anthology ActiveTeach contains a full colour on-screen version of the student anthology. You can quickly and easily launch the available digital resources from the pages of the anthology, making it ideal for whole class teaching. Resources for the introductory lessons can be launched from the contents page of the relevant collection, and those for the final lesson of each collection can be launched from the bottom of the page containing the final poem. All resources are also accessible by using the 'Page Resources' button and within the 'Find Resources' tool.

The resources on the Digital Anthology include:

- Video – watch contemporary poets reading and talking about their poems.

- Audio – an audio recording of every poem in the anthology is provided.

- ResultsPlus activities – these interactive activities help to support grade improvement. See below for more information about using these activities.

- Images – help to set the context for poems with different historical and cultural settings, as well as stimulating discussion.

- Worksheets – editable worksheets are provided to support the activities in the classroom.

- Glossaries – share key words with students on PowerPoint slides for easy reference.

- Multimedia activities – zipped files of video footage which can be downloaded onto your own system and edited using a separate software editing package. Activities are provided which help students to explore the poet's ideas, thoughts and feeling through selection and editing of this footage.

There are also a range of tools available on the Digital Anthology that are designed to support your planning and whole class teaching of the anthology poems:

- Annotation tools – allow you to highlight key words or sections, annotate poems, add notes and save your work.
- My Resources – create your own route through the Digital Anthology and add links to your own resources or to websites, providing the perfect solution for seamless lesson planning and whole class teaching.
- Teacher Guide – here you can access the Word versions of the lesson plans, enabling you to adapt them for the needs of your students. This is also where you will find resources for the Unseen poetry lessons and suggested worksheet answers.

Using the ResultsPlus activities

ResultsPlus interactive activities have been designed to help improve students' answers to exam questions and controlled assessment tasks. These activities are ideal for whole class teaching. They help you to guide your students through sample answers and the mark schemes, exploring student work at different levels so that students can see what they need to do to move up the mark scheme bands.

Improving a sample answer

Learning objective: to show students how to move up a level in the mark scheme.

This activity is an excellent way to show students of all abilities how to improve answers to achieve the next level in the mark scheme. You choose a level of sample answer to set your class and they will suggest improvements you can type up to appear on your whiteboard. You can then see how the examiner would improve the answer and compare the suggestions to those made by the class.

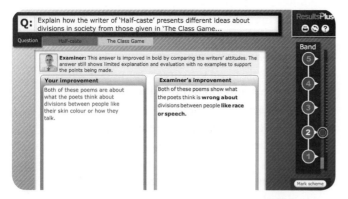

Mark a sample answer

Learning objective: to understand the mark scheme.

This activity will help you and your students to pull apart a sample answer with a highlighting tool. Your students will then assess the strengths and weaknesses of each section by answering a series of questions. At the end of their analysis students can suggest the level of the sample answer. This

activity gives students a chance to be the examiner and really understand how the questions are marked.

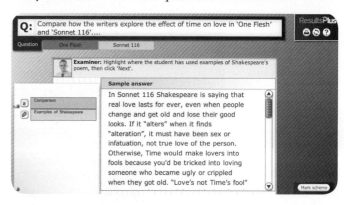

Using the annotation tools

You can access tools to annotate the poems by selecting the 'Pencil' button on the bottom menu bar of the ActiveTeach. This will reveal the annotations palette. Selecting one of the drawing tools lets you draw on the page you are viewing.

If you want to annotate features across the whole poem, for example to explore the rhyme scheme, you should annotate the poem in double-page or single-page view.

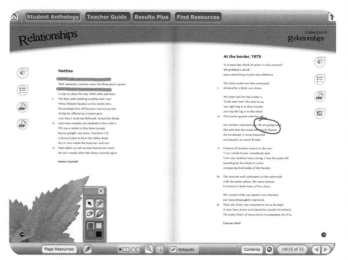

This will allow you to see all of your annotations at once.

If you want to annotate a stanza of the poem in detail you can zoom in on that section by clicking on the selected stanza. You will then be given the option to 'Add space', giving you white space around the poem in which to add annotations. Note, however, that annotations made in this mode cannot be seen when you zoom back out to view the whole poem. However, annotated stanzas are displayed with a keyline around them in both single – and double – page view.

You are able to save your annotations to your ActiveTeach profile, allowing you to pre-prepare annotations for your classes or to return in future lessons to poems that you have annotated.

English as an Additional Language: guidance for teaching poetry

Introduction

A growing number of schools and teachers are now supporting students with English as an Additional Language (EAL). More than one in ten secondary students are, or are becoming, bilingual and over 240 languages are spoken by students in UK schools, the most widely used being Panjabi, Urdu, Bengali, Gujarati, Somali, Polish, Arabic, Portuguese, Turkish and Tamil. This guidance is designed to help your lesson delivery and to give suggestions on how to differentiate materials for your students.

Students learning EAL will vary in their proficiency in their first language *and* in their proficiency in English. Some, but not all, will be fluent in their first language and have age-appropriate academic literacy skills in that language. Some will have age-appropriate skills in English similar to their peers. Others will be at very early stages. Others may be fluent in certain uses of English, but have less secure skills in other areas, for example written academic English. Similarly, students will use their first language skills for different purposes at different times.

For the purposes of this guide, three terms are used to describe students' English language levels:

- *New* to English language and literacy (likely to be new to the UK and unable to participate successfully in curriculum studies without further assistance and support).
- *Exploring* English language and literacy (likely to be able to communicate in everyday and some written English. They may have arrived in the UK during Key Stage 3 and their English is likely to show shortfalls in relation to both academic and social activities).
- *Consolidating* English language and literacy (likely to be competent in spoken English in the classroom and in informal situations, but this fluency may not be reflected in academic reading and writing).
(RBKC, 2006)

The attainment of all these students is likely to vary significantly between speaking and listening, reading and writing, but they often make faster progress than English-speaking peers assessed at the same levels in National Curriculum English.

Broad principles

When faced with the linguistic challenges of a multilingual classroom, you will need to take a broad view of the language development of EAL students. It's not just about developing students' knowledge of items of English vocabulary and grammar, nor about teaching these through 'extra' activities. EAL students will be learning about English as a subject at the same time as they are learning about and through English as a language. They will also be at different stages in this process. Learning a new language requires time, exposure and opportunities to understand meanings through interaction and independent reflection.

Context

Language does not occur in a vacuum, but in a context, and this context affects the way things are written and said. First of all, there is the 'context of culture', where users share common assumptions in relation to the way things are done, whether this is buying some bread or delivering a physics lesson. Secondly, language is used within a 'context of situation'. This means the language used varies according to the relationship of those involved, from speaker to speaker, from topic to topic, according to purpose and situation.

All speakers are instinctively aware of these differences in their first languages. There are also variations in language according to social class, region and ethnic group. In schools, language also varies from subject to subject. For example, the language used in maths is very distinct from that used in English or history. EAL learners need to become familiar with the variations in written and spoken language that are used in subjects, schools and local communities, as well as understanding the cultural expectations, beliefs and practices associated with the language.

Communication

Language is essentially a means of communication. We use language to interact with one another and to express our feelings, viewpoints or our needs and to learn about the world. The functional nature of language in the classroom means an EAL student cannot focus solely on the mastery of grammar or the understanding of vocabulary. Research indicates that language learning is most effective when learners are involved in meaningful situations. Learners acquire language through social interaction but also through activities that offer intellectual challenge.

Practical tip

Aim to give learners the opportunity to engage in social interaction while undertaking activities that offer cognitive challenge. Just as students are marked on the content of their work, EAL students also need to receive feedback on their language use.

Another key principle is the interdependence of speaking, listening, reading and writing. These are often presented as 'four' skills, but in real life contexts they are naturally interdependent. In real life, students acquire the ability to use them simultaneously and interdependently. Their language processes develop as they use multi-modal technologies such as film, video and ICT.

Practical tip

You will need to provide EAL learners with opportunities to develop their language abilities in ways which recognise the interdependence of speaking, listening, reading and writing.

Language learning is not short term. It takes place over time and individual learners acquire language at different rates. There are many contributing factors, such as linguistic or educational backgrounds. Learners' thinking and learning styles, motivation and personality also play a role. You may have seen that EAL learners frequently acquire informal conversational skills more quickly than academic language skills (which may take five to seven years to develop). In order to plan appropriately for the linguistically diverse classroom, it is essential to understand the progression of language from spoken (e.g. playground talk) through to written (e.g. exploratory talk).

It is widely acknowledged that bilingualism is an asset and enhances learners' linguistic and cognitive skills. However, in order for students to benefit fully they need to be very proficient in both languages. This implies that the most effective school environment for EAL learners is one in which the development of the first language for both academic and social purposes is promoted alongside the learning of English. EAL learners who are literate in their first language have many advantages. Literacy in another language helps them to make sense of academic texts in English as they have an understanding of how different kinds of texts work. Importantly, learning a new language also offers them insights into their first language.

Implications for teaching and learning

The principles above have many implications when it comes to planning for and teaching your students. They underpin many aspects of successful teaching in linguistically diverse classrooms, such as:

- Making the most of students' prior knowledge and understanding in their first language and English.
- Encouraging learners to seek meaning through communicative and independent activities.
- Helping students to understand source materials and supporting them to reflect their understanding in their own writing in English.
- Paying attention to culturally and contextually specific ways of using language.
- Activities which focus on specific aspects of English at word, sentence and text level which EAL students may find more difficult.

Some detailed practical suggestions are given in the table below.

EAL insights	Practical implications	Strategies that can be used when teaching poetry in the classroom
Different cultures and languages use different ways of expressing meaning, not just different vocabulary and grammar.	• Make the socio-cultural assumptions in your discussions, tasks and materials explicit. • Give students opportunities to reflect on differences and similarities.	• Amplify the cultural and linguistic background to each poem using visual images, notes and discussions. • Elicit students' feelings, attitudes and opinions and give them the opportunity to compare and contrast the ways ideas are expressed.
EAL learners need to be able to adapt spoken and written language to suit the context. They also need to use spoken or written language in accepted and predictable ways to achieve particular purposes and to communicate meaning.	• Give students a variety of opportunities to engage in understanding, in ways which are appropriate to the subject. • Provide feedback on students' language use.	• Give students opportunities to hear poems read aloud several times. • Model and provide frames at sentence level for students to use, for example in order to discuss literary devices used by poets. • Sentence frames that follow the pattern of PEEE (see pages 12/13) are useful as they can facilitate and build to paragraph writing later on. Examples of sentence frames are provided on page 13.

EAL learners may have strengths and weaknesses within the skill set of speaking and listening, reading and writing.	• Be sensitive to the different skills profiles of learners and the interdependence of speaking, listening, reading and writing. • Groupings based on attainment in reading or writing may not always be appropriate. • EAL learners will benefit from an additional focus on speaking and listening activities as a bridge to reading and writing.	• Provide ample opportunities for students to practise talking about poetry; for example, if discussing onomatopoeia encourage students to repeat the term using different examples. • Encourage oral rehearsal before writing through use of talk partners. • Correct intonation and pronunciation, building on students' ability and confidence to talk about poetry, which in turn will assist them in writing about poetry.
EAL learners will not necessarily acquire English skills in the same order as first language speakers.	• Include strategies which build on students' strengths, for example in spoken English or from their first language. • Where more than one student share a language, opportunities for discussion in that language should be encouraged, as should developing independent translation skills.	• Allow time for students to understand the poem. Two or three readings may be necessary. • Students may make notes using their first language (L1). Encourage use of bilingual and EFL dictionaries. • Students could translate one or two verses of a poem into their L1, which could lead to discussion about meaning and use of language, for example. • Allow students time to reflect on and process their ideas before responding orally.
EAL learners will be acquiring English language skills across the curriculum and will also be using these skills across the curriculum.	• Work to develop learners' oral language skills alongside their literacy skills. • Build on learners' prior knowledge and the resources they bring. • Make links with students' other languages and work across the curriculum to build their language and literacy capacity.	• Where possible, provide opportunities for students to discuss their ideas, attitudes and opinions using key language prior to writing them down. • Give EAL students a chance to learn key poetic terms (such as rhyme and alliteration) with reference to poetry in their first language. • Enable students to see writing as a process which requires constant drafting and redrafting. • Encourage the practice of proofreading and peer proofreading and assessment.
Bilingualism and bi-culturalism are assets and can enhance learners' linguistic and cognitive skills.	• Build in opportunities to promote the use of first languages for academic and social purposes.	• Provide opportunities for students to use their L1, for example by translating a verse of poetry and discussing any insights or variations they come across. • Draw on students' linguistic and cultural backgrounds and knowledge. For example, discuss poetic forms used in other cultures such as Urdu Ghazals.

Rationale for suggested approaches

Reading: poetic form

Poetry can be difficult for students from all cultures to access. However, poetic structure and simile and metaphor cut across all cultures and need to be taught explicitly to all learners. The rhyme patterns and metre of classical English poetry may be different from those of EAL learners' own cultures, although they are more 'natural' to fluent and experienced first-language users of English.

EAL students with limited exposure to different types of poetry in English are at a disadvantage, especially if the practices in their first language are different. However, the similarities of poetic forms across cultures can also be a useful starting point for discussion.

Reading: reading for meaning

Many EAL learners will also be at a disadvantage when trying to interpret clues to predict meanings in texts. This may be because the text describes something which is beyond their current experience.

It is important to remember that most bilingual learners will have been exposed to a range of learning and literacy practices before they come into a UK school. The challenge is to build on these experiences pragmatically.

Reading: going beyond the text

Of course, fluent users of English in your classroom do not simply follow a text to recover meaning from the words and sentences: they have to know how to make use of the information for different purposes. This ability to go beyond the text cannot be taught through just the 'nuts and bolts' of language itself: it has to be supported by increasing familiarity with culturally established ways of seeing, knowing and understanding.

EAL learners with a limited experience of dealing with written texts in English may find this aspect of reading an invisible but constant problem. Similarly, the task of acquiring new vocabulary is not a simple one to be solved by exposing students to 'key words'. Words have multiple meanings and are used with different emphases in different contexts, and students need continued exposure to these meanings.

Writing

Most writing tasks are developed from the curriculum and EAL students may not fully understand the curriculum meanings expressed through spoken English. Words change their meaning according to the context, and the classroom is full of metaphorical and figurative uses of language which are open to misunderstandings. This lack of understanding of content meaning often causes major difficulties in selecting and including appropriate information in writing tasks.

Cameron (2003) identifies some of the following problems that KS4/post-16 EAL students have in writing:

1. Even high level (or **consolidating**) EAL learners may have difficulty in using ideas from source materials in their own writing.
2. **Consolidating** EAL learners may also have difficulty in judging nuances of style, and still experience some of the same problems as their less proficient EAL peers (**new** and **exploring**) with the use of articles, choice of the correct preposition in fixed phrases, and subject-verb agreement.
3. 'Delexical' verbs, i.e. verbs that are 'so frequently used and in so many different contexts that the link between the verb and its meaning become quite weak' (p34), such as 'put', 'do', 'have', 'make' or 'go'. Examples include sentences such as 'make a stop to this' instead of 'put a stop to', and 'they will do more fun' instead of 'they will have more fun'.
4. Difficulties with sentence grammar related to length of clause constituents and use of adverbials and subordination to develop more complex sentence structure.

Although some of these common areas of difficulty may benefit from specific teaching, Gibbons (2002) likens word and sentence level work to focusing a pair of binoculars. Your first gaze is the whole vista and after a while you use the binoculars to home in on a detail of the landscape. You know how to locate this detail because you have already seen it as part of the whole. When you have finished focusing on the detail, you will probably return to the whole panorama again, but with an enhanced sense of what is there. Additional word and sentence level activities need to be compatible with this 'whole vista' approach and provide further opportunities for 'message abundancy'.

Linking reading, writing, speaking and listening

Learning to write in EAL is inextricably linked to learning English and curriculum content through spoken English at the same time. Given that spoken English is not necessarily the same as the written form, it is important to pay attention to bilingual students' writing in English, even when they seem to understand spoken communication reasonably well.

Practical tip

This suggests that reading and writing tasks should start with and be supported by teaching and group activities which use spoken English in conjunction with relevant visual materials, realia and hands-on experiential learning tasks. This will go a long way to making meanings comprehensible. Strategies for this are suggested below.

Practical application

Gibbons (2008) describes what this might look like in practical terms.

If you were a second language learner in that class, you would have had opportunities for participating in an initial shared experience, which is watching the video with everybody else; hearing everyday language alongside academic language in the interactions between teachers and students – the Janus-like talk; seeing the key points written on the board, so you have got a visual representation of what you're hearing; having the difference between everyday and technical language highlighted through the colour-coding; having access to a chart of definitions; getting practice in putting new concepts into practice; and, finally, using the learning in a new context.

Gibbons has used the term 'message abundancy' to describe this sort of teaching sequence – 'So that you have more than one bite of the apple, you don't just get told one thing once.'

A lot of EAL students that I've interviewed in secondary say their teachers talk too quickly. I don't think it's actually the speed of the talk that they're responding to, I think it's the speed at which information is given. If you're a second language learner, it helps enormously to have the time to process a new idea. This kind of recycling of the same idea many times over, I think is one of the most important things about a curriculum. I called it message abundancy because it seemed to me that there was an abundancy of messages there and many opportunities to understand something.

In other words, say less but say it more. For example, rather than aiming for four or five lesson outcomes, accept that two covered thoroughly from several angles with time for independent consolidation and review will be of greater value for an EAL student.

Helping students with exam questions

Examinations require students to be able to read with meaning and answer logically in writing, whatever the subject. You therefore need to teach bilingual students who are still developing their English skills two things:

- How to interpret the requirements of the questions.
- How to write an answer which follows the cues in the questions (in both reading and writing).

These cues are not always made explicit. It is not always the ideas that bilingual learners need, but the language needed for answering the question.

Practical tip

Students need a wide variety of experiences and texts and a formula for how to write in different genres so that they can confidently apply what they know to any unfamiliar context. Some practical strategies relating to specific examples are suggested below.

Experience suggests that EAL learners often encounter difficulties with whole-text genre (which usually gains the highest amount of marks) due to a lack of shared cultural assumptions and experiences. Similarly in reading, inference and deduction, text structure, use of language, and the writer's purpose and effect on the reader may continue to cause problems well beyond the **new** or **exploring** stages of language learning.

Suggested teaching sequence, sample strategies and activities for EAL development

A practical application to use when teaching poetry to EAL learners might look as follows, where the above strategies are applied to the teaching of the poem 'City Jungle'. This approach can also suit monolingual English speakers as the different stages provide a predictable sequence and structure.

Lesson phase	How?
Introduction Set the context to build field knowledge, including concrete experiences, multimedia input, exploratory talk in L1 and L2, reading and note-making. Using different examples, provide opportunities for developing oral language skills of pronunciation, intonation, stress and volume.	The whole vista – helping students to understand the message and viewpoint of the poem 'City Jungle', as well as the reason why the poet wrote the poem, by providing background knowledge and drawing on students' own experience. *For example:* • Discuss the advantages and disadvantages of living in a city. • Visuals – pictures of city life, for example artists' impressions of city life showing the darker side. • Read the poem to the class, asking students to draw any images they see as they listen, then share ideas. • Read the poem again, this time with the class reading too. • Individual/pair reading. Students use bilingual and EFL dictionaries for translating vocabulary and making notes in preferred language L1 or L2.
Modelling Guide students in exploring the genre and the language features. Teacher models and defines the task, making audience, purpose, form and expected language features explicit. Active listening and speaking activities. Exam tasks such as essay-writing are modelled and scaffolded in context with the appropriate language needed.	• Guided questions, for example: Do headlights stare? Do shop doorways keep their mouths shut? Are houses hunched, do they cough? • Students may translate some phrases into their L1. • Discuss the impact of this use of language and the poet's purpose in using it. • Elicit/share the term 'personification'. *The poet uses personification, for example 'Hunched houses cough'. This creates a … effect.*
Joint construction Explain and provide scaffold sequencing and structuring conventions. Teacher guides by asking questions and making suggestions with students' input and re-wording. Students take an increasing role using what they have learnt. Using different examples, provide opportunities for developing oral language skills of pronunciation, intonation, stress and volume.	**Point** *The poet uses personification throughout the poem. Personification is when we give objects human qualities.* **Evidence** *Examples of personification include …* **Explain** *When the poet says, for example 'Streetlights bare their yellow teeth' it has the effect of …* *creating very vivid images …* *bringing the poem to life …* *making the city seem to be a menacing and scary place …* **Explore** *Alternative interpretations of this poem include…* At this stage, repetition may be used to ensure students pronounce the words correctly. Elicit the intonation of certain words, e.g. per'sonifi'cation. The more confident and competent students are in using the language orally the better they will be able to write about it.

Lesson phase	How?
Independent construction Task broken down into smaller tasks. Planning a number of paragraphs in a logical sequence. Independent construction should be scaffolded by a range of grouping strategies, frames and aids, planning a number of paragraphs in a logical sequence. Pair and group work. EAL students will need to have several practices and opportunities to peer-assess, edit and rewrite before they become competent.	• Students write their own paragraph on personification using the scaffold frame (see example scaffold frame on page 13). These stages can be repeated for other techniques, such as the poet's use of onomatopoeia, writing a good introduction, writing a good conclusion, etc., to build up to answering the exam question: 'Explain how Corbett uses poetic techniques to present an unusual image of the city.' • Students read their work aloud in pairs or groups, providing further opportunities for oral practice of structure and language. • Using white boards to practise linking sentences with key connectives. • Students are encouraged to see writing as a process consisting of two or more drafts. • Proofreading – reading aloud for meaning, individual/peer assessment: have I used paragraphs, quotation marks, PEEE? etc.
Assessment and consolidation Provide individual feedback on errors/development points unless these apply to large numbers of students. Sentence level difficulties for EAL learners may include: subject/verb, noun/pronoun agreements and some plurals; use of articles; endings for tense/person and modal verbs. Give oral and written feedback on both content and language assessing both holistically *and* separately. Implement assessment strategies which require students to communicate with their peers and provide further opportunities to recycle and consolidate language. Provide an exemplar answer followed by a test which shows how the marks awarded increase if certain features are included in the answer. Making assessment criteria explicit may help students to realise what they have to do to reach higher levels in examinations and progress in their language learning.	• Using examples of students' writing, pool typical errors for sentence level grammar correction, for example students might make errors using the articles 'a' and 'the'. • Using a written response by a student, model the marking process pointing out the strengths and weaknesses of the piece. • Provide simplified assessment criteria written in language that is easily accessible. • Provide ample opportunities for students to read good model answers. • Using the assessment criteria, encourage students to grade responses prior to knowing the marks achieved. • Encourage individual and peer assessment by grading their own work, prior to teacher assessment. Same nationality students may give each other feedback using L1.

The following are example scaffold frames for writing about literary techniques:

- *The poet uses personification, for example ... The impact of this on us, the readers, is ...*
- *Another example of this technique is ... This is effective because ...*
- *The poet uses personification because ...*
- *A further technique used by the poet is ..., for example ... The effect of this is ...*
- *Another example of this technique is ... This makes an impact because ...*
- *Ultimately, the use of these techniques helps to get the poet's message or theme across because ...*

EAL students may have difficulty in expressing the impact or effect of the literary device in L2. They could be encouraged to use their L1 to try and express these ideas first. It may also be helpful to prepare a list of relevant sentence endings that they could use, for example:

… *adds impact.*
… *adds to the tone or mood of the poem.*
… *adds to the flow and rhythm of the poem.*
… *brings the poem to life.*
… *provides vivid images which absorb the reader.*
… *appeals to our feelings.*

Further resources and reading

Cameron, L. (2003) *Writing in English as an additional language at Key Stage 4 and post-16*. London: OFSTED.

Cummins, J. (1984) *Bilingualism and Special Education: Issues in assessment and pedagogy*. Clevedon, England: Multilingual Matters.

Cummins, J. (2001) *Negotiating Identities: Education for Empowerment in a Diverse Society* (2nd ed.). Los Angeles: CABE.

DfEE (2001) 'Literacy across the curriculum' (DfEE Ref 0235/2001).

Excell, D. (2006) 'Key Stage 3: Observations on Baseline Reading Tests and Formal Assessments for EAL Learners' in *NALDIC Quarterly 4.2* Reading: NALDIC.

Gibbons, P. (2002) *Scaffolding Language, Scaffolding Learning: Teaching Second Language Learners in the Mainstream Classroom*. Portsmouth, NH: Heinemann.

Gibbons, P (2008) 'Challenging Pedagogies: More than just good practice' in *NALDIC Quarterly 6.2* Reading: NALDIC

Halliday, M.A.K. (1975) *Learning how to mean*. London: Edward Arnold.

Leung, C. (2004) *English as an Additional language – Language and Literacy Development*. Royston: UKLA.

McWilliam, N. (1998) *What's in a Word: Vocabulary Development in Multilingual Classrooms*. Stoke-on–Trent: Trentham.

Mohan, B. (1986) *Language and Content*. Reading, MA: Addison-Wesley.

OFSTED (2005) 'Could they do even better? The writing of advanced bilingual learners of English at Key Stage 2: HMI survey of good practice'. London: Office for Standards in Education.

RBKC (2006) *English Language and Literacy in Curriculum Learning*. London: RBKC.

NALDIC with adaptations by Sabishna Hasan

Relationships

Relationships

Lesson A1
Relationships introduction

Learning objectives
- To consolidate students' understanding of the features of poetry and a range of poetic devices.
- To think about what issues poems with a 'relationships' theme might explore.
- To understand the assessment objectives for this unit.

Resources
- Glossary A1
- Worksheet A1.1
- Worksheet A1.2
- Worksheet A1.3
- Interactive A1

---

1 Starter activity: whole class work

- Ask the class to give examples of some devices that can be used by poets to help convey meaning. If they can, ask them to provide an example of how these devices might be used, and explain how they can be effective.
- Complete the activity in Interactive A1 as a class. The icons to open the resources for this lesson can be found on the contents page for Collection A, on page 1 of the ActiveTeach. This activity involves matching the following poetic devices with the correct definitions: alliteration, assonance, metaphor, onomatopoeia, rhyme, rhythm, personification, simile. Ask individuals to come up to the board and make what they think is the correct connection, or ask the whole class to complete the activity against the clock.

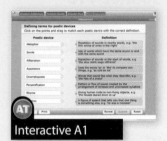
Interactive A1

- Hand out Glossary A1 for students to look at the correct definitions. Remind students that they can return to this glossary to refresh their memory at any point during their study of this collection of poems.

2 Identifying poetic devices: pair work

- Hand out Worksheet A1.1, which gives students examples of different poetic devices from the poems in the collection. They are asked to identify the poetic device used in a second set of quotations from the poems.
- Ask students to swap work with another pair and mark each other's work. Explain that if they make a mistake, each pair must explain to the other pair why they are wrong.

Worksheet A1.1

3 Looking at imagery: independent work

- Provide students with Worksheet A1.2, which gives a list of phrases from the collection that include particularly vivid imagery.
- Ask each student to choose one of these phrases and draw a picture of the item described. Tell them to think about how the words used help them to understand what the poet is trying to communicate and what the item should look like. Ask them to label the picture or write at least two sentences beneath it to explain why they have chosen to draw the image in this way, pinpointing particular words from the phrase.

Worksheet A1.2

- Ask for volunteers to share their pictures with the rest of the class. Ask students to explain why they have illustrated the phrase in this way and why they think the poet's use of imagery is effective.

4 Making inferences from shape: whole class work

- Hand out Worksheet A1.3, which indicates just the shapes of two poems: 'Our Love Now' and 'Rubbish at Adultery'.

Worksheet A1.3

- Discuss how students know that these are poems and what they can infer from the shape of them.
- Ask pairs of students to devise a list of five to ten features that differentiate prose from poetry (this should be familiar to them from KS3 work). These might relate to line length, rhyme, rhythm, standard punctuation, grammar and stanzas.
- Ask pairs to feed back to the class and compare and contrast their ideas. Encourage them to think about how each of these aspects of poetry might help a poet convey meaning. For example, if a poem was written using the language of SMS, without any standard punctuation, what impression might this give of the poet or what message s/he is trying to communicate?

5 Exploring ideas: whole class work

- Introduce students to the theme of the collection of poems they are going to study. Ask students what they expect poems in a collection with this title will be about.
- Compile a class list of the types of issues students suggest these poems might explore on the board. To prompt students you could ask them to consider books or films that they have enjoyed with a similar theme.

6 Plenary

Introduce students to the assessment objectives for this unit, according to which course they are following. Explain the skills that they will need to develop while studying these poems, in preparation for their assessment.

English

AO2:

i) Read and understand texts, selecting material appropriate to purpose, collating from different sources and making comparisons and cross-references as appropriate;

ii) Explain and evaluate how writers use linguistic, grammatical, structural and presentational features to achieve effects and engage and influence the reader.

English Literature

AO2: Explain how language, structure and form contribute to writers' presentation of ideas, themes and settings.

AO3: Make comparisons and explain links between texts, evaluating writers' different ways of expressing meaning and achieving effects.

7 Further work

Ask students to find a copy of a poem and annotate it explaining what they liked or didn't like about it. Did they like the topic? Was there something particularly memorable about it? Why? They should think about language and vocabulary, any rhyme pattern, line length and form and imagery covered in the lesson. What effect did each of these have and why was it effective (or not) in their view? You might wish to guide them to use a PEEE structure. This terminology is used throughout the scheme of work for the collection and can help to guide students in their writing by ensuring they have made a Point, found Evidence for this, Explained the reasoning and finally Explored alternative interpretations and implications.

Suggested answers

Answers to worksheets are provided in the editable Word lesson plans on the ActiveTeach.

5 Exploring ideas
Suggested ideas for topics on the theme of 'relationships' might include love, family heritage, culture, or a variety of ideas on linkage.

Relationships

Lesson A2
Valentine
Carol Ann Duffy

Learning objective
To understand how Duffy uses imagery and language to portray her understanding love.

Resources
• Edexcel GCSE Poetry Anthology, page 2
• Audio A2
• Glossary A2
• Worksheet A2.1
• Worksheet A2.2
• Multimedia A2

1 Before reading: whole class work

• Brainstorm ideas associated with Valentine's Day, e.g. cards, flowers, a romantic meal, poetry, chocolates, hearts, the colour red.

• Ask the class what gifts they have received in the past from people they love. Why were these gifts significant? Why did they appreciate them (or not)?

• If possible, bring in an onion and chop and peel it at the front of the class. Ask the class what they would think if a member of their family or a boy/girlfriend gave them an onion as a gift. Explain that Duffy is arguing that an onion is an appropriate gift for a lover. Why might this be? What effect does the chopped onion have on students?

2 First reading: whole class work

• Listen to Audio A2 and ask students to follow the poem in their anthologies.

• Ask students to highlight the references to traditional images of Valentine's Day and love.

• Encourage them to consider the context in which these references are used. Draw out that these traditional things are often dismissed ('not…') or related to aspects of the onion ('platinum loops', 'cling', 'possessive and faithful'). Guide students to understand that Duffy is drawing parallels between love and relationships, and the characteristics of an onion.

Access

• Check that students know what metaphors and similes are (refer to Glossary A1 as necessary). Ask them to identify one metaphor and one simile in this poem and to draw an image representing each one.

• Discuss how and why this imagery is used and what Duffy is trying to suggest.

3 Exploring ideas: independent work

• Introduce the idea that although an onion does not appear to be a very romantic gift, Duffy is using it as an extended metaphor for aspects of love.

• Ask students to identify the parallels that Duffy has drawn between the onion and love. What senses does she make use of (sight, hearing, touch, smell, taste)?

• Ask them to write an explanation of why they think these parallels are effective. What impression of love do they give the reader? Refer them to Glossary A2 as necessary.

• Students should feed back to the class and ideas should be compared in discussion.

4 Exploring ideas: pair work

• Hand out Worksheet A2.1, which asks students to select comparisons to the onion that convey positive and negative attitudes towards love.

• Ask students whether the overall impression of love given in the poem is positive or negative. Why?

Worksheet A2.1

5 Multimedia activity: group work

• Divide students into groups and hand out Worksheet A2.2 which briefs them on how to complete a short multimedia activity using the downloadable footage provided on the ActiveTeach. When Multimedia A2 is opened, you will be prompted to save the file somewhere on your system. The multimedia clips can then be accessed by extracting them from the zip file, and then opened in editing software for

Worksheet A2.2

students to use and modify. The aim of the activity is to encourage students to interpret the poet's ideas, thoughts and feelings through selection and editing of the material provided. Students will require access to editing software and up to an hour to complete the task.

Extend

Ask students to look again at the lines that stand alone as well as the one-word lines and explain why, in their opinion, Duffy has used this form for the poem. How does it help to convey her understanding of love?

6 Independent writing

Ask students to write a PEEE paragraph in response to the following question: How does Duffy use language and imagery to explore a variety of unusual ideas on love within this poem?

7 Peer assessment

- Ask students to swap their answers to the independent writing above with a partner. Invite the students to mark each other's work. Students should assess how well their partner's responses:
  - show an understanding of Duffy's use of imagery and language to explore her ideas about love;
  - demonstrate the ability to make relevant connections between the techniques used and the presentation of themes;
  - use the 'PEEE' technique to show the link between form and point of view.
- Students should award up to five marks, deciding which of the five bands the work falls into. You may want to refer them to Resource A17.2 (English Literature Higher Tier mark scheme), A17.3 (English Literature Foundation Tier mark scheme) or A17.4 (English mark scheme).
- Students should comment on how the answer could have been improved, looking at the importance of supporting points with good examples.

8 Plenary

- Recap and ensure that students have:
  - understood how Duffy has used language and imagery to achieve effects;
  - grasped how she has engaged the reader
  - responded to this - unusual - poem.
- Discuss how everyday items or objects could be used in a similar way in a poem (e.g. a brick: strong, long-lasting; a paper clip: linking, connecting, keeping together).
- For English Literature, ask students to find another poem in Collection A that shows love in a more conventional way, and ask them to suggest ways in which they could compare the two poems.

9 Further work

Ask students to look at the last three lines of the poem and write a paragraph exploring why the poet decided to end on this chilling note. What effect does this have on the poem as a whole? How do these lines help to convey the complexity of relationships?

Suggested answers

2 First reading
red rose, satin heart, photo, cute card, kissogram, kiss, faithful, wedding ring.

3 Exploring ideas
- *'It is a moon wrapped in brown paper' – a plain brown cover conceals something wonderful – the moon is often associated with romantic evenings.*
- *'It promises light / like the careful undressing of love' – light colour inside, naked body/emotions.*
- *'Blind you with tears / like a lover' – love can make you cry, like an onion when it is peeled.*
- *'It will make your reflection / a wobbling photo of grief' – love can cause sadness and tears, like an onion when it is peeled.*
- *'Its fierce kiss' – strength of feeling, and perhaps bitterness as well.*
- *'Its platinum loops shrink to a wedding-ring' – the ring symbolises love and commitment.*

Relationships

Lesson A3
Rubbish at Adultery
Sophie Hannah

Learning objective
To explore how Hannah uses structure, tone and language to paint a humorous picture of an unfaithful relationship.

Resources
- Edexcel GCSE Poetry Anthology, page 3
- Audio A3
- Glossary A3
- Worksheet A3.1
- Worksheet A3.2
- Video A3.1
- Video A3.2

1 Before reading: whole class work

- This poem deals with a potentially sensitive subject which teachers should approach carefully and with an awareness of the needs of their students.
- Give students a dictionary definition of adultery: 'being unfaithful to one's husband or wife'. Ask students whether they think that adultery is acceptable. Are their responses similar? Does gender affect their viewpoint?
- Draw students' attention to the title. What are their initial reactions to this? Do they think that it's a good or bad thing to be 'rubbish' at adultery? Ensure they understand that adultery is normally seen as a negative thing.

2 Before reading: pair work

- Hand out Worksheet A3.1, which presents the poem as a letter, written in prose form.
- Ask pairs to read through it together and discuss how to sequence the text as a poem. Encourage them to think about rhythm and rhyme.
- You may wish to stagger giving the following information about the poem to the students: it has 24 lines, 4 stanzas, 6 lines per stanza.

Worksheet A3.1

3 First reading: whole class work

- Watch Video A3.1 of Hannah reading the poem or listen to Audio A3, asking students to follow it in their anthologies.
- Ask students to identify the rhyming pattern of the poem – which lines rhyme? The pattern is abcbdb. How many beats does each of the lines have?

Video A3.1

- Discuss what this use of rhyme and rhythm helps to convey about the tone and mood of the persona. Ideas might include a nagging, lecturing, repetitive tone, a predictable pattern. Note that lines 2, 4 and 6 of each stanza rhyme, yet the others don't, suggesting a conflict and lack of harmony between the couple.

4 Exploring ideas: independent work

- Having established the fact that the persona is complaining to her partner, refer students to the title. Ask students to write down three reasons why she is unhappy. What does she want? What does she want her partner to do? They should pick out text to support their answers. Refer them to Glossary A3.
- Students feed back to the class. Ask students whether it is typical for people to complain about their partner being faithful. Establish that the tone of the poem is humorous as our expectations of relationships are reversed.

5 Discussing meaning: whole class work

As a class, watch Video A3.2 and discuss the ideas which Sophie Hannah raises. Particularly relevant is the first section where the poet talks about her use of rhyme and rhythm.

Video A3.2

Access

Students should complete Worksheet A3.2 which lists various phrases that they should sort into the correct column, either 'The persona – for adultery' or 'The persona's love – wants to be faithful'.

Worksheet A3.2

6 Looking at character: group work

- Give students the following words: sensual, thoughtful, impatient, unsympathetic, philosophical, angry, selfish, understanding, fun-loving. Explain that these adjectives can be used to describe different characteristics of people.
- Working as a group, ask them to discuss and annotate the poem with these words, linking each characteristic to a phrase in the poem that supports the use of the word to describe the persona. They should be prepared to justify their decisions when giving feedback to the class.

7 Exploring language and tone: pair work

- Ask students to re-read the poem with a partner, making sure they understand all the vocabulary, and discuss any elements they do not understand.
- Pairs should role-play a conversation between the persona and a friend, where the persona explains the situation and problems she or he has, and what her or his emotions and feelings are. Encourage them to draw on the language and information in the poem and to think about an appropriate tone of voice.
- Draw students' attention to the questions in the poem and ask them how they help us to understand the persona's frame of mind. Ideas might include: to express exasperation; to highlight the isolation of the speaker; or to make implicit criticism effective.
- Select pairs to share their role-plays with the class.

8 Peer assessment

- Ask students to write a comment about another pair's work based on whether they have:
  - shown an understanding of the use of humour, ideas and emotions within the poem;
  - demonstrated the ability to explain, develop and support ideas, making relevant connections between the techniques used and the presentation of themes.
- Students should then award up to five marks, deciding which of the five bands the work falls into. You may want to refer them to Resource A17.2 (English Literature Higher Tier mark scheme), A17.3 (English Literature Foundation Tier mark scheme) or A17.4 (English mark scheme).
- Ask students to comment on how the response could have been improved, assessing how well understanding of the ideas within the poem has been communicated.

Extend

Ask students to write about the use of humour and/or irony in the poem and consider to what extent it sheds light on the two lovers' characters and the nature of the relationship. To what extent is the accusation of being 'rubbish at adultery' being used as a defence mechanism? Could the roles of man and woman be seen as reversed? You might particularly want to draw their attention to the following phrases:

How terribly grim you feel

A tortured, wounded soul

Trouble is, at fidelity you're also slightly crap

I'm after passion, thrills and fun

You say you'll never leave/Your wife and children. Fine

I think you ought to quit

9 Plenary

- Recap and ensure that students have:
  - understood how structure and language have been used and their effects;
  - engaged with Hannah's tone and use of humour/irony.
- Ask students to offer suggestions as to how humour can be used in poetry to introduce important themes.
- For English Literature, ask students to work in groups and find one other poem in Collection A that surprises the reader with unexpected ideas. Discuss which you find more effective and why.

10 Further work

Ask students to write a reply to this poem in the form of a letter from the persona's lover. They should show their own understanding of the nature of the relationship, particularly how the lover's perception of the situation may differ from that of the persona's.

Relationships

Lesson A4
Sonnet 116
William Shakespeare

Learning objective
To understand how Shakespeare uses form, structure, language and imagery to explore the nature of love.

Resources
- Edexcel GCSE Poetry Anthology, page 4
- Audio A4
- Glossary A4
- Worksheet A4.1
- Worksheet A4.2
- Worksheet A4.3
- Image A4.1
- Image A4.2
- Image A4.3
- Interactive A4

1 Before reading: whole class work

- Write the words 'True love' on the board. Ask students to come up to the board in turn to add a word that they would associate with this.
- Discuss ideas students have contributed, particularly anything connected with eternal or constant love.
- Explain that in this poem Shakespeare believes that true love is constant and unchanging. Do students agree with this view of love? They should support their argument with reasons, perhaps referring to their own experiences or examples that they have read about.

2 First reading: pair work

- Distribute Worksheet A4.1, which provides a copy of the poem with certain words removed.
- Ask them to read through the poem together slowly, using Glossary A4 as necessary.
- They should suggest words that could be used to fill the spaces, bearing in mind the context and the rhyme pattern.

Worksheet A4.1

3 Looking at form: whole class work

- Ask students to feed back to the class and give reasons for their choices.
- Provide the correct missing words and discuss how this might alter their understanding of meaning.
- Encourage them to identify the rhyme pattern within the poem (abab, cdcd, etc.). Remind them that rhyme depends on the pronunciation and sound of the word rather than spelling. Help them where the rhyme is only partial.
- Linking back to the title, ask students what this rhyme pattern suggests about the genre of the poem. Remind them that the subject matter (the nature of love) is typical of this form. Draw their attention to the classic rhyming couplet at the end of the sonnet.

Access

- Hand out Worksheet A4.2, which asks students to match words into rhyming pairs and to identify whether each is perfect or imperfect rhyme.

Worksheet A4.2

- Discuss the answers, emphasising that rhyming words do not necessarily look similar, and words that look similar do not necessarily rhyme – it is the pronunciation and sound of the words that matter. Use an example from the poem to reiterate.
- Ask students to pick out examples from the poem that are partial rather than full rhymes. Does this have an effect on their reading of the poem?

4 Exploring meaning: whole class work

- Listen to Audio A4 or read the poem to the class, asking students to follow it in their anthologies. You could pause every four lines to explore the meaning of each section.

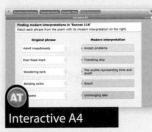

Interactive A4

- You might want to use Interactive A4 and support students as they match archaic phrases from the poem with modern meanings.

5 Exploring meaning: independent work

Hand out Worksheet A4.3. Ask students to write five explanations for what love is and four for what it is not, according to the poem. Emphasise that they should use their own words.

Worksheet A4.3

6 Exploring imagery: whole class work

- Ask students to identify a reference in the poem to a pair of joined hearts.
- Display Images A4.1, A4.2 and A4.3 and ask them to find references to each of these images.
- Discuss why Shakespeare might have used these images, focusing on the relationship between love and time.

Image A4.1

Image A4.2

Image A4.3

Extend

Ask students to identify the example of personification within the poem (Time) and decide what effect this has in helping them to understand Shakespeare's thoughts on love and relationships.

7 Looking at the overall message: pair work

- Draw students' attention to the final rhyming couplet and ask them to work in pairs to suggest their own explanation of what Shakespeare is saying here.
- Ask pairs to feed back to the class. How do the two lines relate to the rest of the poem? How does Shakespeare make the message of his poem persuasive in these two lines?

8 Independent writing

Ask students to explore, writing about half a page, how the poem uses imagery, structure and form to present ideas about relationships.

9 Peer assessment

- Ask students to swap their answers to the independent writing with a partner. Invite the students to mark each other's work. Students should assess how well their partner's responses:
  - show an understanding of the use of imagery, structure and form in the presentation of a relationship;
  - demonstrate the ability to make relevant connections between the techniques used and the presentation of themes.
- They should award up to five marks, deciding which of the five bands the work falls into. You may want to refer them to Resource A17.2 (English Literature Higher Tier mark scheme), A17.3 (English Literature Foundation Tier mark scheme) or A17.4 (English mark scheme).
- Students then comment on how the answer could have been improved, looking at the importance of supporting points with good examples.

10 Plenary

- Recap and ensure that students have:
  - understood the use of form, structure, language and imagery to achieve effects;
  - responded to the theme presented.
- Ask students to make a chart, grid or list that they can add to while studying the poems from Relationships, subdividing poems into different groups and making links between them. Show how the first poems studied might fit into this.
- For English Literature, compare the use of the sonnet form in 'Pity me not because the light of day' with that in this poem. How does each writer's use of this form contribute to the effect of the poem?

11 Further work

Ask students to write a paragraph considering whether Shakespeare's views still hold true today. Encourage them to compare the views in this poem with the views expressed by contemporary poets in some of the other poems in this collection, e.g. 'Valentine' or 'Rubbish at Adultery'.

Relationships

Lesson A5
Our Love Now
Martyn Lowery

Learning objective
To investigate how Lowery uses structure and imagery to explore different perspectives on the changes within a relationship.

Resources
• Edexcel GCSE Poetry Anthology, page 5
• Audio A5
• Glossary A5
• Worksheet A5.1

1 Before reading: whole class work

• Display the poem at the front of the class using the ActiveTeach. Draw students' attention to the title and explain that this is a poem that explores different perspectives on a long-term relationship.

• Ask them to look at the structure of the poem. Do they recognise a pattern in the way in which each stanza begins? Why might the poet have used this structure?

• Establish that it gives two different views on a relationship. Draw attention to the gender of the poet. Do students think that men and women view love and relationships differently?

2 First reading: pair work

• Working in pairs, students should decide how to read the poem, either from left to right, or one column at a time. They should look at the content and sense to help them make their decision, and perhaps read sections out loud.

• Choose one or more pairs to explain their decision about how to read the poem to the rest of the class. What is the effect of their choice? (How does their decision about how to read the poem affect its meaning and the impression it makes on the reader?) Encourage them to pick out particular lines to support their arguments.

• Listen to Audio A5 and compare their readings to this audio reading. How does it differ? What might be the reasons for this? The poem is read from left to right on Audio A5.

3 Exploring metaphor: group work

• Check that students understand the use of metaphor, referring to Glossary A1 as necessary.

• Divide students into small groups and ask them to identify the various images that Lowery uses to represent the relationship, e.g. a wound, hair, a raging storm. Through discussion, ask them to suggest two reasons why the poet might have chosen each image. Are the images inherently negative or positive? How are they used?

• Ask students to feed back to the class. Highlight the way in which the same image is used in opposite stanzas but in a different way to make a contrasting point. Ask them to identify precise ways in which the metaphor has been changed in each case (addition or removal of words or change of tense). How is this effective?

Access

• Support students in identifying the positive and negative images in the poem.

• Discuss their choices and whether the images are predominantly negative or positive. How are these distributed within the poem? Is there a pattern? If so, why might this be?

4 Exploring points of view: pair work

• Hand out Worksheet A5.1, which asks students to write a script for a conversation between the couple based on the poem.

Worksheet A5.1

• Ask pairs to feed back to the class with sections of their scripts and discuss them as a class. They should then swap their completed worksheets with another pair and write a comment on how well the scripts convey the contrasting emotions and perspectives on the relationship, as expressed within the poem.

Extend

Ask students to explore further the effect of the repeated phrase of 'such is our love (now)'. Where does this appear? In each instance, how is it used and why? Does the meaning change as the poem progresses or when a different 'voice' uses it? Why is the word 'now' used in some places and not elsewhere?

5 Independent writing

Ask students to write at least one PEEE paragraph exploring the poet's use of metaphor and structure to show the two sides of a changing relationship.

6 Peer assessment

- Ask students to swap their answers to the independent writing task with a partner. Invite the students to mark each other's work. Students should assess how well their partner's responses:
  - show an understanding of the use of metaphor and structure;
  - demonstrate the ability to make relevant connections between the techniques used and the presentation of themes.
- Students should award up to five marks, deciding which of the five bands the work falls into. You may want to refer them to Resource A17.2 (English Literature Higher Tier mark scheme), A17.3 (English Literature Foundation Tier mark scheme) or A17.4 (English mark scheme).
- Ask students to comment on how the answer could have been improved, looking at the importance of supporting points with good examples.

7 Plenary

- Recap and ensure that students have:
  - understood the ways in which Lowery has used form, structure and imagery to explore changes in a relationship;
  - connected with the different attitudes of the man and the woman.
- Discuss how successfully the poet conveys what has happened between the couple.
- Ask students to update the chart, grid or list that they created in the previous lesson, incorporating this poem. Guide students in deciding which group(s) this poem might fall into, and linking it with other poems on the basis of theme or techniques used.
- For English Literature, find another poem in Collection A that uses metaphor, and ask students to compare the use of this device in the two poems.

8 Further work

Ask students to write a conclusion to their scripted conversation, showing whether the relationship did in fact end. They should draw on evidence from the poem.

Suggested answers

Access

Positive: *wound heals, skin slowly knits, the cut will mend, our beauty together, our love, the breach is mended.*

Negative: *the scab of the scald, red burnt flesh is ugly, incomplete, raging storm, damages the trees, not the same, always a scar, the skin remains bleached, numbness prevails, the style will be different, leaves damage in its wake which can never be repaired, the tree is forever dead.*

Relationships

Lesson A6
Even Tho
Grace Nichols

Learning objective
To explore how Nichols conveys the nature of a relationship through language and structure.

Resources
- Edexcel GCSE Poetry Anthology, page 6
- Audio A6
- Glossary A6
- Worksheet A6.1
- Image A6.1
- Video A6.1

1 Before reading: whole class work

- Give students the following words, explaining that they are from the poem: watermelon, starapple, plum, banana, avocado, carnival, sweet. What impression of the poem do the students get from these words? Refer them to Glossary A6 as necessary.
- Tell them that the poet, Grace Nichols, grew up in Guyana, on the northern coast of South America, facing onto the Caribbean. Play Video A6.1 where Nichols discusses the influences of both England and Guyana on her poetry, and show them Image A6.1, explaining that this poem explores the nature of a relationship in this type of environment.

Video A6.1

Image A6.1

2 Looking at language: whole class work

- Listen to Audio A6, read the poem to the class, or ask selected students to read lines out loud.
- Ask them if they notice anything unusual about the use or spelling of words (e.g. 'tho', 'we', 'leh' and 'de'). How were they pronounced in the reading?
- Why has the author used these spellings? Students may suggest that it is to convey a Caribbean accent. What effect does this Caribbean accent have on students' impression of the atmosphere and tone within the poem?

Access

Give students extra support in understanding the meaning of words that are not Standard English and/ or those which suggest a Caribbean dialect.

3 Exploring imagery: pair work

- Display the poem at the front of the class using the ActiveTeach.
- Re-read the first two lines of the poem and brainstorm meanings of the word 'devour'. Guide students towards the idea of consuming completely, greedily, etc., and that the word is normally connected with food. It can create quite a destructive image.
- Hand out Worksheet A6.1 and ask students, working in pairs, to complete it. They identify an image connected with eating and/or taste and think about why it might have been used.

Worksheet A6.1

- Ask pairs to feed back to the class. Establish that the fruit in the second stanza is used as a metaphor for the poet herself ('I'm all...'). How does this relate to the first stanza? What do the images connected with taste or food suggest about the couple's relationship?

4 Exploring meaning: group work

- Ask groups to re-read the poem from line 15 onwards and discuss the images of 'hug up', 'brace-up' and 'sweet one another up' as well as 'break', 'break free' and finally 'person/ality'. What do these phrases suggest about the relationship between the couple? Are they together or separate all the time or only sometimes? Ask them to write down two PEEE points about the relationship.
- Ask groups to feed back to the class. Discuss the ideas the poet is expressing about the role of an individual within a couple. Look at the ways in which the use of the punctuation in 'person/ality' helps to convey this. Do the ideas expressed about a relationship here mirror those of students' own experiences of relationships with people they love?

5 Looking at structure: individual work

- Display the poem on the ActiveTeach. Ask students to look at the beginning of the stanzas and see if they can identify a pattern ('even tho', 'Come', 'but then'). Ask how this structure helps the poem's message.
- Using the highlighting tool, highlight line 1 ('Man I love') in one colour and line 2 ('but won't let you devour') in a different colour. Explain that this first two-line stanza suggests two contrasting feelings – the first the idea of love and togetherness, the second the fact that this closeness shouldn't be destructive and the individuals need to maintain their own identities. Work through the rest of the poem, asking students to come up and highlight each stanza in one of these two colours, depending on whether it links back to line 1 or 2. Invite others to comment.
- Ask students to suggest why the poet has decided to break with the pattern of four-line stanzas at the end of the poem. Why might there be a break after line 21 and before line 22?

Extend

Ask students to think about the rhythm of the poem. Is there a fixed rhythm? How might the rhythm (or lack of it) help with our understanding of the poet's message about relationships?

6 Individual writing

Ask students to write a PEEE paragraph exploring how the poet uses language, form and punctuation to convey the nature of the relationship.

7 Peer assessment

- Ask students to swap their answers to the question above with a partner. Invite the students to mark each other's work. Students should assess how well their partner's responses:
  - show an understanding of the use of language, form and punctuation;
  - demonstrate the ability to make relevant connections between the techniques used and the presentation of the nature of the relationship;
  - use the 'PEEE' technique to show the link between form and point of view.

- They should then award up to five marks, deciding which of the five bands the work falls into. You may want to refer them to Resource A17.2 (English Literature Higher Tier mark scheme), A17.3 (English Literature Foundation Tier mark scheme) or A17.4 (English mark scheme).
- Ask students to comment on how the answer could have been improved, looking at the importance of supporting points with good examples.

8 Plenary

- Recap and ensure that students have:
  - understood the ways Nichols has used language and structure to convey the nature of her relationship;
  - connected with the different attitudes presented.
- Ask students to update their grid/list of sub-groups within the collection, discussing why they should put this poem in a particular group.
- Discuss how successfully the poet conveys the balance of being close and yet still needing freedom within a relationship.
- For English Literature, find another poem in Relationships that explores a relationship between a woman and a man through one (or more) strong personal voice. Ask students to compare the impact that the relationship has on them as readers.

9 Further work

Ask students to find one other poem within the collection that explores the sensations and feelings connected to being in a relationship. They should write down three ways in which the two poems are similar, and three ways in which they are different, thinking about use of imagery and language as well as topic and theme.

Suggested answers

Access

tho – though; leh we – let us; de – the; I be – I will be; hug up – cuddle; brace-up – embrace; sweet one another up – whisper sweet nothings.

Relationships

Lesson A7
Kissing
Fleur Adcock

Learning objective
To understand how Adcock uses structure and the concept of kissing to explore the nature of relationships at different ages.

Resources
• Edexcel GCSE Poetry Anthology, page 7
• Audio A7
• Glossary A7
• Worksheet A7.1
• Worksheet A7.2
• Image A7.1
• Image A7.2

1 Before reading: whole class work

• Display Images A7.1 and A7.2 of different couples kissing in public and discuss students' reactions to them. Draw out whether they have any age or gender bias in their opinions about relationships at different ages.

Image A7.1

Image A7.2

2 Before reading: pair work

• Hand out Worksheet A7.1. Ask students to think about the meaning of the poem and then decide where punctuation and capital letters are needed.

Worksheet A7.1

Access

Help students to understand the meaning of long sentences by breaking them down and clarifying any relative clauses. You could do this by asking them to re-read selected sections again with a partner and exchanging ideas on meaning.

3 First reading: whole class work

• Listen to Audio A7 or read the poem to the class. Ask students to follow it in their anthologies, noting where Adcock places punctuation, and thinking about the pauses and emphasis this creates.

• Draw attention to the long first sentence, followed by four much shorter sentences. What effect does this have? Point out the slightly awkward grammatical construction on line 5 and discuss the possible effects of this. Awkward convoluted sentences might suggest the awkwardness of kissing in public, or of other people witnessing public displays of affection. Do any particular lines stand out? Why?

4 Looking at structure: group work

• In groups, students should discuss why the poet has split the poem into two stanzas. What does each of the stanzas explore?

• Draw students' attention to the final sentences in each stanza. How do they compare? What is the poet saying about the two different age groups?

• Ask groups to feed back to the class and discuss their thoughts.

5 Exploring ideas: pair work

• Hand out Worksheet A7.2. Model exploring the first phrase, 'a nest of some kind', discussing with students how the image of a nest might imply a wish for privacy or a home.

Worksheet A7.2

• Take feedback and discuss students' responses to these phrases, sharing with them the ideas in the Suggested answers section as appropriate.

Extend

Ask students to explore the implications of the phrase 'Seeing's not everything' in line 11. How does this relate to the message that Adcock is trying to convey about relationships at different ages?

6 Independent writing

Ask students to write a PEEE paragraph in response to the following question: How does the poet use the idea of kissing to explore the nature of relationships at different ages?

7 Peer assessment

- Ask students to share their responses, comparing their own views with those of the poet. They should then swap their answers to the question above with a partner. Invite the students to mark each other's work. Students should assess how well their partner's responses:
  - show an understanding of the use of kissing to communicate thoughts and feelings about relationships;
  - use the 'PEEE' technique to show the link between form and point of view effectively;
  - demonstrate the ability to make relevant connections between the techniques used and the presentation of the nature of relationships at different ages.
- They should award up to five marks, deciding which of the five bands the work falls into. You may want to refer them to Resource A17.2 (English Literature Higher Tier mark scheme), A17.3 (English Literature Foundation Tier mark scheme) or A17.4 (English mark scheme).
- Finally, they should comment on how the answer could have been improved, looking at the importance of supporting points with good examples.

8 Plenary

- Recap and ensure that students have:
  - understood the ways Adcock has used structure to convey relationships at different stages of life;
  - responded to the language and emotions of the poem.
- Discuss how successfully the poet explores the ways the couples of differing ages react and behave.
- In full class, discuss how we think of the way that the passage of time influences our view of life and the way we live. In two columns, list on the board some attitudes and views that we think of as characteristic of young people and older people.
- For English Literature, look at other poems in Collection A that consider the relationship between Love and Time. Discuss how this link might be expressed in students' chart, grid or list.

9 Further work

Students should select another poem from the collection, or a poem of their choice from another source, which also explores relationships at different ages. They should write three points about how the two poems are similar, either in content or the way in which they are written, and three points about how they are different.

Relationships

Lesson A8
One Flesh
Elizabeth Jennings

Learning objective

To explore how Jennings uses structure and linguistic features to describe the autumn years of a relationship.

Resources
- Edexcel GCSE Poetry Anthology, page 8
- Audio A8
- Glossary A8
- Worksheet A8.1
- Worksheet A8.2
- Interactive A8

1 Before reading: Whole class work

- As a class, complete Interactive A8, which gets students to match up different phrases to create the lines of the first stanza of the poem. Ensure students justify their decisions and focus on how they can use context and rhyme pattern to determine which sections go together.

Interactive A8

2 First reading: whole class work

- Listen to Audio A8 or read the poem to the class, asking students to follow it in their anthologies.
- Ask them to describe their initial reactions to the poem.
- Ask them to compare their version of the first stanza created in Interactive A8 to the original and consider whether all the lines of the poem split clearly into two parts.

3 Exploring language: pair work

- Divide students into pairs and ask them to identify a line containing two contrasting images. Ask each pair to analyse the two separate images within their line. Model an answer using line 7: 'Tossed up like flotsam' is an image of abandonment and 'passion left far behind' expresses the powerful emotion that was previously felt. Another example is line 13, which conveys the idea that they are unusual in their distance and unusual in their proximity; the repetition of 'strangely' emphasises the idea of strangers; the whole line implies awkwardness in the relationship, emphasised by the use of the comma.
- Take feedback from the class. Focus discussion on the theme of separation and the passing of time within the relationship. Note how this theme is demonstrated by Adcock's use of separate images within one line.

Access

Help students to find words in the poem that suggest separation or lack of feeling.

Then guide them to look at words which suggest togetherness, warmth and feeling.

Ask them to think about how these words are used, guiding them towards the fact that words such as 'passion' or 'feeling' are often paired with 'former' or 'little'. You might want to draw their attention to positioning of words and also look at contrasting words such as 'fire' and 'cold' in line 18. How does the poet's use of vocabulary help with the tone and mood of the poem?

Extend

Ask students to identify the rhyme scheme in the poem. Why do they think the poet has used this rhyme scheme? How does it contribute to the tone and mood of the poem? They might decide that it helps to lend emphasis to some lines (e.g. the last two lines of both the first and second stanzas) or particular words (e.g. particularly in the last stanza where 'hold', 'old' and 'cold' all rhyme and stand out for a reader).

4 Exploring ideas: pair work

- Hand out Worksheet A8.1 and ask students, working in pairs, to decide what is implied by each of the similes and metaphors and why they think they are effective. (Refer to Glossary A1 to revise definitions of similes and metaphors if necessary.)

Worksheet A8.1

- Take feedback from the pairs. What did students agree/disagree on?

5 Exploring ideas: group work

- Display Worksheet A8.2. Ask students to work in groups to discuss the statements and decide whether they agree or disagree with each one. Ask them to write down reasons for their decisions and be prepared to feed these back to the class.

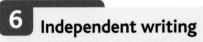

Worksheet A8.2

- Take feedback, encouraging students to comment on what this poem says about relationships.
- Ask students how they respond to the poem and the ideas it contains. What effect does it have on them as a reader?

6 Independent writing

Ask students to write a PEEE paragraph exploring how Jennings uses structure and linguistic features to explore the late years of a relationship.

7 Peer assessment

- Ask students to swap their answers to the question above with a partner.
- Invite the students to mark each other's work. Students should assess how well their partner's responses:
  - show an understanding of the use of structure and linguistic features;
  - use the 'PEEE' technique to show the link between form and point of view;
  - demonstrate the ability to make relevant connections between the techniques used and the presentation of the late years of a relationship.
- They should then award up to five marks, deciding which of the five bands the work falls into. You may want to refer them to Resource A17.2 (English Literature Higher Tier mark scheme), A17.3 (English Literature Foundation Tier mark scheme) or A17.4 (English mark scheme).
- Finally they should comment on how the answer could have been improved, looking at the importance of supporting points with good examples.

8 Plenary

- Recap and ensure that students have:
  - understood the ways in which Jennings has used structure and linguistic features to discuss the 'autumn years' of a relationship;
  - responded to the images created.
- Discuss how successfully the poet conveys what has happened between the couple.
- Ask students to think about the effect of describing the relationship through the eyes of the daughter.
- For English Literature, find another poem in Collection A that has striking images of contrast, and ask students to compare the use of this device in the two poems, making close reference to the language of the poems.

9 Further work

Ask students to explain why the poem is called 'One Flesh'. Students should support their answers with references to the poem.

Relationships

Lesson A9
Song for Last Year's Wife *Brian Patten*

Learning objective
To evaluate how Patten uses language, viewpoint and comparison to convey a sense of loss.

Resources
- Edexcel GCSE Poetry Anthology, page 9
- Audio A9
- Glossary A9
- Worksheet A9.1
- Worksheet A9.2
- Resource A9.1
- Image A9.1
- Image A9.2

1 Before reading: whole class work

Display Resource A9.1, explaining that it shows the first one and a half lines of the poem. Ask students to suggest what they think the poem is about. They may suggest death, divorce, a child leaving home, the end of a relationship, etc.

> **Alice, this is my first winter of waking without you**
>
> Resource A9.1

2 First reading: pair work

- Distribute Worksheet A9.1. Ask students to decide on words that could be used to fill the gaps based on their understanding of the context.
- Take feedback, asking students to explain the reasons for their choices.

Worksheet A9.1

Access

Distribute Worksheet A9.2. Students should use the word bank to select the missing words. Ask them to think about how these words contribute to their understanding of the poem.

Worksheet A9.2

3 First reading: whole class work

- Listen to Audio A9, or read the poem to the class, asking students to compare it with their own versions.
- Recap on the suggestions in the first activity on what the poem might be about. How do the words used help their understanding of meaning?
- Draw attention to the last two lines, which reveal that the poem is about loss of the persona's wife, and ask students what in the poem adds to the idea of loss. Examples might include the direct address and the use of hypothetical questions.

4 Exploring language and viewpoint: pair work

- Working in pairs, ask students to find words in the poem that suggest the persona's feelings.
- Take feedback and draw attention to the monologue style, which provides just one point of view.
- Ask pairs to find all the references to winter and determine how these relate to the persona's feelings.
- Take feedback from the pairs, ensuring that students understand the connection between winter and loss. Do they think that this pairing is effective? Why or why not?

5 Exploring ideas: independent work

- Display Images A9.1 and A9.2, which show a winter landscape and a torn wedding photo.

Image A9.1

Image A9.2

- Ask students to rewrite the poem in the third person, as if it were the opening to a novel. They should use their own ideas and any others that the images stimulate. Remind them to include the fact that the poem is being written on an anniversary.

6 Peer assessment

- Ask students to swap stories with a partner and write one comment about something that has been done well and another about something they think could be improved. They should assess how well their partner's responses:
  - show an understanding of images used by the poet
  - demonstrate the ability to make relevant; connections between the techniques used and the presentation of the theme.
- Ask them to award up to five marks, deciding which of the five bands the work falls into. You may want to refer them to Resource A17.2 (English Literature Higher Tier mark scheme), A17.3 (English Literature Foundation Tier mark scheme) or A17.4 (English mark scheme).
- Finally, they should comment on how the answer could have been improved, looking at the importance of supporting points with good examples.

Extend

Ask students to write two paragraphs in response to the following question: How does Patten use language, viewpoint, and comparison to convey a sense of loss? What does the poem tell us about relationships?

7 Exploring language: pair work

- Discuss the sympathetic view of the persona that students have probably developed so far.
- Ask the students, working in pairs, to find phrases that suggest the persona is a less sympathetic character, such as the title, 'Song for Last Year's Wife', and to discuss the extent to which this alters their thoughts about the poem.
- Take feedback from the pairs. Have these lines changed students' attitudes towards the persona?

8 Plenary

- Recap and ensure that students have:
  - understood the ways in which Patten has used language, viewpoint and comparison to convey a sense of loss;
  - responded to the strong personal voice and to the contrasts of warmth and cold.
- Discuss how far the poem appeals to the senses in order to evoke the feelings of loss experienced by the speaker.
- For English Literature, ask students to update their chart, grid or list, deciding which category to put this poem into; compare it with one other poem from Collection A which explores a relationship that changes or ends.

9 Further work

Ask students to continue writing the next page of their 'novel', either in prose or poetry form, still on the day of the anniversary. Encourage them to show that they empathise with the persona and the situation described in the poem, and to consider how the persona might mark the occasion.

Suggested answers

4 Exploring language and viewpoint

winter, without, hard, empty, isolation, ghost, loss.

7 Exploring language

song for last year's wife; wake with another mouth feeding from me; love had not the right to walk out of me; I send out my spies; as when they knew you first.

Relationships

Lesson A10
My Last Duchess
Robert Browning

Learning objective
To explore how Browning uses language and structure to portray the Duke's character, in relation to the Duchess.

Resources
- Edexcel GCSE Poetry Anthology, pages 10–11
- Audio A10
- Glossary A10
- Worksheet A10.1
- Worksheet A10.2
- Image A10.1
- Image A10.2

1 Before reading: whole class work

- Display Image A10.1.
Explain to students
that this poem is based
loosely on historical
events. The persona
is Alfonso II, Duke of
Ferrara, in the sixteenth
century. He married
Lucrezia de Medici
when she was 14 years
old. She died three
years later, perhaps as a result of poisoning. In this
poem the Duke describes a painting of his dead
wife to a messenger from the nobleman who is
arranging his second marriage.

Image A10.1

2 First reading: whole class work

- Explain to students that this poem is a dramatic
monologue spoken by the Duke. Check their
understanding of 'monologue' (see Glossary A1).
- Listen to Audio A10 or read the poem to the class,
asking students to follow it in their anthologies.
- Ask them to describe their impressions of the tone
of the poem.

3 Understanding language: group work

- Give each group a section of the poem to rewrite
in modern English. Refer them to Glossary A10
as necessary.
- Ask groups to read out their modern versions to
the rest of the class in sequence.
- Ask each group to write a summary of the events
in the poem.
- Take feedback and consolidate their understanding
of the narrative of the poem.

Access

Use Worksheet A10.1 to help
students understand some
of the archaic language in
the poem by asking them to
match phrases to modern
versions.

Worksheet A10.1

4 Exploring ideas: whole class work

- Display Image A10.2 of
the Duke of Ferrara.
- Ask students to describe
their initial impressions
of the Duke's character
from reading the poem
and begin to compile
a class list of ideas.
- Annotate the poem
using the annotation
tool on the ActiveTeach to keep track of aspects
of the poem that portray the Duke's character.

Image A10.2

5 Exploring ideas: pair work

- Hand out Worksheet A10.2
and ask students working in
pairs to discuss the Duke's
relationship with the Duchess.
What do they think it was like
being married to him? What
might he have thought when
he married her? Does it sound
like a good relationship or
not? Students should be able
to justify their ideas with details from the poem.
- Ask pairs to discuss the role of the silent person in
the poem (the listener). What would it be like to be
in that position, listening to this monologue?

Worksheet A10.2

6 Exploring structure: pair work

- Ask students to look at the structure of the poem. What do they notice?
- Point out that there are three main structural techniques used in this poem: rhyming couplets, iambic pentameter and enjambement. Explain these techniques and make sure that students understand them.
- Ask students, working in pairs, to look at the techniques and write a sentence commenting on the effect of each one. Take feedback from pairs.
- Working in pairs again, ask them to examine sentence lengths. What do they notice?
- Take feedback. Explain that the different lengths and structures build tension in the Duke's diatribe until the climax in lines 46–47.

Extend

Ask students to examine how the poet uses parentheses (i.e. brackets or paired dashes) to convey subtle implications about the persona.

7 Independent writing

Ask students to write a PEEE paragraph in response to the following question: How does Browning use language and structure to portray the Duke's personality, as seen in his relationship to the Duchess?

8 Peer assessment

- Ask students to swap their answers to the question above with a partner. Invite the students to mark each other's work. Students should assess how well their partner's responses:
  - show an understanding of the use of language and structure;
  - demonstrate the ability to make relevant connections between the techniques used and the presentation of the character of the Duke.
- Students should award up to five marks, deciding which of the five bands the work falls into. You may want to refer them to Resource A17.2 (English Literature Higher Tier mark scheme), A17.3 (English Literature Foundation Tier mark scheme) or A17.4 (English mark scheme).
- They should then comment on how the answer could have been improved, looking at the importance of supporting points with good examples.

9 Plenary

- Recap and ensure that students have:
  - understood the ways how Browning has used language and structure to portray the Duke's character;
  - seen the importance of the dramatic monologue form.
- Discuss in small groups the qualities of the Duchess, compared with those of the Duke. Comment on how the Duke gradually reveals more and more about her as the poem progresses.
- For English Literature, find another poem in Collection A with a strong narrative voice, and ask students to compare the use of story-telling in the two poems.

10 Further work

Ask students to write the Duchess's account, in diary form, of her last few days before she died. They should pay attention to evidence from the poem in writing this account, but remind them that they may want to communicate a different impression of the Duchess from the one communicated by the persona of the Duke.

Suggested answers

6 Exploring structure

Rhyming couplets: *rigidity of Duke's personality, might emphasise the concept of husband and wife partnership.*

Iambic pentameter: *rhythm, rigidity of Duke's personality.*

Enjambement: *draws attention away from the rhyme and towards the speaker's voice.*

Relationships

Lesson A11
Pity me not because the light of day *Edna St. Vincent Millay*

Learning objective
To explore how Edna St. Vincent Millay uses language and structure to show the effects of time and age on love in a relationship.

Resources
• Edexcel GCSE Poetry Anthology, page 12
• Audio A11
• Glossary A11
• Worksheet A11.1
• Image A11.1
• Image A11.2
• Image A11.3
• Image A11.4

1 Before reading: whole class work

• Ask students to think of a relationship that has changed over time – it could be with a friend or relative. How do they feel about this relationship?

• Explain that this is a poem about the loss of love and the breaking down of a relationship.

2 First reading: pair work

• Listen to Audio A11, or read the poem to the class, asking students to follow it in their anthologies.

• Allocate each pair of students one of the following: lines 1–2; lines 3–4; line 5 or line 6. Ask them to read the whole poem again, but to concentrate on their allocated line(s). They should think about the imagery used in their section, discuss what it means and why the poet might have used it.

• Pairs should feed back their ideas for each section to the class. Establish that much of the imagery is to do with nature.

• Display Images A11.1–A11.4, which match up to each of the sections. Work towards the idea that each of these images signifies the end of something, but is also part of a cycle.

Image A11.1

Image A11.2

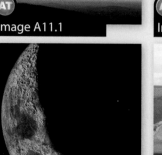
Image A11.3

Image A11.4

• Draw their attention to lines 7 and 8 where the poet draws a parallel between the decrease of love in her relationship and these images of nature.

3 Close reading: group work

• Ask students, working in groups, to look at the beginning of lines 1–8 and identify patterns in the structure of this part of the poem. They should be able to find 'Pity me not…'

• Ask students to feed back to the class. What effect does the repetition of this phrase have? How do they think the persona feels?

• Ask students to look at lines 9–12 and think about why the poet doesn't want pity. Explain that these lines are a definition of what the poet sees as love. Ask them to discuss these lines, identify what type of imagery is used and what the poet's message is.

• Ask students to feed back to the class. Discuss the aspects of love created by these images. Ideas might include that love is uncertain and shifting, and that it can be destructive. What might this suggest about the poet's state of mind? Draw attention to the start of line 9: 'This have I known always…'

4 Looking at structure and rhyme: individual work

• Ask students to identify the rhyme pattern in the poem. What type of poem is it? (It is a sonnet.)

• Recap the features of sonnets (refer to Glossary A1 as necessary).

• Draw attention to the last two lines (the rhyming couplet) and the use of 'Pity me', which is now in the affirmative rather than the negative.

• Ensure that students understand the meaning of these two lines. What is their tone? What do these lines tell us about the poet's feelings? How do her feelings differ from her knowledge and experience of love as expressed in the preceding four lines? How do the adjectives help to convey this?

Access

Ask students to draw illustrations of the images in lines 9–12 and write a sentence to explain what the poet is trying to communicate about love by these images.

5 Exploring language: pair work

- Working in pairs, ask students to read the sonnet again and look for examples of alliteration and onomatopoeia.
- Hand out Worksheet A11.1. Students should identify examples of these literary devices and comment on how they contribute to the meaning of the poem.
- Take feedback and discuss the effects that these techniques have on the reader.

Worksheet A11.1

Extend

Students should think about why the author has used the sonnet form here. How does it help the poet to explore the loss of love and what effect does this have on the reader?

6 Independent writing

Ask students to write two paragraphs in response to the following question: Explain how the poet uses language and imagery to present her ideas about love in a relationship. Emphasise that they should refer to the last two lines in their answer.

7 Peer assessment

- Ask students to swap their answers to the question above with a partner. Invite the students to mark each other's work. Students should assess how well their partner's responses:
  - show an understanding of the use of word choice and imagery;
  - demonstrate the ability to make relevant connections between the techniques used and the presentation of the theme of a relationship over time.
- They should then award up to five marks, deciding which of the five bands the work falls into. You may want to refer them to Resource A17.2 (English Literature Higher Tier mark scheme), A17.3 (English Literature Foundation Tier mark scheme) or A17.4 (English mark scheme).
- Finally, they should comment on how the answer could have been improved, looking at the importance of supporting points with good examples.

8 Plenary

- Recap and ensure that students have:
  - understood the ways in which Millay has used language and the sonnet form to show how relationships change with time and age;
  - responded to the natural imagery used, discussing the most powerful and effective images.
- Discuss how successfully the poet conveys what has happened between the couple.
- Update the 'connections' chart, grid or list, linking this poem with others with which the students can see close connections in theme or treatment.
- For English Literature, find another poem in Collection A that uses natural imagery, and ask students to compare the effect of this imagery in the two poems, analysing the examples chosen and making brief, appropriate references to the texts.

9 Further work

Ask students to imagine that they are the other person mentioned in this sonnet and to write a paragraph explaining their point of view about the relationship. They should draw on evidence from the poem.

Relationships

Lesson A12
The Habit of Light

Gillian Clarke

Learning objective
To explore how Clarke uses language and imagery to create a Clarke character.

Resources
• Edexcel GCSE Poetry Anthology, page 13
• Audio A12
• Glossary A12
• Worksheet A12.1
• Worksheet A12.2

1 Before reading: whole class work

Write the word 'light' on the board and brainstorm words and ideas connected with this concept. Ideas might include daytime, sunshine, happiness, etc.

2 First reading: whole class work

• Listen to Audio A12 or read the poem to the class. Ask students to focus on the impression created by the poem as they listen. Refer them to Glossary A12 as necessary.
• Ask students to share their initial thoughts about the poem. Draw out any links to the discussion about light in the starter activity.

Access

Hand out Worksheet A12.1 and ask students to decide which of the words they would use to describe the impression created by the poem. Encourage them to justify their choices.

Worksheet A12.1

3 Exploring ideas: whole class work

• Ask students to find words in the poem that suggest light, annotating these using the annotation tool on the ActiveTeach.
• Discuss the strength of these images, and draw out that they create a mysterious and beautiful atmosphere, e.g. 'cloud-lit' and the association of light with beeswax.

4 Exploring character: pair work

• Ask pairs to underline all the words and phrases in the poem that they feel create a sense of place.
• Next, have students annotate these words and phrases with what they convey about the character in the poem.
• Ask students to circle all words or phrases that specifically describe the character (e.g. bright red hair).
• Hand out Worksheet A12.2, which provides various phrases from the poem. Explain that students should discuss the phrases and decide what each one tells them about the character in the poem.
• Compare the two activities about character. Ask students why we know more about the character than is specifically described. Help students understand that the character is built through description of a sense of place.

Worksheet A12.2

Extend

Ask students to write a PEEE paragraph exploring how the poet has created a relationship between the character and her home (sense of place). Students should support their answer with evidence from the poem.

5 Exploring theme: individual work

- Have students refer back to their references of light from Activity 3 and complete the following sentence: 'The references to light in the poem are significant because…'
- Take feedback from the students, having them read their answers to the class to form a discussion on light.
- Students should understand that the light imagery adds to the sense of place and description of character. It may be useful to discuss how the light reflects the domestic routine of the character.

6 Independent writing

Give students the two definitions of the word 'habit': customary behaviour and attire/dress. Ask them to write a PEEE paragraph considering how the poet has interpreted this word in the poem. Emphasise that they should support their answer with evidence from the poem.

7 Peer assessment

- Ask students to swap their answers to the question above with a partner. Invite the students to mark each other's work. Students should assess how well their partner's responses:
  - show an understanding of the use of the concept of 'habit';
  - use the 'PEEE' technique to show the link between form and point of view;
  - demonstrate the ability to make relevant connections between the techniques used and the presentation of the importance of habit and customary practices.
- They should then award up to five marks, deciding which of the five bands the work falls into. You may want to refer them to Resource A17.2 (English Literature Higher Tier mark scheme), A17.3 (English Literature Foundation Tier mark scheme) or A17.4 (English mark scheme).
- Students should finally comment on how the answer could have been improved, looking at the importance of supporting points with good examples.

8 Plenary

- Recap and ensure that students have:
  - understood the ways in which Clarke has used language and imagery to create a vivid character;
  - grasped the connection between the character and her home, considering how the description of the home sheds light on the person who lives there;
  - responded to the sense of warmth and light and to the feeling of pride and love of home created in the poem.
- For English Literature, find another poem in Collection A that creates a detailed character. Explore the language used in both and give brief quotations to support your points.

9 Further work

Explore the possible relationship between the poet and the character in the poem. What clues are provided about who the character might be?

Suggested answers

3 Exploring ideas
lamps, brass, silver, glass, dawn, glimpse, cloud-lit, flickered, bright, palest.

4 Exploring character
lamps in corners, polished furniture, glimpse of the… sea, oak floors, kitchen, saucepans, kettle, Aga, smells of supper, old windows, blackbird, details of fruit and vegetable garden.

Relationships

Lesson A13
Nettles
Vernon Scannell

Learning objective
To explore how Scannell uses imagery and metaphor to convey his feelings about parenthood.

Resources
• Edexcel GCSE Poetry Anthology, page 14
• Audio A13
• Glossary A13
• Worksheet A13.1
• Resource A13.1

1 Before reading: whole class work

• Display the last line of the poem using Resource A13.1.

My son would often feel sharp wounds again

AT
Resource A13.1

• Ask students to speculate about what might have happened to the son. Prompt them by asking: How old is the son? What has 'wounded' him? How badly? What are the persona's feelings?

2 First reading: whole class work

• Listen to Audio A13 or read the poem to the class, asking students to follow it in their anthologies.

• Ask students to describe their first impressions of the poem. How does it compare with what they thought it might be about based on the last line? Are they surprised? What did they notice most about the poem? Did they get a good picture of what the poet is describing?

3 Close reading: independent work

• Distribute Worksheet A13.1. Ask students to draw images to tell the narrative of the poem.

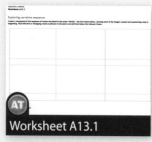

AT
Worksheet A13.1

• Students should then find words or phrases from the poem that they found particularly effective or intriguing and add them to the appropriate storyboard frames to summarise what is happening.

• Ask them to swap storyboards with a partner and discuss whether they have represented the sequence of the narrative effectively.

• Take feedback from the class. Which words or phrases did students find effective? Explain that the poet uses imagery and metaphor to 'draw' his storyboard within the poem.

4 Identifying metaphors: pair work

• Ask students, working in pairs, to find as many metaphors as possible in the poem.

• Ask pairs to look at the list of metaphors in the poem and determine what the link is between the words. Each pair should pick a word or two that suggests or explains the link between the metaphors.

• Take feedback from the pairs. What links did they find? Make sure that students understand that the metaphors are linked with military/war/painful images.

• Ask pairs to discuss, and be prepared to report back on, what this link tells the reader about the persona's feelings towards the nettles.

• Take feedback from the pairs. What did most pairs think the father felt about the nettles? What does this say about the father's relationship with his son?

Access

Recap on metaphor. Support students in finding the metaphors in the poem, perhaps by giving them line references: 2, 3, 11, 13, 13, 15, 16. Help them to appreciate how a word, such as 'spears', is used to represent something else, like 'nettles', and the overall impact of such imagery on the poem.

5 Exploring relationships: group work

• Ask students, working in groups, to identify and discuss the different aspects of fatherhood depicted in the poem and decide which is the most prominent. They should be prepared to justify their answers.

• Take feedback from the whole class. What aspects of the poem led groups to their conclusions?

• Look at the last three lines of the poem and point out the shift that occurs here. Ask students what they think the poet is saying and how this section represents the persona's feelings.

Extend

Ask students to write an answer to the following question: How does the poet express his views about his relationship with his son in this poem? Are you able to sympathise with him? Why?

6 Independent writing

Ask students to write a PEEE paragraph explaining why Scannell has chosen to use military images to explore ideas about parenthood in this poem.

7 Peer assessment

- Ask students to swap their answers to the question above with a partner. Invite the students to mark each other's work. Students should assess how well their partner's responses:
  - show an understanding of the use of military imagery;
  - use the 'PEEE' technique to show the link between form and point of view;
  - demonstrate the ability to make relevant connections between the techniques used and the exploration of parenthood.
- They should then award up to five marks, deciding which of the five bands the work falls into. You may want to refer them to Resource A17.2 (English Literature Higher Tier mark scheme), A17.3 (English Literature Foundation Tier mark scheme) or A17.4 (English mark scheme).
- Finally, ask them to comment on how the answer could have been improved, looking at the importance of supporting points with good examples.

8 Plenary

- Recap and ensure that students have:
  - understood the ways Scannell has used imagery to convey his feelings about parenthood;
  - responded to the battle metaphors used to convey the savagery he perceives in their 'attack' on his son.
- Brainstorm ideas, using two columns, about when parents are showing necessary care to protect children and when they can become over-protective. How should children respond to what they see as over-protective behaviour (for example, severe restrictions on their movements)?
- For English Literature, find another poem in Collection A that shows anger, and explore how each poem conveys, through language devices, the strength of these feelings.

9 Further work

Ask students to explain what the 'sharp wounds' in line 16 might refer to. Ask them to use evidence from the rest of the poem to justify their answers.

Suggested answers

4 Identifying metaphors

Metaphors: *green spears, regiment of spite, fierce parade, funeral pyre, fallen dead, tall recruits, sharp wounds.*

Links: *military, soldiers, war, violence, pain/injury.*

6 Independent writing

Anger (fierce, dead, fury), protective (seeking comfort, tender, soothed; regular rhyme suggests a nursery rhyme sung to comfort a child), communication between father and son (language is reminiscent of young boys' 'soldier' games, monosyllabic words).

Learning objective
To understand how Hardi uses narrative structure to explore her relationship with her home country.

Resources
• Edexcel GCSE Poetry Anthology, page 15
• Audio A14
• Glossary A14
• Worksheet A14.1
• Image A14.1

Lesson A14
At the border, 1979
Choman Hardi

---

1 Before reading: whole class work

• Display Image A14.1. Explain poet Choman Hardi's background to students. She was born in Iraqi Kurdistan in 1974. Her family fled to Iran, but returned to Iraq after the amnesty in 1979, when she was five years old. This poem describes the poet and her family's returning to Iraq over the border.

Image A14.1

• Ask students how they think Hardi might have felt about returning to Iraq when she was only five years old.

2 First reading: whole class work

• Listen to Audio A14 or read the poem to the class, asking students to follow it in their anthologies.
• Take feedback from the students. Ask them if reading the poem led them to change their opinions about how Hardi might have felt.

3 Close reading: group work

• Ask students to re-read the poem closely and, in groups, develop a dramatisation of the events described, using dialogue from the poem.
• Ask groups to act out their drama (or present their work) to the class, focusing on demonstrating their understanding of the events described in the poem.

4 Exploring structure: whole class work

• Ask students to study the structure of the poem. What do they notice about it?
• Identify that this is a narrative poem and explain that narrative poems tell a story, often to prove a point.
• Explain that narrative poems sometimes incorporate speech or dialogue. Ask students to find examples of speech in the poem. What are the effects of these? Students may suggest they help make the narrative seem real and emphasise emotion.
• Ask students to think about why stanzas might be different lengths. They might decide this gives emphasis to particular lines.

5 Exploring language: pair work

• Ask students to work in pairs to highlight ten words or phrases from the poem that they feel are the most significant or important, annotating each with an explanation of its significance. (Refer them to Glossary A14 as necessary.)
• Have pairs feed back to the class, comparing and discussing choices.

Access

• Hand out Worksheet A14.1, which highlights 15 words and phrases in bold. Ask students to select the ten they feel are most significant.

Worksheet A14.1

• Identify the most popular choices and discuss why students think they are significant.
• Identify any other unusual choices and encourage students to justify their choices. Are there any other words in the poem which students felt were important or unusual? Why?

6 Exploring theme: pair work

- Ask students, working in pairs, to identify the different relationships explored in the poem. Encourage them to think not only of personal relationships but the relationship to land and home.
- Ask pairs to feed back to the class. Discuss which relationships seem most important to Hardi and why.
- Draw attention to the last line of the poem. Ask students what they think it means. Point out the change of tense that occurs here and discuss how it contributes to the overall meaning of the poem.

Extend

Ask students to write a paragraph about how the poem explores the relationship between the poet as an adult and as a five-year-old child.

7 Independent writing

Ask students to write a PEEE paragraph in response to the following question: How does the poet use narrative structure to express her views about her relationship to her homeland?

8 Peer assessment

- Ask students to swap their answers to the question above with a partner. Invite the students to mark each other's work. Students should assess how well their partner's responses:
  - show an understanding of the use of narrative structure;
  - use the 'PEEE' technique to show the link between form and point of view;
  - demonstrate the ability to make relevant connections between the techniques used and the poet's views on her homeland.
- Students should then award up to five marks, deciding which of the five bands the work falls into. You may want to refer them to Resource A17.2 (English Literature Higher Tier mark scheme), A17.3 (English Literature Foundation Tier mark scheme) or A17.4 (English mark scheme).
- Finally, ask them to comment on how the answer could have been improved, looking at the importance of supporting points with good examples.

9 Plenary

- Recap and ensure that students have:
  - understood the ways Hardi has used narrative structure to explore her relationship with her home country;
  - grasped the importance of the use of direct speech in the poem.
- Ask the students, in groups, to imagine themselves having to live in a different country for a long time. Invite them to draw up a list of the feelings they would have on return, and pool them. If time permits, compare these feelings with those they think adults would have in similar circumstances. Are these different? Why?
- For English Literature, ask students to update their chart, grid or list of connections, and discuss in pairs whether other poems connect relationships with descriptions of places. How do these poems compare in making this link?

10 Further work

Ask students to write a paragraph about the significance of the line 'It rained on both sides of the chain'. Emphasise that they should use details from the rest of the poem to justify their answer.

Relationships

Lesson A15
Lines to my Grand-fathers *Tony Harrison*

Learning objective
To explore the ways in which Harrison conveys thoughts and feelings about his grandfathers through the use of structure, form and imagery.

Resources
• Edexcel GCSE Poetry Anthology, pages 16–17
• Audio A15
• Glossary A15
• Worksheet A15.1
• Image A15.1

1 Before reading: independent work

• Ask students to draw their own family trees including grandparents, if possible.
• Select some students to share their family trees, and to talk about where their parents or grandparents are from and/or their jobs.
• Prompt discussion about memories, shared characteristics and how family ties and bonds show themselves. For example, do they share any particular traits with their relatives, either of personality or appearance? Do they have any vivid memories of shared experiences with relatives?

2 Before reading: pair work

• Display Image A15.1 and the first two lines of the poem using the ActiveTeach (you might want to zoom in on the first stanza).

Image A15.1
• Discuss the kind of place suggested by these lines. Draw out how the image is created, annotating the lines; for example, the simile 'as print' and the personification of the stone walls implied by the verb 'defy'.

3 First reading: whole class work

• Listen to Audio A15 or read the whole poem to the class, asking students to follow it in their anthologies.
• Ask students for feedback. What did they notice about the poem? What parts stood out? Draw their attention to the division of the poem into two parts – why do they think the poet has done this? (Remind them that everyone has two grandfathers.) What are their initial ideas on why the second stanza is presented differently from the rest of the poem?

Access

It may be necessary to help students with unfamiliar vocabulary and lead them through the poem, stanza by stanza. You could ask them to discuss each grandfather in turn as you do this.

4 Exploring ideas: group work

• Hand out Worksheet A15.1. Ask students to discuss the questions and write down answers in their groups.
• Take feedback from the whole class.

Worksheet A15.1

5 Exploring meaning: group work

• Working in groups, ask students to read the whole poem and discuss the significance of the first two lines. Why is the place important for the poet? How does he relate the nature of the place to his relationships with his grandfathers?
• Ask students to think about who Wilkinson might be, if Horner and Harrison are the persona's grandfathers. Ideas might include great uncle (brother of grandfather), neighbour, stepfather, etc. Why is he significant for the poet, in relation to his grandparents, and how is his job important?
• Ask groups to feed back to the rest of the class, comparing and contrasting their ideas.

6 Looking at imagery: pair work

- Ask students to work in pairs to highlight all the references to 'lines' in the poem and discuss their significance. Take feedback and explore how images of lines are used to represent connections within a family. What, for example, is the significance of the word 'connections' in line 31?

Extend

Encourage students to link the significance of the imagery connected with 'lines' and 'connections' within the poem to the form and structure. For example, the layout of the second stanza and the division of the poem into two parts with Roman numerals is significant. They could also trace the progression of the use of the imagery within the structure of the poem.

7 Independent writing

Ask students to write a PEEE paragraph in response to the following question: How does the poet use the imagery of 'lines' to present ideas about relationships between the various members of his family? Remind them to look at structure and form in the poem as well as language.

8 Peer assessment

- Ask students to swap their answers to the question above with a partner. Invite the students to mark each other's work. Students should assess how well their partner's responses:
  - show an understanding of the use of the imagery of 'lines';
  - use the 'PEEE' technique to show the link between form and point of view;
  - demonstrate the ability to make relevant connections between the techniques used and the presentation of the family relationships.
- Students should award up to five marks, deciding which of the five bands the work falls into. You may want to refer them to Resource A17.2 (English Literature Higher Tier mark scheme), A17.3 (English Literature Foundation Tier mark scheme) or A17.4 (English mark scheme).
- Finally, ask students to comment on how the answer could have been improved, looking at the importance of supporting points with good examples.

9 Plenary

- Recap and ensure that students have:
  - understood the ways in which Harrison has conveyed thoughts and feelings about his grandfathers through the use of structure, form and imagery;
  - responded to the description and the vivid pictures that are built up of Grandfather ('grampa') Horner and Grandfather Harrison.
- Discuss, as a group, how important family ties and bonds are for the writer, and pick out lines which show this clearly.
- For English Literature, find two other poems in Collection A that explore relationships by including reminiscences or memories, or comparing the past with the present. Think about how each uses a range of techniques and devices to convey the importance of time passing.

10 Further work

Ask students to write a character profile of both Horner and Harrison, including pictures if they wish. They should select lines from the poem to support their profile. How can we tell what the persona's feelings are towards his two grandfathers?

Suggested answers

2 Before reading
alliteration to emphasise 'straightness' and precision (parallel, straight); 'stony' and 'stone' to suggest a harsh, unrelenting landscape; 'defy' suggests a battle to survive; the simile 'parallel as print' may link with the author's profession and indicate his distance or may convey his feeling of familiarity with the landscape.

6 Looking at imagery
title, parallels, straight, straight and narrow, rail tracks, straight lines, direct and straight, connections.

Relationships

Lesson A16
04/01/07

Ian McMillan

Learning objective
To explore how McMillan uses imagery and structure to communicate emotions related to the loss of his mother.

Resources
• Edexcel GCSE Poetry Anthology, page 18
• Audio A16
• Glossary A16
• Video A16.1
• Video A16.2

1 Before reading: whole class work

• Ask students to write down examples of things they are aware of in their current surroundings using each of the five senses (sight, sound, touch, taste and smell).

• Discuss what is meant by 'heightened senses'. What circumstances might cause this? Examples could include the heightened smell and taste you experience if you are very hungry; or heightened hearing if you have a headache or are in the dark.

• Lead students towards the idea that extreme feelings or emotions can also heighten the senses, e.g. sadness, euphoria, anticipation, apprehension.

2 First reading: whole class work

• Listen to Audio A16 of McMillan reading the poem or watch Video A16.1. Ask students to listen for references to the senses.

• Ask students to read through the poem a second time on their own and write down a word or phrase describing how the poem makes them feel.

Video A16.1

• Take feedback from the class. What are their initial reactions to the poem? Does it provoke an emotional response?

3 Exploring imagery: independent work

• Ask students to highlight all the references to the senses in the poem.

• Take feedback. Why do students think there are so many references to the senses? What is the effect of this? This should lead, through discussion, to the idea that visual images are implied because of the night's darkness.

• Ask students to use a different colour to highlight visual images in the poem.

• Ask them to represent each of these images pictorially and then surround each one with words, suggesting the thoughts and feelings it creates.

• Take feedback. What images within the poem are most effective and meaningful to them?

4 Exploring interpretations: pair work

• Show students Video A16.2, where Ian McMillan talks about his reasons for writing the poem. You may want to pause the video and discuss ideas as you go. The poet talks about the theme and ideas behind the poem, the title, imagery, rhythm and the sonnet form from.

Video A16.2

• Bearing in mind the points raised in the video, ask students to work in pairs to prepare a reading of the poem to present to the class. Students should focus on presenting emotion.

• Take feedback from the class. Which pairs of students gave particularly effective readings of the poem? What made their readings effective? Have they picked up on any of the ideas highlighted by the video?

5 Exploring structure: whole class work

• Ask students to look at the structure and length of sentence in the poem. Point out, particularly, that lines 5–9 are one sentence while line 10 is two sentences. Ask students what effect this has and draw out the increase in tension in the poem.

• Ask students if they are in a state of suspense while waiting to hear what happened to the persona. Did his news come as a surprise? Why or why not?

6 Exploring the sonnet form: pair work

- Remind students of the definition of a traditional sonnet (see Glossary A1).
- Ask them to re-read the poem and, in pairs, discuss the extent to which the poem fits the sonnet form, giving reasons for their comments.
- Take feedback. You might want to re-watch part of Video A16.2, the video interview with Ian McMillan. What effect does the use of the sonnet form have on the poem? Why does the author use it?

Accesss

Ask students to work in pairs and identify any unusual language, imagery or ideas used in the poem. Why is 'new year' not capitalised? Why does he describe his face as 'torn'? What is the significance of the 'stream dried up'? What do these tell us about the poet and/or his feelings? You might want to replay parts of Video A16.1 to help them.

Extend

Ask students to explain why they think the poet has used a date as the title of the poem. You might want to re-watch Video A16.2 to help students.

7 Independent writing

Ask students to write two PEEE paragraphs in response to the following question: How does the poet use structure and imagery to convey his feelings about the news of his mother's death?

8 Peer assessment

- Ask students to swap their answers to the question above with a partner. Invite the students to mark each other's work. Students should assess how well their partner's responses:
  - show an understanding of the use of structure and imagery;
  - demonstrate the ability to make relevant connections between the techniques used and the expression of his feelings about his mother's death.
- They should then award up to five marks, deciding which of the five bands the work falls into. You

may want to refer them to Resource A17.2 (English Literature Higher Tier mark scheme), A17.3 (English Literature Foundation Tier mark scheme) or A17.4 (English mark scheme).
- Finally, ask students to comment on how the answer could have been improved, looking at the importance of supporting points with good examples.

9 Plenary

- Recap and ensure that students have:
  - understood the ways in which McMillan has used imagery and structure to explore emotions experienced on the loss of his mother;
  - engaged with the way time seems to stand still and the accentuation of the senses so that they are more acute.
- Discuss whether McMillan has successfully conveyed the moment and his emotions. Think of times when you have experienced such heightened feelings. You may invite students to close their eyes for a minute and concentrate on the sense of hearing.
- This poem can be seen to be very economical in its way of expressing ideas. For English Literature, find one other poem in Collection A which uses brief yet striking images and sounds. Compare how effects are achieved.

10 Further work

Ask students to explain the final couplet in their own words. What is the effect of these lines? Why do they think the author ended the poem in this way?

Suggested answers

3 Exploring imagery

Sound: *telephone, brother's voice, milk float, plane, light clicks on.*

Touch: *feel you there, feel the tears.*

Visual images: *night's dark glass; night's dark blue; my torn face; the stream dried up; the smashed glass clear.*

6 Exploring the sonnet form

- *The poem has 14 lines but is divided into stanzas, perhaps to reflect the separation of mother and son.*
- *The rhyme pattern is regular and fits the traditional form, apart from lines 5 and 7, which could suggest the speaker's disorientation.*
- *The rhyming couplet at the end fits the traditional definition as it comments on the rest of the poem.*

Relationships

Lesson A17
Understanding the assessment

Learning objective
- To reinforce how poems link with the theme of the collection.
- To find links and comparisons between the poems in the collection.
- To develop the skills needed to write about poems in the assessment.

Resources
- Worksheet A17.1
- Resource A17.1
- Resource A17.2
- Resource A17.3
- Resource A17.4
- ResultsPlus interactives

1 Starter activity: whole class work

- As a class, brainstorm all of the ideas about the theme 'relationships' that are explored in the poems in this collection. Record ideas using a spider diagram.
- Ask students to come up with at least one way each poem in the collection relates to the theme. You might want to focus on particular lines or imagery from poems and discuss different responses to the same poem and reasons for these.

Access

Ask students to choose one image that could be used to represent each of the poems in the collection. They could write a description of the image, draw it or find an image from a magazine or online. Each student should share their ideas with others, explaining the reasons why they have selected each image and how it links to the theme of the collection.

2 Practising writing in the exam or controlled assessment: pair work

- Divide the class into pairs. Ask pairs to draw a flow diagram showing the process of planning and writing a response to an assessed question. What will they do first in the exam or controlled assessment? What kind of things will they include in their response? How will they conclude their response?
- Hand out Resource A17.1 and ask students to compare the guidance on this sheet to their flow diagrams. Ask them to amend their diagrams accordingly and highlight areas on the Resource sheet which they feel are particularly important for them to remember.

Resource A17.1

3 Preparing for part a) of the English Literature question: whole class work

- Open a ResultsPlus interactive on the ActiveTeach which is relevant to Section B part a) of the Unit 2 English Literature exam, where students have to answer on a single poem. You

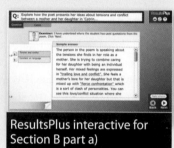
ResultsPlus interactive for Section B part a)

may want to ensure that it is the relevant tier (either Higher or Foundation) for your students. Sample questions from other collections can often be tailored to your own needs as necessary. ResultsPlus is a unique resource designed to help students achieve their best with sample questions, graded answers and examiner tips. A sample exam question is provided alongside a sample student answer. Each answer is annotated with examiner comments to make clear why the mark has been given, and showing where and how the essay could have been improved to gain a mark in a higher band. See page 5 for guidance on using these activities.
- Use the interactive with the class, encouraging and supporting them to explore what mark might have been given and/or how the sample answer could have been improved. You may also want to make use of the mark scheme provided in Resource A17.2 or Resource A17.3 to help students understand how their essays will be marked.

4 Comparing poems in English Literature: pair work

- Explain to students who will be taking the English Literature exam that they will be required to compare and contrast the poems they have studied. They will need to think about the different ways in which the poets have approached the theme of the collection, and the ways in which they have communicated their ideas.

- Hand out Worksheet A17.1. Tell students to work in pairs and think about links between the poems in terms of a) the topic explored and the poet's ideas, and b) the use of poetic devices (such as form, language and imagery) and their effects.

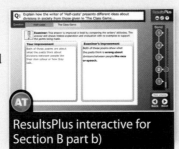
Worksheet A17.1

- Take feedback as a class, exploring differences of opinion and asking students to record their thoughts. You might want to compile class spider diagrams which can be used to support students' revision later on.

5 Preparing for part b) of the English Literature question: whole class work

- Open a ResultsPlus interactive on the ActiveTeach which is relevant to Section B part b) of the Unit 2 English Literature exam, where students will be required to compare two poems.

- Use the interactive with the class, encouraging and supporting them to explore what mark might have been given and/or how the sample answer could have been improved. You may also want to make use of the mark scheme provided in Resource A17.2 or Resource A17.3 to help students understand how their essays will be marked.

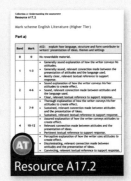
ResultsPlus interactive for Section B part b)

6 Preparing for the English controlled assessment: whole class work

- Open the ResultsPlus interactive for English controlled assessment. It will help students understand how a sample response can be improved.

- Use the interactive with the class, encouraging and supporting them to explore how the sample answer could have been improved. You may also want to make use of the mark scheme provided in Resource A17.4 to help students understand how their essays will be marked.

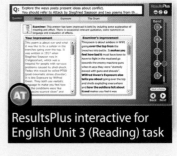
ResultsPlus interactive for English Unit 3 (Reading) task

7 Assessed question: individual work

- Ask students to think of an appropriate question for a particular poem, justifying how this would allow a student to demonstrate understanding and analysis of the poem(s).

- Ask students to swap essay questions with a partner and plan their essay in bullet points.

8 Peer assessment

Ask students to work in groups of four, share their plans with the group and assess each other's plans using the relevant mark scheme on Resource A17.2, Resource A17.3 or Resource A17.4.

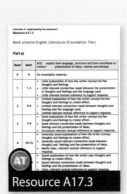
Resource A17.2

Resource A17.3   Resource A17.4

9 Further work

Ask students to plan and write an answer to one assessed question within the sample assessment material provided by Edexcel. You may like to direct students to specific questions to suit their ability.

Collection B

Clashes and Collisions

Lesson B1
Clashes and collisions introduction

Learning objectives
- To consolidate students' understanding of the features of poetry and a range of poetic devices.
- To think about what issues poems with a 'clashes and collisions' theme might explore.
- To understand the assessment objectives for this unit.

Resources
- Glossary B1
- Worksheet B1.1
- Worksheet B1.2
- Worksheet B1.3
- Interactive B1

1 Starter activity: whole class work

- Ask the class to give examples of some devices that can be used by poets to help convey meaning. If they can, ask them to provide an example of how these devices might be used, and explain how they can be effective.
- Complete the activity in Interactive B1 as a class. The icons to open the resources for this lesson can be found on the contents page for Collection B, on page 19 of the ActiveTeach.

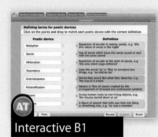
Interactive B1

  This activity involves matching the following poetic devices with the correct definitions: alliteration, assonance, metaphor, onomatopoeia, rhyme, rhythm, personification, simile. Ask individuals to come up to the board and make what they think is the correct connection, or ask the whole class to complete the activity against the clock.
- Hand out Glossary B1 for students to look at the correct definitions. Remind students that they can return to this glossary to refresh their memory at any point during their study of this collection of poems.

2 Identifying poetic devices: pair work

- Hand out Worksheet B1.1, which gives students examples of different poetic devices from the poems in the collection. They are asked to identify the poetic device used in a second set of quotations from the poems.
- Ask students to swap work with another pair and mark each other's work. Explain that if they make a mistake, each pair must explain to the other pair why they are wrong.

Worksheet B1.1

3 Looking at imagery: independent work

- Provide students with Worksheet B1.2, which gives a list of phrases from the collection that include particularly vivid imagery.

Worksheet B1.2

- Ask each student to choose one of these phrases and draw a picture of the item described. Tell them to think about how the words used help them to understand what the poet is trying to communicate and what the item should look like. Ask them to label the picture or write at least two sentences beneath it to explain why they have chosen to draw the image in this way, pinpointing particular words from the phrase.
- Ask for volunteers to share their pictures with the rest of the class. Ask students to explain why they have illustrated the phrase in this way and why they think the poet's use of imagery is effective.

4 Making inferences from shape: whole class work

- Hand out Worksheet B1.3, which indicates just the shapes of two poems: 'Conscientious Objector' and 'The Class Game'.

Worksheet B1.3

- Discuss how students know that these are poems and what they can infer from the shape of them.

- Ask pairs of students to devise a list of five to ten features that differentiate prose from poetry (this should be familiar to them from KS3 work). These might relate to line length, rhyme, rhythm, standard punctuation, grammar and stanzas.

- Ask pairs to feed back to the class and compare and contrast their ideas. Encourage them to think about how each of these aspects of poetry might help a poet convey meaning. For example, if a poem was written using the language of SMS, without any standard punctuation, what impression might this give of the poet or what message she/he is trying to communicate?

5 Exploring ideas: whole class work

- Introduce students to the theme of the collection of poems they are going to study. Ask students what they expect poems in a collection with this title will be about.

- Compile a class list of the types of issues students suggest these poems might explore. To prompt students you could ask them to consider books or films that they have enjoyed with a similar theme.

6 Plenary

Introduce students to the assessment objectives for this unit, according to which course they are following. Explain the skills that they will need to develop while studying these poems, in preparation for their assessment.

English

AO2:

i) Read and understand texts, selecting material appropriate to purpose, collating from different sources and making comparisons and cross-references as appropriate;

iii) Explain and evaluate how writers use linguistic, grammatical, structural and presentational features to achieve effects and engage and influence the reader.

English Literature

AO2: Explain how language, structure and form contribute to writers' presentation of ideas, themes and settings.

AO3: Make comparisons and explain links between texts, evaluating writers' different ways of expressing meaning and achieving effects.

7 Further work

Ask students to find a copy of a poem and annotate it, explaining what they liked or didn't like about it. Did they like the topic? Was there something particularly memorable about it? Why? They should think about language and vocabulary, any rhyme pattern, line length and form and imagery covered in the lesson. What effect did each of these have and why was it effective (or not) in their view? You might wish to guide them to use a PEEE structure. This terminology is used throughout the scheme of work for the collection and can help to guide students in their writing by ensuring they have made a Point, found Evidence for this, Explained the reasoning and finally Explored alternative interpretations and implications.

Suggested answers

Answers to worksheets are provided in the editable Word lesson plans on the ActiveTeach.

5 Exploring ideas

Suggested ideas for topics on the theme of 'clashes and collisions' might include racism, rich v. poor, war and relationships.

Lesson B2
Half-caste
John Agard

Learning objective
To understand how Agard uses linguistic and grammatical features to influence the reader and challenge perceptions of race.

Resources
- Edexcel GCSE Poetry Anthology, page 20
- Audio B2
- Glossary B2
- Worksheet B2.1
- Image B2.1
- Image B2.2
- Image B2.3
- Video B2.1
- Video B2.2

1 Before reading: whole class work

- Share your background (anything which helps create your identity, e.g. religion or birthplace, not just race). Emphasise positive things you get from this.
- Ask students to volunteer to share similar information and explain what they like about their background.
- Discuss how people's differing backgrounds can cause conflict. You might give an example of how you have experienced prejudice or discrimination.
- What might motivate name-calling? Explain that the poem's title, 'Half-caste' comes from the fact that people see the poet as being from two different backgrounds – one parent was from Portugal and another from Guyana, a Caribbean country.

2 First reading: whole class work

- Watch Video B2.1 of Agard reading 'Half-caste'. You may want to explain that Agard performs his poetry dramatically, which accounts for the differences between the printed text and his reading. Ask students to think about his tone as they watch. How does he feel about the term 'half-caste'?

Video B2.1

- Display the poem and draw students' attention to repeated phrases such as 'explain yuself'. What effect does this repeated phrase have? Guide students towards the idea that Agard is challenging the use of the term 'half-caste'.

3 Exploring ideas: group work

- Split the class into small groups and allocate each group a section of the poem: lines 4–9 ('half-caste canvas'), lines 10–22 ('half-caste weather') or lines 23–30 ('half-caste symphony').

- Ask groups to write out these lines in Standard English. Refer students to Glossary B2 if needed.
- Groups should work out why Agard has used the term 'half-caste' for these things (canvas, weather or symphony).

Access

Recap on the features of Standard English. Model how to rewrite one or two lines of the poem in Standard English prose. Ask pairs to complete Worksheet B2.1.

Worksheet B2.1

4 Exploring ideas: whole class work

- Ask groups to feed back to the class on the phrase they have been given. Display Image B2.1, a Picasso painting, for lines 4–9. Agard is ridiculing the idea of a mixture being negative by pointing out that a masterpiece like this is made up of two different colours.

Image B2.1

- Display Image B2.2, British weather, and Image B2.3, piano keys, to demonstrate the same point for lines 10–22 and lines 23–30.
- Ensure students have understood that Agard is ridiculing the idea

Image B2.2

that mixtures are negative and is reinforcing instead the idea that they are positive, using references to the West (Western cultural figures and proverbial British weather) to emphasise the point.

Image B2.3

Extend

Ask students to write three to four paragraphs answering the question: How does Agard use language and form to put forward his point of view? They could mention inclusion of Western cultural icons to illustrate the benefits of 'mixture', and use of punctuation, spelling and vocabulary to convey dialect, show his heritage, etc.

5 Exploring ideas: pair work

- Ask students to work in pairs and identify all references to 'half' and 'whole' that Agard uses in lines 31–50.
- What do these references refer to? What tone of voice is Agard using in this section? What significance does the term 'whole' take on in lines 48–50?
- Ask pairs to feed back to the class. Establish that Agard is using a sarcastic tone in saying that because people are called 'half-caste' they must only have half an ear, half an eye, half a hand, etc. Play Video B2.1 again to establish this tone of voice. In asking the reader to use the whole of their eye, ear and mind, Agard is asking them to be more open-minded and accepting in thinking about background.

6 Looking at language: whole class

- Show Video B2.2 of Agard talking about his poem.
- Discuss why Agard might have used non-standard English in his poem (representation of dialect) and unusual punctuation marks such as '/'. What effect does

JOHN AGARD

Video B2.2

this have on the reader? Do we see Agard differently because of the way the poem sounds?
- Why did he use lower case for Picasso, Tchaikovsky and England? Refer to the video for guidance.

8 Peer assessment

- Ask students to swap work with a partner. Students should write a comment on their partner's work based on how well their partner has:
  - understood Agard's use of language to achieve effect;
  - been able to explain, develop and support their comments, making relevant connections between the techniques used and how the ideas and themes are presented.
- Students should then decide which of the five bands the work falls into. You may want to refer them to Resource B17.2 (English Literature Higher Tier mark scheme), B17.3 (English Literature Foundation Tier mark scheme) or B17.4 (English mark scheme).
- Finally they should write a comment on how the answer could have been improved, looking at the importance of supporting points with good examples.

9 Plenary

- Ensure that students have understood:
  - the ways Agard conveys his ideas about race;
  - how he uses tone to make the reader react.
- Ask pairs to contribute one key point about Agard's ideas and theme and/or the language, structure and form, explain it and support it with an example.
- Suggestions should be pooled and used as a basis for inviting an overall response to and evaluation of the poem, with reference to the learning objective.
- For English Literature, find another poem in Collection B that deals with prejudice, and ask students to compare the way the subject is treated.

7 Independent writing

- Model writing one paragraph to begin to explain the reasons Agard gives for 'half-caste' being a hurtful and unacceptable term.
- Ask students to write their own paragraph.

10 Further work

Ask students to write a version of 'the other half of my story' using the last three lines of the poem as inspiration. They might like to consider the clashes and collisions which they have encountered themselves and how they might convey these to a reader, thinking particularly about the tone and language of their writing.

Lesson B3
Parade's End
Daljit Nagra

Learning objective
To explore how Nagra uses vocabulary and narrative structure to engage the reader and explore issues of racial and cultural tension within a community.

Resources
• Edexcel GCSE Poetry Anthology, page 21
• Audio B3
• Glossary B3
• Worksheet B3.1
• Worksheet B3.2
• Worksheet B3.3
• Interactive B3

1 Before reading: whole class work

• Brainstorm all the ideas associated with the words 'gold' and 'brown' so that students begin to gain an understanding of the poem's message. Possible ideas might include:

Gold – precious metal, wealth, beauty, jewellery, shiny, exciting.

Brown – dull, mud, winter, boring, ugly.

• Draw out the contrast between the associations with these two colours and explain that these two colours will be important in the poem.

2 First reading: whole class work

• Listen to the reading of 'Parade's End' on Audio B3 and ask students to think about the sequence of events.

• Look at the poem on the ActiveTeach and clarify any unknown vocabulary (see Glossary B3).

• Ask students to explain what happens in the poem. Note the use of punctuation marks (e.g. the colon in line 25) and how these aid understanding. You might want to create a class flow diagram of the key events on the board.

• Ask students to imagine themselves in the position of the narrator. How would they feel if this happened to them? What would their reaction be to seeing their car ruined (again)? Would they respond calmly or angrily?

Access

Students work on Worksheet B3.1, either individually or in pairs, writing down the events described in each stanza of the poem.

Worksheet B3.1

3 Close reading: whole class work

• Open Interactive B3 on the ActiveTeach, and ask the class to decide which of the words and phrases from the poem are images of poverty and which are images of success. They should justify their decisions with evidence from the poem.

Interactive B3

• Take feedback, focusing on what this might tell us about the community.

4 Analysing imagery: pair work

• Model the analysis of two images from the poem:

– 'The few who warmed us a thumbs-up' – this suggests friendliness through the metaphorical use of 'warmed' and reinforces it with the colloquial phrase 'thumbs-up'; however, it also emphasises the lack of support by the use of the word 'few', thus implying that they are not really part of the community.

– 'Spread trolleys at ends of the darkened aisles' – this suggests a threatening atmosphere by the use of the word 'darkened', and the 'trolleys' take on an ominous tone as they create deliberate barriers and are 'spread' out just as an army might be deployed.

• Hand out Worksheet B3.2. Working in pairs, ask students to analyse the images listed. The models given above are also provided on the worksheet.

• Take feedback, looking in particular at the use and effect of metaphors.

Worksheet B3.2

5 Looking at themes: whole class work

- Discuss the idea of contrasts, particularly the idea of 'us' and 'them' (e.g. how these terms are used: teachers and pupils; parents and children; old and young; rich and poor; black and white races, etc.). Ask what instances of 'us' and 'them' students have experienced. Ideas could be recorded on the whiteboard.
- Ask students to work in pairs, look closely at the second stanza and identify the 'us' and 'them' referred to here, using phrases from the stanza. How does this idea in the poem link to their own ideas? They should be prepared to feed back to the class.
- Ask them to explain the lines written in phonetic Yorkshire accent.
- Students should feed back to the rest of the class.

6 Looking at themes: individual work

- Hand out Worksheet B3.3. Ask students to fill in the answers to the questions on the language and imagery that are used to explore the key theme of conflict.

Worksheet B3.3

7 Peer assessment

- Ask students to swap their work on Worksheet B3.3 with a partner. Go through the answers, asking students to mark each other's work, awarding two marks per answer. Students should assess how well their partner's responses:
  - show an understanding of Nagra's use of language and structure to convey ideas about cultural tensions;
  - demonstrate the ability to explain, develop and support ideas, making relevant connections between the techniques used and how the ideas, themes and setting are presented.
- Students should then decide which of the five bands the work falls into. You may want to refer them to Resource B17.2 (English Literature Higher Tier mark scheme), B17.3 (English Literature Foundation Tier mark scheme) or B17.4 (English mark scheme).
- Then ask students to comment on how the answer could have been improved, looking at the importance of supporting points with good examples.

8 Plenary

- Recap and ensure that students have understood:
  - the ways Nagra has conveyed his ideas about cultural tensions;
  - how Nagra uses physical and mental barriers to explore the theme of conflict.
- Each pair should be asked to contribute one key point about Nagra's ideas and theme and/or language, structure and form of the poem, explain it and support it with an example from the poem.
- Ideas should be pooled on the board and used as a basis for inviting an overall response to and evaluation of the poem, with reference to the learning objective above.
- For English Literature, find another poem in Collection B that deals with a different form of prejudice (e.g. 'Half-caste'), and ask students to compare the way the subject is treated.

9 Further work

Ask students to write a response to the following prompt: Comment on how effectively Nagra uses imagery to describe the racist attack on his father's car.

Extend

Ask students to discuss how Nagra uses metaphors as a way of exploring the difficult topic of racism.

Clashes and collisions

Lesson B4
Belfast Confetti
Ciaran Carson

Learning objective
To understand how Carson has used punctuation and form to create an image of war.

Resources
- Edexcel GCSE Poetry Anthology, page 22
- Audio B4
- Glossary B4
- Worksheet B4.1
- Worksheet B4.2
- Worksheet B4.3
- Worksheet B4.4
- Image B4.1
- Image B4.2
- Video B4.1
- Video B4.2
- Multimedia B4

1 Before reading: whole class work

- Write the following punctuation marks on the board: exclamation mark, asterisk, hyphen, full stop, colon, semi-colon, question mark.
- Ask students to suggest ideas or emotions that could be associated with each punctuation mark, e.g. exclamation marks suggest surprise, excitement, danger, etc.
- Next, brainstorm the connotations of the word 'confetti', e.g. used for celebrations such as weddings.

2 First reading: whole class work

- Watch the video reading of 'Belfast Confetti' on Video B4.1.
- Ask students about their reactions to the poem. What stood out to them? Did they find the references to punctuation engaging? Interesting? Strange?

Video B4.1

- Make sure students understand the references in the poem using Glossary B4.
- Now watch the alternative reading on Video B4.2. How does this compare to the first reading? What are the tone and atmosphere of each reading? Which

Video B4.2

reading do students prefer and why? You may want to come back to these videos later in the lesson.

3 Close reading: pair work

- Ask students to discuss the references to punctuation marks in the poem with their partner. Why do they think the poet has used this vocabulary?
- Hand out Worksheet B4.1, which asks students to fill in the chart with words from the poem that they associate with writing and with fighting. Ask student pairs to discuss their choices.

Worksheet B4.1

- Take feedback, discussing the ambiguity and the fact that some words might fit both sides.
- Hand out Worksheet B4.2, asking student pairs to discuss the images created by the words/phrases in the table.

Worksheet B4.2

Extend

Draw students' attention to the phrases below, asking them to make notes on what each one implies:
- 'a fount of broken type' – visual image of the shrapnel-like broken bits of letters from a typewriter
- 'complete a sentence' – make sense of what was happening
- 'every move is punctuated' – stopped, prevented, impeded by something.

4 Setting the context: whole class work

- Identify the language connected with war. Give explanations as necessary, using the glossary.
- Explain to students the context of the 'Troubles' in Northern Ireland – the conflict between Roman Catholics and Protestants. Emphasise how long the Troubles lasted. Explain how the fighting would commonly impact the everyday lives of citizens and

how schools and streets were (and to an extent still are) divided – either Catholic or Protestant. You may wish to show Images B4.1 and B4.2 to support this discussion.

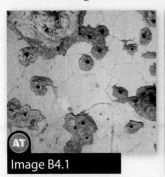

Image B4.1

Image B4.2

Access

Hand out Worksheet B4.4, which models the writing of sentences to explain how Carson links the ideas of writing and war, using the PEEE format, and asks them to find three further examples and write a sentence on each.

Worksheet B4.4

5 Multimedia activity: group work

- Divide students into groups and hand out Worksheet B4.3 which briefs them on how to complete a short multimedia activity using the downloadable footage provided on the ActiveTeach. When Multimedia B4 is opened, you will be prompted to save the file somewhere

Worksheet B4.3

on your system. The multimedia clips can then be accessed by extracting them from the zip file, and then opened in editing software for students to use and modify. The aim of the activity is to encourage students to interpret the poet's ideas, thoughts and feelings through selection and editing of the material provided. Students will require access to editing software and up to an hour to complete the task.

6 Independent writing

Ask students to write a paragraph explaining how Carson has linked the ideas of writing and war in the poem. Encourage them to write about the meaning of the poem's title as well.

7 Peer assessment

- Ask students to swap their independent writing with a partner and then give an assessment of and write a comment on each other's work. Students should assess how well their partner has:
  - understood Carson's use of language, writing and punctuation to convey his ideas about war;
  - been able to explain, develop and support ideas, making relevant connections between the techniques used and how the ideas, themes and setting are presented.
- They should decide which of the five bands the work falls into. You may want to refer them to Resource B17.2 (English Literature Higher Tier mark scheme), B17.3 (English Literature Foundation Tier mark scheme) or B17.4 (English mark scheme)
- They should then comment on how the answer could have been improved, looking at the importance of supporting points with good examples.

8 Plenary

- Recap and ensure that students have understood:
  - the ways Carson has conveyed images of war linked to writing;
  - the impression of the Troubles created in the reader's mind.
- Each pair should be asked to contribute one key point about Carson's use of language and punctuation to create images of war, to explain it and support it with an example from the poem.
- Ideas should be pooled on the board and used as a basis for inviting an overall response to and evaluation of the poem, with reference to the learning objective above.
- For English Literature, find another poem in Collection B that deals with a time of conflict (e.g. 'Invasion') and ask students to compare the way the subject is treated.

9 Further work

Students should research the Irish 'Troubles' looking at the conflict between Protestants and Roman Catholics in Belfast. How does this help their understanding of the poem? How might they have felt living in Belfast during the 'Troubles'.

Lesson B5
Our Sharpeville
Ingrid de Kok

Learning objective
To understand how de Kok uses vocabulary and imagery to explore alternative points of view on a significant event in South Africa's history.

Resources
• Edexcel GCSE Poetry Anthology, page 23
• Audio B5
• Glossary B5
• Worksheet B5.1
• Resource B5.1
• Image B5.1
• Video B5.1
• Video B5.2

1 Before reading: whole class work

• Ask students how they would feel if some students needed special permission to move around the school but other students could come and go as they pleased.

• Explain that this poem is set during the apartheid era in South Africa and that apartheid was a system of racial segregation. The Pass Laws meant that black people had to carry a pass wherever they went and their movements were restricted. Explain that the Sharpeville Massacre took place in March 1960, when the South African police opened fire on a group of black protestors during a protest against the Pass Laws. More than 180 people were injured and 69 were killed.

• Show Image B5.1 to illustrate the impact on everyday life of apartheid and discuss how this links to the theme of 'clashes and collisions'.

Image B5.1

• Play Video B5.2 which shows Ingrid de Kok discussing her memories of the Sharpeville massacre; afterwards discuss students' reactions to the points raised. How do they feel about discrimination on this scale? What would their reaction be if something like this happened in Britain today?

Video B5.2

2 First reading: pair work

• Watch Video B5.1 and ask students to think about what they know about the context while they listen to the reading of the poem.

• Have students work in pairs to read the poem again, look up unfamiliar words in Glossary B5 and write a brief summary of what the poem is about.

• Ask pairs to feed back to the class. Clarify the action taking place in the poem for students where necessary.

Video B5.1

Access

• Revise what metaphors and similes are, and agree on appropriate definitions.

• Hand out Worksheet B5.1, asking students to fill in the agreed definitions and to complete the examples of similes and metaphors.

Worksheet B5.1

3 Close reading: group work

Ask students to work in groups to identify the metaphors and similes in the poem and record them in a list. Then ask the groups to explore the meanings of the metaphors and similes that have been identified and feed back to contribute to a class discussion. Students gain credit for suggesting more than one possible effect of using these literary devices.

4   Exploring themes: pair work

- Ask pairs of students to find words and phrases that:
  - define the narrator's life as a child, e.g. 'hopscotch', 'oasis', 'Sunday school';
  - suggest the danger and violence at which the poem hints, e.g. 'dangers of the mission', 'pool of blood', 'do things'.
- Take feedback and discuss how these words and worlds contrast. Why is the narrator, the little girl, confused? What are her instincts? Why is it effective that the poet decides to show the massacre through young white eyes? You might find it effective to highlight the relevant words in the poem using the annotation tool in the ActiveTeach. Alternatively, you can hand out Resource B5.1.

Resource B5.1

5   Independent writing

Ask students to write a paragraph explaining how and why de Kok has used certain vocabulary and images to describe the child's life clearly but has left the threat of danger deliberately vague.

6   Peer assessment

- Ask students to swap work with a partner and then give an assessment of and write a comment on each other's work. Students should assess how well their partner has:
  - understood de Kok's use of language, writing and punctuation to convey her ideas about a divided society;
  - been able to explain, develop and support ideas, making relevant connections between the techniques used and how the ideas, themes and setting are presented.
- Ask students to decide which of the five bands the work falls into. You may want to refer them to Resource B17.2 (English Literature Higher Tier mark scheme), B17.3 (English Literature Foundation Tier mark scheme) or B17.4 (English mark scheme).
- Students should then comment on how the answer could have been improved, looking at the importance of supporting points with good examples.

7   Plenary

- Recap and ensure that students have understood:
  - the ways de Kok has conveyed her ideas about apartheid through the eyes of a child;
  - how she uses imagery to make the reader react to the theme and to setting.
- Each pair should be asked to contribute one key point about de Kok's ideas, theme or setting and/or her language, structure and form, explain it and support it with an example from the poem.
- Ideas should be pooled on the board and used as a basis for inviting an overall response to and evaluation of the poem, with reference to the learning objective above.
- For English Literature, find another poem in Collection B that deals with divisions in society (e.g. 'The Class Game'), and ask students to compare the way the subject is treated.

Extend

Ask students to answer the following question: How and why does the poet emphasise the idea of being separated in some way in the last stanza?

8   Further work

Students should research in more detail the Sharpeville Massacre and the Pass Laws in order to gain a greater understanding of the background to the poem. How does this help their understanding of the poem? Do they see the people featured within the poem any differently (e.g. the little girl, the protestors, or the grandmother)?

Suggested answers

3 Close reading

Metaphors: *miners roared; signals at a crossing; hot arteries; deep jade pool; fearful thing; living name; the day lengthened; buried in voices.*

Similes: *like the call and answer of road gangs; like a great caravan; grew like a shadow.*

5 Independent writing

Paragraph might include: *the positioning of the metaphor 'roared' directly underneath the phrase 'playing hopscotch' seems to interrupt the carefree nature of childhood games; the alliterative juxtaposition of 'foreign' and 'familiar' to emphasise the security of the child's world; the 'silver stars just like the ones / you got for remembering your Bible texts' linking the night sky to simple childhood connections.*

Lesson B6
Exposure
Wilfred Owen

Learning objective
To explore how Owen uses poetic devices to reflect the horror of war, and what effect these have on a reader.

Resources
- Edexcel GCSE Poetry Anthology, pages 24–25
- Audio B6
- Glossary B6
- Worksheet B6.1
- Worksheet B6.2
- Worksheet B6.3
- Image B6.1
- Image B6.2

1 Before reading: whole class work

- Explain to students that Wilfred Owen signed up to fight in World War I at the age of 22. You might want to remind students of the recruitment posters from 'The Drum', if this poem has already been studied. Owen wrote much poetry about his experiences during the war, talking frankly about the suffering and horrors, which contrasted with the positive and patriotic images of war propaganda which was encouraged in Britain. He was killed one week before the end of the war at the age of 25.

Image B6.1

- Show students Images B6.1 and B6.2 of soldiers in World War I which help to illustrate what the living conditions were like in the trenches.
- Discuss students' impressions based on the information and images, focusing particularly on the conditions the soldiers experienced.

Image B6.2

2 First reading: whole class work

- Remind students of the title of the poem, and get them to think about the open trenches in winter, with very few clothes, the mud, etc.
- Listen to the reading of the poem on Audio B6 or read the poem as a class. Ask students to try to visualise what is happening in the poem as they listen to it being read.

3 Exploring imagery: pair work

- Ask students to close their anthologies and, in pairs, note down or draw as many images as they can recall from the poem.
- Take feedback, drawing out which were the most common images selected.
- Discuss why students found these particular images the most powerful.

Access

Ask students to try to work out the meanings of the words on Worksheet B6.1 in the context of the poem. Give assistance sooner or later, depending on time constraints. Refer students to Glossary B6 for the answers.

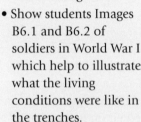
Worksheet B6.1

4 Analysing imagery: group work

- Hand out Worksheet B6.2 and allocate one of the phrases on the sheet to each group of students.
- Model a response to the first phrase for students, e.g. 'mad gusts tugging on the wire' – personification, despair, violence, helplessness, alliteration – short, sharp, reflects jerkiness of action.
- Ask each group to analyse their phrase and write a response to it in the same way. They should be prepared to

Worksheet B6.2

feed back their ideas to the class. Emphasise that they should focus on the effect of language, imagery and poetic devices, such as metaphor, simile, personification and alliteration.

5 Evaluating imagery: class discussion

- Take feedback from the group work, focusing on the image that each phrase creates and how it is created. Encourage references to personification and metaphor.
- Look at what effect this imagery has and how it helps to reinforce the sense of conflict in war.

6 Close reading: independent work

Hand out Worksheet B6.3, which asks students to study the last three stanzas of the poem and answer a series of questions on the language used here.

Worksheet B6.3

7 Peer assessment

- Ask students to swap work with a partner and discuss their answers, deciding which are the most detailed and perceptive comments. They should assess how well their partner has:
  - understood Owen's use of language to convey the setting and his ideas;
  - been able to explain, develop and support ideas, making relevant connections between the techniques used and how the ideas, themes and setting are presented.
- Students should then decide which of the five bands the work falls into. You may want to refer them to Resource B17.2 (English Literature Higher Tier mark scheme), B17.3 (English Literature Foundation Tier mark scheme) or B17.4 (English mark scheme).
- Finally all students should use the best comments to annotate the poem in their anthologies.

8 Looking at structure: pair work

Ask pairs to look again at the final line of each stanza. They should write down their ideas about what the author is trying to show through his use of repetition. Prompt them to consider the following questions: What are the narrator's feelings and emotions? How does this use of repetition help us to understand the idea of 'exposure'?

Extend

Ask students to explain how Owen has used adjectives and adverbs to highlight conflict in the poem.

9 Plenary

- Recap to ensure that students have understood:
  - the ways Owen conveys his thoughts and ideas on the horrors of war;
  - how he uses imagery, rhetorical questions, repetition and other poetic devices to make the reader reflect on conditions in war and on the theme.
- Pick out examples of approaches to the theme of 'clashes and collisions' in the poems already studied. On the basis of these examples, discuss how poetry can create vivid scenes and strong feelings.
- For English Literature, encourage comparison of different ideas on conflict, drawing on other poems in the collection.

10 Further work

Ask students to write three paragraphs in response to the question: How has Wilfred Owen explored the idea of 'exposure' in this poem?

Suggested answers

3 Exploring imagery

Images might include: *Knives, barbed wire, clouds, blackbird, ghosts, etc.*

Lesson B7
Catrin
Gillian Clarke

Learning objective
To explore how Clarke uses language and structural features to present the mixed feelings involved in the parent–child relationship.

Resources
• Edexcel GCSE Poetry Anthology, page 26
• Audio B7
• Glossary B7
• Worksheet B7.1
• Worksheet B7.2
• Image B7.1
• Image B7.2

1 Before reading: group work

- Hand out Worksheet B7.1. Allocate one of the phrases from the poem on the worksheet to each group of students.

- Ask students to generate initial ideas about their given phrase, using the spider diagram on the worksheet if they wish, and then feed back to the whole class.

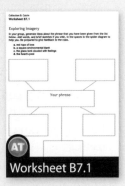

Worksheet B7.1

Access

Show students Images B7.1 (of a hospital ward) and B7.2 (of a mother with her baby) and ask them to brainstorm all the words they would associate with these images. They should record these ideas on a spider diagram and keep them to help them later in the lesson (i.e. Activity 5). Possible ideas for the maternity room include: clean, disinfected, white, bare, detached, calm; for the mother with her baby, students might think of love, contentment, bond, amazement, miracle, protection.

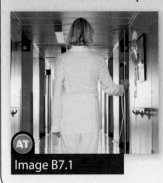

Image B7.1

Image B7.2

2 Before reading: whole class work

- Before students open their anthologies, listen to the poem being read on Audio B7, or read the poem to the class. As they listen to the poem, students should focus on visualising the images Clarke creates.

- Go through the worksheet phrases again and ask students if their understanding of the images has changed. It may be necessary to explain the meaning of the phrases in the context of the poem at this point. Ask how close students' ideas about the phrases in the pre-reading exercise were, now that they have heard them in context. Alternatively, ask students how the pictures at the start link with their impressions of the poem.

3 First reading: pair work

- Hand out Worksheet B7.2, asking students to fill in the missing words. Explain that they must choose words that fit the context and alliterate with the neighbouring emboldened word.

- Recap on alliteration while looking at the poem in the anthology to see which words were used by Clarke in these places, perhaps focusing on particular examples.

Worksheet B7.2

- Through discussion with their partner, students should annotate a copy of the poem, referring to the effect created by the alliteration, e.g. 'window watching' creates a feeling of separation; 'first fierce confrontation' suggests a power struggle, etc. Encourage them to pick up on any other effects, such as assonance and onomatopoeia and analyse these as well.

4 Close reading: pair work

- Ask students to work in pairs to decide how to divide the poem into four sections. Ask them to give each of the sections a title. Students should use Glossary B7 if they need to check the meanings of any words in the poem.
- Take feedback, comparing results.
- Ask students to highlight, in two different colours:
  - words associated with conflict;
  - words that suggest love/affection.
- Take feedback.
- Ask students to think about possible links between these two sets of words.
- Draw out the conclusion that the central theme is the conflicting emotions in the parent–child relationship.
- Relate this to the collection's theme of 'clashes and collisions'. How is this similar to, and different from, the clashes and collisions described in other poems in this collection that students have studied so far?

Extend

- Recap on the meaning of 'oxymoron' if necessary.
- Ask students to create five oxymorons around the theme of parent–child relationships.

5 Independent writing

- Model writing one paragraph to discuss how Clarke explores the conflicting emotions involved in the relationship between a parent and child. Make sure students realise the importance of giving evidence and exploring the impact on the reader.
- Ask students to write two or three paragraphs of their own about the different stages of the poem.

6 Peer assessment

- Ask students to swap their paragraphs and assess how well their partner has:
  - understood Clarke's use of language, imagery and structure to present the parent–child relationship; they might have picked up on some of the points in the Suggested answers panel but credit should be given to other valid points as well;
  - been able to explain, develop and support ideas, making relevant connections between the techniques used and how the ideas, themes and setting are presented.

- Students should decide which of the five bands the work falls into. You may want to refer them to Resource B17.2 (English Literature Higher Tier mark scheme), B17.3 (English Literature Foundation Tier mark scheme) or B17.4 (English mark scheme).
- They should then comment on how the answer could have been improved, looking at the importance of supporting points with good examples.

7 Plenary

- Recap and ensure that students:
  - have an appreciation of the feelings of both the parent and the child;
  - have thought about how their feelings differ and why.
- Discuss the overall impression they have formed of the relationship. Is it more positive than negative? Ask for a show of hands and discuss.
- For English Literature, find another poem in Collection B that deals with difficulties in family relationships, and ask students to compare the way the subject is treated.

8 Further work

Ask students to write the mother's diary entry for this event in two to three paragraphs. They should include emotions as well as narrative, focusing on the imagery within the poem.

Suggested answers

4 Close reading

Suggested divisions: end of line 4, end of line 17, end of line 20 to end of poem.

Words associated with conflict: hot, fierce, white (with rage), confrontation, fought, wild, struggle, separate, won, lost, struggle, changed, fighting, defiant, tightening, conflict.

Words that suggest love/affection: remember, love, tender, feelings, heart.

6 Peer assessment

The 'hot white room' suggests a sterile environment that is alien to the mother; the 'tight red rope of love' seems to make the umbilical cord into a power struggle as well as something restricting; the use of the words 'won' and 'lost' make direct reference to a fight; the use of the oxymorons 'rosy', 'defiant' and 'love and conflict' highlight the ongoing struggle.

Lesson B8
Your Dad Did What?
Sophie Hannah

Learning objective
To explore how Hannah uses language, grammatical features and form to depict misunderstanding between adult and child.

Resources
- Edexcel GCSE Poetry Anthology, page 27
- Audio B8
- Glossary B8
- Worksheet B8.1
- Worksheet B8.2
- Video B8.1
- Video B8.2

1 Before reading: independent work

- Hand out Worksheet B8.1, asking students to fill in the answers to the questions about what they did last weekend.
- Ask students what stage in their school life this activity reminds them of. Draw out that they might have been asked to write 'news' like this when they were at primary school.
- Explain that this is a poem written from a teacher's perspective and that the teacher has set work like this for the students.

Worksheet B8.1

2 First reading: whole class

- Watch Video B8.1 of Sophie Hannah reading the poem.
- Ask students what happened in the poem. What was the misunderstanding? At what point in the poem did they realise what was meant by the boy's response?

Video B8.1

3 Close reading: pair work

- Hand out Worksheet B8.2, which presents the poem as a prose passage.
- Review the purpose of rhyme and rhythm in poetry and discuss the possible positions of line breaks to turn the prose passage into a poem.
- Ask pairs of students to write out the passage as a poem and be prepared to feed back to the whole class. Emphasise that students need to consider the role of rhyme and rhythm.

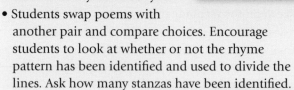
Worksheet B8.2

- Students swap poems with another pair and compare choices. Encourage students to look at whether or not the rhyme pattern has been identified and used to divide the lines. Ask how many stanzas have been identified.
- Facilitate a class discussion comparing their poems with Hannah's. Point out the rhyme pattern and structure she used in the poem. Ask students what they notice about Hannah's rhyme pattern and why she may have used this type of rhyme and form in her poems (i.e. simplistic rhyme to pair with the primary school setting).

4 Close reading: pair work

- Ask pairs to look at the poem and highlight any short sentences and also phrases that are presented as sentences, e.g. 'What did his Dad?'
- Discuss the use of this technique and the effect. You might identify that the incomplete sentence of 'My Dad did' led to the mark of an 'E'. The short incomplete sentences could also be seen to represent a child's voice and/or the teacher's instruction to the child; they give a sense of abruptness that implies a lack of patience, and contrast with the longer, complex sentences representing the teacher's thoughts.

5 Close reading: independent work

- Ask students to re-read the last stanza carefully and explore the double meaning of the letter 'E'.
- Ask students to write one or two sentences to explain the use of the letter in both places in this verse (it is both the grade given as a result of misunderstanding through misspelling, and also the very letter which is missing from the misspelt word). Encourage them to think about how Hannah uses this to create a sense of poignancy. What is the effect of gradually and only finally making clear to the reader the reason for the misunderstanding? Can students identify any parts of the poem which are particularly poignant once we understand the confusion, on a second reading (e.g. 'you who can count and spell')?

6 Discussing meaning: whole class work

Sophie Hannah Interviewed

Video B8.2

- As a class, watch Video B8.2 which shows Sophie Hannah discussing the use of rhyme and rhythm, the subject-matter and the interpretation of her poetry. How do her points link to the poem 'Your Dad Did What?'? How do they help students' understanding of the poem? You may wish to stop the video at various points to give an opportunity for discussion.

Extend

Explain why Hannah has used first, second and third person in the poem and what effect this has on the reader's response.

7 Independent writing

Ask students to write a response to the question: How does Hannah use language and structure to create a sense of sadness in the poem?

Encourage them to cover the following points in their writing:

- the use of short sentences;
- the variation in language;
- the phrase 'doesn't want to add anything';
- the phrase 'my dad did';
- the phrase 'no change';
- the idea of the poem building to a climax.

8 Peer assessment

- Ask students to swap their independent writing with a partner and then give an assessment of and write a comment on each other's response. Students should assess how well their partner has:
  - explored Hannah's use of language and form in the poem to convey the sense of sadness;
  - been able to explain, develop and support ideas, making relevant connections between the techniques used and how the ideas, themes and setting are presented.
- Students should then decide which of the five bands the work falls into. You may want to refer them to Resource B17.2 (English Literature Higher Tier mark scheme), B17.3 (English Literature Foundation Tier mark scheme) or B17.4 (English mark scheme).
- Ask students to comment on how the answer could have been improved, looking at the importance of the detailed analysis. They should then join up with another pair to discuss their answers.

9 Plenary

- Recap and ensure that students have understood:
  - how form and grammatical features can influence the presentation of the subject matter;
  - how Hannah uses short phrases and comments gradually to unfold the situation and make the reader react poignantly to the misunderstanding between the teacher and the boy.
- Each group of four students should be asked to contribute one key point to general discussion about how attitudes change throughout the poem and what their group consider to be the most powerful short phrase/comment.
- For English Literature, find another poem in Collection B that conveys a sense of sadness (e.g. 'August 6, 1945'), and ask students to compare the way the subject is treated.

10 Further work

Explain how you think this poem relates to the theme of 'clashes and collisions'. You might guide the students to get them to think about the sadness or poignancy of the poem and how the teacher might have felt as a result of the misunderstanding. Also, what was the reason for the 'clash'? Are literacy and spelling important?

Clashes and Collisions

Lesson B9
The Class Game
Mary Casey

Learning objective
To evaluate how effectively the poet has used vocabulary and poetic devices to portray differences in social class and her attitudes towards these.

Resources
- Edexcel GCSE Poetry Anthology, page 28
- Audio B9
- Glossary B9
- Worksheet B9.1
- Worksheet B9.2
- Image B9.1
- Image B9.2

1 Before reading: pair work

- Ask students to discuss in pairs what the word 'posh' means to them and how they feel about the concept. Encourage them to list examples of things that might be described as 'posh'.
- Take feedback, focusing in particular on stereotypes, and on whether class matters, i.e. does it define a person; should we be proud or ashamed of our background?
- Show students Images B9.1 and B9.2 and ask for their immediate reactions to them. How would they 'class' these people or places? What background information do they think would fit with them? Do they think they have been guilty of stereotyping them?

Image 9.1

Image 9.2

2 First reading: pair work

- Listen to the reading of the poem on the audio or read the poem to the class, while students follow the text in their anthologies. Ask students to think about the initial discussion about class while they listen.
- Hand out Worksheet B9.1, asking students to fill in one column with words or phrases from the poem which suggest ideas that are posh, and another column with words or phrases which suggest ideas that aren't posh.

Worksheet B9.1

- If possible, ask students to place the 'persona' words/ phrases opposite the linking 'reader' words/phrases to bring out contrasts drawn within the poem.
- Take feedback, asking why students made these decisions.
- Ask pairs to discuss which words and phrases represent differences in dialect and which differences in lifestyle and then to highlight their anthologies accordingly, perhaps using colour-coding and a key.

3 Close reading: whole class work

- Recap on the different types of rhyme (full rhyme, internal rhyme and rhyming couplets) as well as assonance and consonance. Brief definitions are available in Glossary B1.
- Ask students to underline in different colours the examples of full rhyme, internal rhyme and assonance/consonance in the poem.
- Discuss the effect of these, asking students to annotate their anthologies, and leading on to make the link with the theme and poem title. Students might decide that the assonance highlights the difference in speech between classes, e.g. 'mouth'/'scarf', or that the full rhyme accentuates Received Pronunciation, e.g. 'card'/ 'yard'. The rhythm and rhyme create a sense of light-heartedness connecting with the notion of a 'game'.

Access

Ensure students understand rhyme, assonance and consonance by handing out Worksheet B9.2. Ask them to match up the appropriate pictures or words. Then go on to ask them to find examples of these in the poem and help them to discuss what effect they have.

Worksheet B9.2

4 Exploring ideas: whole class discussion

- Explain that this poem is a monologue. Discuss the effects of writing a poem as a monologue, e.g. one voice giving personal feelings, views and emotions can present a biased viewpoint.
- Ask students to pick out words or phrases which suggest a biased viewpoint.
- What do students feel about the persona's point of view? Do they share her feelings? Or perhaps they feel as if she's attacking the reader and/or a group of people unjustifiably?

5 Independent writing

- Model writing one paragraph about the effectiveness of using monologue in this poem. A suggested opening could be: 'The monologue form is used in "The Class Game" to show clearly the attitude of the persona. The very first line sounds aggressive because… This has the effect of showing that she believes…'
- Ask students to write their own paragraph on the same subject.

6 Peer assessment

- Students exchange their independent writing with a partner. They should assess how well their partner has:
  - given a creative or individual interpretation and explored the features of the monologue;
  - understood Casey's use of language to convey his ideas;
  - been able to explain, develop and support ideas, making relevant connections between the techniques used and how the ideas, themes and setting are presented.
- They should then decide which of the five bands the work falls into. You may want to refer them to Resource B17.2 (English Literature Higher Tier mark scheme), B17.3 (English Literature Foundation Tier mark scheme) or B17.4 (English mark scheme).
- Ask them to comment on how the answer could have been improved, looking at the importance of supporting points with good examples.

7 Plenary

- Recap and ensure that students have understood:
  - the attitudes to social class shown in the poem;
  - the ways in which the language and use of contrast present these attitudes.
- Discuss students' ideas on why Casey might have written this poem and what she is hoping to achieve by writing it. Do they think this poem says something important?
- Ideas should be pooled on the board and used as a basis for inviting an overall response to and evaluation of the poem, with reference to the learning objective above.
- For English Literature, find another poem in Collection B where the use of dialects or accents is important and ask students to compare the way the subject is treated.

Extend

Ask students to explore the use of questions in the poem. They should write two or three paragraphs explaining why Casey has used questions and what effect they have on the reader. Answers might include:
- they involve the reader;
- they ask the reader to think about what defines class;
- they emphasise the persona's voice in the poem, challenging the reader to object to her sense of self (the reader is assumed to be 'upper class');
- they remind the reader that the persona's point of view may be biased.

8 Further work

Ask students to generate a list of words that feature in their local dialect (whether this is regional, religious or to do with class), as well as some words which they associate with a different group of people. Ask students to write a poem about differences, thinking about the theme of the collection, using some of these words. They might focus on relationships with parents, a peer group, people in authority, etc.

Clashes and Collisions

Lesson B10
Cousin Kate
Christina Rossetti

Learning objective
To understand how Rossetti has used narrative form and language in the poem to explore relationships and evoke sympathy in the reader.

Resources
• Edexcel GCSE Poetry Anthology, page 29
• Audio B10
• Glossary B10
• Worksheet B10.1
• Worksheet B10.2
• Worksheet B10.3
• Image B10.1
• Image B10.2
• Interactive B10

1 Before reading: independent work

• Recap on rhyme, specifically full rhyme, if this has not been done in previous lessons.

• Hand out Worksheet B10.1 which requires students to complete the poem by filling in the blanks with words from the boxes. This will help them to focus on the rhyme pattern, rhythm and its effect.

Worksheet B10.1

2 First reading: whole class work

• Students should listen to the poem being read on Audio B10, while following in their anthology. Ask students to listen out particularly for the rhyme and its effect.

• Briefly discuss the effect of the regular rhyme pattern. Answers could include the creation of a rhythm, sounds like a ballad, is a traditional style, etc.

• Set the context of the poem by showing Images B10.1 and B10.2. Ask students for their impressions of the time/era of the poem. They should keep this in mind during the rest of their work on the poem.

Image B10.1

Image B10.2

3 Understanding language: pair work

Hand out Worksheet B10.2, which lists modern interpretations of eight phrases from the poem. Ask students to find the equivalent phrase in the poem for each modern phrase and to annotate their anthologies to help them understand the meaning.

Worksheet B10.2

Access

Help students to complete Interactive B10, perhaps against the clock, which gives the original phrases as well as the interpretations for students to match them up before annotating their copy of the poem.

Interactive B10

4 Close reading: group work

• Divide students into groups and allocate each group either stanzas 1 and 2, 3 and 4, or 5 and 6. Ask them to produce an explanation of the actions and emotions expressed in their section, writing down a couple of sentences as a group to summarise this.

• Ask groups to feed back to the class, in order of the stanzas studied, ensuring that the whole class understands the narrative and emotions expressed. How many people are involved? What are their relationships? Who did what? Who is speaking?

5 | Looking at themes: pair work

- Hand out Worksheet B10.3 to student pairs. Explain that, through discussion and reference to the poem, they need to pair up the words on the sheet which contrast and then decide how the pairings are important in the poem overall. You could model the following example: the contrasting pair 'shameless/shameful', which is significant in showing that while the persona has been shamed through living with the lord, it is not her fault and she should not be ashamed. It might also reflect that the lord himself did not feel any shame and others do not see his actions as shameful.

- Take feedback, focusing particularly on the effect these paired contrasting words have on the reader.

AT
Worksheet B10.3

Extend

- Draw students' attention to lines 23–24 and the contrast drawn between 'mean' and 'high' here. Discuss with them the concept of social status, shame and the different roles of men and women in the Victorian era.

- Bearing this information in mind, students should discuss what they think Rossetti's intentions are and what she wished to convey in this poem – is it just a pretty ballad, or does it have some sort of moral? Do we feel sorry for the woman in the poem?

6 | Independent writing

- Write the following words on the board: bitter, regretful, angry, happy, triumphant, uncaring, jealous, sad, vindictive, proud.

- Ask students to choose the two or three of the words that they think best describe the tone of the poem and the woman's emotions. They should then write a paragraph justifying their choices (with evidence from the poem) and evaluating the overall message delivered by the poet.

7 | Peer assessment

- In pairs, students should evaluate each other's paragraph, assessing how well their partner has:
  - understood Rossetti's use of language and structure to present her ideas about relationships;
  - has been able to explain, develop and support ideas, making relevant connections between the techniques used and how the ideas, themes and setting are presented.

- They should then decide which of the five bands the work falls into. You may want to refer them to Resource B17.2 (English Literature Higher Tier mark scheme), B17.3 (English Literature Foundation Tier mark scheme) or B17.4 (English mark scheme).

- Ask them to comment on how the answer could have been improved, looking at the importance of supporting points with good examples.

8 | Plenary

- Recap and ensure that students have understood:
  - the ways Rossetti has conveyed her ideas;
  - how Rossetti uses poetic devices to develop these.

- Each group of four should present for one minute to the whole class on their agreed 'best words' (from the independent writing activity) and the reasons for them.

- Lead a class discussion on the similarities and differences in the groups' responses, with reference to the overall learning objective.

- For English Literature, find another poem in Collection B that gives a woman's view on a relationship, and ask students to compare the way the subject is treated.

9 | Further work

Ask students to write a prose narrative telling the story in the poem from the point of view of either 'the great lord' or 'Cousin Kate'. You might want to ask students to think about how they can use structure and language to make an impression on their reader.

Lesson B11
Hitcher
Simon Armitage

Learning objective
To understand how Armitage uses first-person narrative and vocabulary to build up detailed character profiles and explore motivation.

Resources
• Edexcel GCSE Poetry Anthology, page 30
• Audio B11
• Glossary B11
• Worksheet B11.1
• Video B11.1
• Video B11.2

1 Before reading: whole class work

• Discuss sources of annoyance and irritation in everyday life, asking students to supply specific examples. Does the level of annoyance depend on mood, circumstance, etc.? What are their reactions to these annoyances?

• This poem is about a person who gives a lift to a hitchhiker. What do students associate with the word 'hitchhiking'? Answers might include cheap, liberating, free-living, dangerous.

• Students should keep these ideas in mind when they read the poem.

2 First reading: whole class work

• Watch the poem being read on Video B11.1, available on the ActiveTeach.

Video B11.1

• Ask students to determine what is going on. Did the events come as a surprise? It will probably be necessary to read the poem in their anthologies as well.

• Explore the meanings and associations of the words in Glossary B11 with students where necessary, including the use of brand names and the allusion to Bob Dylan lyrics. You may want to play the song 'Blowin' in the wind' to students if they don't know it, explaining that it's a song which raises moral questions about peace and freedom.

3 Close reading: pair work

• Hand out Worksheet B11.1 which provides a list of metaphorical phrases in the poem. Students should discuss and fill in what each one tells us about the persona and the hitchhiker within the poem so that they can build up a character profile of both.

• Pairs should feed back to the whole class. Discussion should take place around how the poet wished the reader to see each character, what each character might have thought about the other (considering that the poem is a first-person narrative), and the possible motivation of the persona for his actions, linking back to the ideas from the starter activity.

Worksheet B11.1

Access

• Ask students to work in pairs to make a list of words or phrases that they would use to define the persona of the poem, citing evidence for them in the poem. Suggested ideas: takes lots of time off work, is ill or feigns illness, jealous, angry, selfish, vicious, immoral. Students could annotate relevant sections of the poem in their anthologies with these words.

• They should then do the same for the hitchhiker, drawing on the poem to justify their choice of words/phrases.

4 Looking at themes: whole class work

• Show students Video B11.2 in which Simon Armitage discusses some of the themes in the poem 'Hitcher'.

Video B11.2

• Discuss some of the issues raised within this video, including the possible character and motivations of the persona of the poem.

5 Role-play: group work

- Divide students into small groups and ask them to imagine the court case that might have followed this incident and to role-play the scene. They should think about circumstances and motivation. Ask them to use evidence from the poem (imagery/language, etc.) in their role play.
- Select groups to share their role plays with the class. Ask other students to comment on what ideas the group have drawn out of the poem. Discuss how creating these role plays has developed students' understanding of the poem.

Extend

- Encourage students to find examples of ambiguity in the poem. Possible responses: 'you're finished' (refers to boss's attitude to the persona, but could also describe the persona's attitude to hitchhiker later on), 'round the next bend' (either simple road description or sense of impending doom in turn of events), 'I let him have it' (either reference to generosity with lift, or reference to violence).
- Suggest to students the idea that the hitcher is possibly an alter ego of the persona. Look at the phrases which might suggest this: the persona also 'thumbs a lift'; 'we were the same age, give or take a week'. What implications does this have for our understanding of the poem?
- Ask students to record their thoughts in their independent writing.

6 Independent writing

Ask students to write a paragraph answering the question: How does Armitage create a sense of violence in this poem? Prompt them to comment on language, rhyme, positioning of words/phrases and line length. They might include the ansaphone 'screaming', the phrase 'you're finished', the ominous 'round the next bend', the placing of 'I let him have it', 'with the head', 'in the face' and 'bouncing off the kerb'.

7 Peer assessment

- Ask students to swap their independent writing with a partner and then to compare their interpretations of the events, the motivation of the narrator and what they have given as evidence of violence in the poem. Students should assess how well their partner has:
  – explored Armitage's ideas about the situation;
  – been able to explain, develop and support ideas, making relevant connections between the techniques used and how the ideas, themes and setting are presented.
- Students should then decide which of the five bands the work falls into. You may want to refer them to Resource B17.2 (English Literature Higher Tier mark scheme), B17.3 (English Literature Foundation Tier mark scheme) or B17.4 (English mark scheme).
- They should then comment on how the answer could have been improved, looking at how well the examples are used and how points could be developed and linked.

8 Plenary

- Recap and ensure that students have understood:
  – how the first-person narrative and the tone influence the way the incident is built up;
  – how the language, structure and form contribute to the presentation of the characters and how the reader reacts to the ambiguities.
- Ideas should be pooled in class discussion about how surprising or shocking the poem is and how our views change throughout the poem.
- For English Literature, find another poem in Collection B that has a first-person narrator, and ask students to compare the way the speaker conveys his or her thoughts to the reader.

9 Further work

Encourage students to look further at the form (basic shape) and structure (detailed composition) of the poem. Why has the poet chosen to arrange the poem on the page in this way? What effect do the line lengths have? Why has the poet used enjambement between lines and sometimes stanzas? How does the form link to the rhyme pattern and why? Ask them to use the PEEE format to write roughly half a page on this.

Lesson B12
The Drum
John Scott

Learning objective
To understand how Scott uses form and vocabulary to encourage the reader to see recruitment and military in a negative light.

Resources
- Edexcel GCSE Poetry Anthology, page 31
- Audio B12
- Glossary B12
- Worksheet B12.1
- Worksheet B12.2
- Worksheet B12.3
- Image B12.1
- Image B12.2
- Image B12.3

1 Before reading: whole class work

- Show students Images B12.1, B12.2 and B12.3 which are recruitment posters from World War I, World War II and the present, respectively.

Image B12.1

- Discuss and compare the messages conveyed by the posters. How has the message changed and why? What do students think being a soldier is like?

Image B12.2

- Give students the first two lines of the poem: 'I hate that drum's discordant sound, Parading round, and round, and round' Explain that the drum was often beaten in the army before going into attack, in military processions and exercises.

Image B12.3

- Ask students for their initial ideas on why the persona might hate this sound.

2 First reading: whole class work

Listen to the audio reading of the poem, asking students to think about what they have already learned as they listen. Do they have any further thoughts on the meaning of the first two lines of the poem?

3 Close reading: pair work

- Ask students, in pairs, to compare stanzas 1 and 2, explaining that they give two contrasting views of life as a recruit.
- Hand out Worksheet B12.1, which asks students to categorise the vocabulary in the poem as representing the positive things that Scott thinks recruits would get out of life in the army, and then the negative things which recruits would experience.

Worksheet B12.1

- Take feedback and discuss their ideas. Is the poem clearly negative or positive in their view? Make sure students can justify their views with examples from the poem (e.g. 'tawdry lace' isn't really positive, and 'glittering arms' suggests superficiality).
- Lead the discussion on to the personification of 'Ambition' and 'Misery' and why the poet has chosen to personify these two words.

Access

Hand out Worksheet B12.2, which asks students to identify any unfamiliar words. They should write these down and work together to come up with possible meanings based on the context in the poem. They can then take it in turns to look up these words using a dictionary

Worksheet B12.2

(or provide them with Glossary B12), and explain the actual meaning to their partner, comparing how close they were to their original meaning. Finally, they should think how the actual meaning of the word changes their understanding of the poem.

4 Exploring meaning: independent work

- Hand out Worksheet B12.3, which asks six questions to deepen students' understanding of the poem. Refer students to Glossary B1 for definitions of terminology and to Glossary B12 as necessary.
- Take feedback and discuss suitable responses, while students self-assess their work.

Worksheet B12.3

5 Peer assessment

- Ask students to swap their responses to Worksheet B12.3 with a partner, comparing their answers to each of the six questions. Students should:
  - decide which of the two answers for each question is a more detailed and relevant response and annotate the poem in their anthologies accordingly;
  - look for further examples to support the points raised in each question to develop the writer's interpretation;
  - continue to annotate the poem with examples of effective use of contrast.
- Ask students to assess how well their partner has
  - understood Scott's use of negative language to convey his ideas about war;
  - been able to explain, develop and support ideas, making relevant connections between the techniques used and how the ideas, themes and setting are presented.
- They should then decide which of the five bands the work falls into. You may want to refer them to Resource B17.2 (English Literature Higher Tier mark scheme), B17.3 (English Literature Foundation Tier mark scheme) or B17.4 (English mark scheme).
- Ask students to comment on how the answer could have been improved, looking at the importance of supporting points with good examples.

6 Plenary

- Recap and ensure that students have understood:
  - Scott's negative reactions to the army and the effects of conflict;
  - how Scott uses contrasts within the structure and form of the poem to convey the tone and theme.
- Ask students to find examples of how sound effects, rhythm and human voices are linked to the theme of the misery of war and help to create strong feelings.
- For English Literature, compare this poem with other war poems already studied, seeing what different aspects of the effects of war each poet focuses on.

7 Further work

Ask students to design an anti-recruitment poster of which Scott might have approved. Encourage them to use some of the devices he uses, such as negative vocabulary, alliteration and repetition.

Extend

Ask students to write a speech for or against joining the armed forces. Encourage them to use some of the devices Scott uses, such as positive/negative vocabulary, alliteration and repetition.

Suggested answers

1 Before reading

Wartime posters: *fight for your country, loyalty, duty, honour.*
Modern poster: *excitement, travel, trade, experience.*

Lesson B13

O What is that Sound *W.H. Auden*

Learning objective

To understand how Auden uses dialogue and the narrative form to build tension, explore repercussions and express emotions connected with war.

Resources

- Edexcel Poetry Anthology, pages 32-33
- Audio B13
- Glossary B13
- Worksheet B13.1
- Resource B13.1
- Resource B13.2
- Image B13.1

1 Before reading: whole class work

- Read aloud the short traditional ballad, 'She moved through the fair' to students from Resource B13.1. They may be familiar with this ballad. Ask students to focus on the key features of rhyme, rhythm and repetition as you read.

Resource B13.1

- Explain that ballads are traditional poems and/or songs that tell a story. They originated as part of the oral tradition when few people could read and write and so were entertained by tales passed on by word of mouth.

- Ask students what effect this rhyming and rhythm pattern has. Make clear that the poem they are about to study is part of the same tradition and has the same type of rhythm and rhyme.

2 First reading: whole class work

- Display Image B13.1 of a soldier crying on the battlefield.

Image B13.1

- Discuss the tragic side of war. What are people's feelings during periods of war? What might they experience? Discuss how families can be divided, friends fight against one another, etc. Elicit responses from students about current situations that might reflect this.

- Read the poem aloud, having students follow along in their anthologies. Explain that this poem is about two people who are experiencing war and ask them to think about the personas' emotions and attitudes.

3 Close reading: pair work

- Ask students to decide on the number and gender of the speakers in the poem and to use highlighters to show which lines are spoken by each speaker.

- Next, in pairs, students should produce a dramatic reading of the poem (they could use mime and suitable actions, if appropriate), each taking one persona. As they read, they should think about what tone of voice should be used.

- Ask them to join with another pair and peer-assess each other's readings, focusing on clarity of presentation and understanding of the action within the poem and the personas' emotions and attitudes as the poem progresses. Groups should be prepared to feed back to the class.

- Ideas can be collated at the front of the class using the annotation tools on the ActiveTeach and highlighting lines according to speaker. Alternatively you can use Resource B13.2. How do students' interpretations differ? Is there a man and a woman? If so, which way round? Who is speaking in the last stanza? What is the changing tone of voice in the poem? Increasing anxiety as the army approaches? Bewilderment? What effect do the questions have for the reader?

Resource B13.2

- Ensure students understand that one of the characters has deserted and betrayed their lover. What are students' reactions to this? Listen to Audio B13 on the ActiveTeach.

Access

- Hand out Worksheet B13.1, on which the question marks in the poem have been changed to full stops. Ask students to replace eight of the full stops with question marks. This activity should help students to focus on how the word order of the sentence implies a question.

- Discuss their choices. What effect do the questions within the poem have? What do they suggest about the characters? What is the tone of voice suggested by the questions? How does the tone of the questions change as the poem progresses?

Worksheet B13.1

Extend

- How does Auden portray this act of deception and betrayal? Is it justified in the context of war?
- You might also want to introduce the idea that Auden wrote the poem in 1936, at the start of the Spanish Civil War. This was a war that raged between two political groups in Spain from 1936 to 1939 (when the Second World War began). Many civilians were killed, injured or raped simply because of their political beliefs. Many others died of starvation or malnutrition. The war split up communities, families, friends and relationships. W.H. Auden's work may well have been influenced by this war, and could be seen as an exploration of advancing danger and possible betrayal, an allegory for the advancement of Fascism within Europe.

4 Exploring vocabulary: independent work

- Ask students to list all the words in the poem that link with war and conflict.
- Ask them to pick three particularly effective words and write a paragraph explaining how Auden uses words and phrases to explore this theme.
- Explain that the soldiers and images of war provide the obvious clash in this poem but that there is also a second conflict between the personas. Ask students to find words to suggest the clash between the two people featured, and write a paragraph to suggest how Auden portrays their emotions and reactions to war.
- Guide students in thinking about how W.H. Auden's ideas on war compare to those of John Scott in 'The Drum'. How do the messages of the two poets compare? Do they communicate strongly negative or positive messages on war? Or perhaps the poems are left open to a reader's own interpretation? What are the similarities and differences in the ways in which these messages are communicated?

5 Peer assessment

- Ask students in pairs to evaluate each other's paragraph and assess how well their partner has:
  - understood Auden's use of words and phrases and dialogue between two characters to convey his ideas in an unusual way;
  - been able to explain, develop and support ideas, making relevant connections between the techniques used and how the ideas, themes and setting are presented.
- They should then decide which of the five bands the work falls into. You may want to refer them to Resource B17.2 (English Literature Higher Tier mark scheme), B17.3 (English Literature Foundation Tier mark scheme) or B17.4 (English mark scheme).
- Ask them to comment on how the answer could have been improved, looking at the importance of supporting points with good examples.

6 Plenary

- Recap and ensure that students have understood:
  - the ways Auden has conveyed his story through dialogue;
  - how Auden has used the poetic devices of rhyme, rhythm and repetition to develop his ideas.
- Discuss how they feel about the two characters and why.
- Invite reflections on what makes one person betray another. For example, ask students how they would feel if betrayed by someone very close to them. How does Auden bring out these emotions within his poem?
- For English Literature, find another poem in Collection B that has regular stanzas, and ask students to compare the way these are connected to the poem's effect.

7 Further work

Students should write a diary entry from the point of view of the persona who has betrayed their lover, explaining the reasons behind this. They should think about the context of war and the theme of Collection B and use evidence from the poem within their work.

Lesson B14
Conscientious Objector
Edna St. Vincent Millay

Learning objective
To evaluate the effectiveness of the personification of Death within the poem to help convey the persona's stance as a conscientious objector.

Resources
- Edexcel GCSE Poetry Anthology, page 34
- Audio B14
- Glossary B14
- Worksheet B14.1
- Image B14.1
- Image B14.2
- Image B14.3

1 Before reading: whole class work

- Ask students what they know about conscientious objectors (they may have learnt about them in History lessons). Ensure students understand that they are people who object to war and participating in military service for either moral or religious reasons.
- Explain that this poem is written from the view of a conscientious objector and uses personification as one of its key poetic devices.
- Recap on the device of personification and ask students to identify which of the following sentences use personification:
  - The sea raced up the beach.
  - The angry shoulders of the mountain raged.
  - He was swallowed by the enormous armchair.
  - The plant grew like wildfire.
  - The gate creaked in the wind.
- Discuss the image created in each of the examples of personification and clarify why the others are not personification.

2 First reading: whole class work

Listen to Audio B14. Ask students to identify what is being personified as they listen (Death on horseback). Discuss the evidence in the poem for their ideas.

Access

- Hand out Worksheet B14.1, explaining that they should write a paragraph to explain what impression of death is given by the phrases used in the poem.
- Ask students to swap work with a partner and compare their comments.
- Clarify, as necessary, that Death is personified, depicted as a horseman (perhaps reference threatening and ghostly images on horseback from stories such as the Harry Potter novels or *Lord of the Rings*, as an aid).

Worksheet B14.1

3 Looking at imagery: pair work

- Remind students that conscientious objectors refuse to participate in warfare and conflict for moral or religious reasons. They often wish to prevent killing and death.
- Draw students' attention to lines 4–7. Ask them to work in pairs and decide how the poet uses the personification of Death and horse-riding imagery to show the role of the conscientious objector effectively. They may look at the poem as a whole if they wish.
- Ask pairs to feed back to the whole class. Establish that the first-person narrator/persona is the conscientious objector. Look at the intimidating tactics of Death (flicking of whip, hoof on breast) and suggest that this may represent the social pressures to sign up to the army (perhaps link to Scott's poem 'The Drum').

4 Exploring themes: independent work

- Ask students to identify the issues that Death is pursuing in the poem, where he 'has business', i.e. areas where conflict and death are involved. If they have problems, draw their attention to lines 3, 6 and 7.
- Ask them to think about what specific type of conflict these areas of Death's business are.
- Ask students to feed back to the class. Show Image B14.1 of US/international warfare in Cuba during the poet's lifetime. Discuss the fact that this, and the war in the Balkans, were major and controversial conflicts when the poet was writing.

Image B14.1

- Show Images B14.2 and B14.3, of fox hunting and slavery in the US. What is the author's message by including all the above references in her poem?

Image B14.2

Image B14.3

Extend

Draw attention to the repetition of the first line in the poem in line 8. Ask students to explain what they think the line means and to comment on the significance of its repetition in the poem. What might the 'pay-roll' refer to?

5 Independent writing

Ask students to write a paragraph in response to the following question: How does St Millay create a voice and persona to convey the idea of conscience in this poem? Students might like to refer to the first-person narration within the poem, alongside the personification of Death as an intimidating horseman.

6 Peer assessment

- Ask students to swap work with a partner and assess how well their partner has:
  - understood St. Vincent Millay's use of language to create an effective voice to talk about war;
  - been able to explain, develop and support ideas, making relevant connections between the techniques used and how the ideas, themes and setting are presented.
- They should then decide which of the five bands the work falls into. You may want to refer them to Resource B17.2 (English Literature Higher Tier mark scheme), B17.3 (English Literature Foundation Tier mark scheme) or B17.4 (English mark scheme).
- Ask students to go on to comment on how the answer could have been improved, looking at the importance of supporting points with good examples.

7 Plenary

- Recap and ensure that students have understood:
  - the attitudes to war and fighting which are shown in the poem;
  - the ways in which the personification of death presents these attitudes.
- Is it right for individuals to be able to refuse to fight for their country? Conduct a quick discussion followed by a vote.
- For English Literature, find another poem in Collection B that shows strong personal feelings, and ask students to compare the way these feelings are conveyed.

8 Further work

Ask students to re-read the last line and answer the following question: What promises might Death be making and what might 'mapping the route to any man's door' entail? They should present their response as a piece of writing perhaps accompanied by illustrations or digital media.

Clashes and Collisions

Lesson B15
August 6, 1945
Alison Fell

Learning objective
To explore the Fell's use of imagery, vocabulary and form to convey the horror of nuclear attack.

Resources
- Edexcel GCSE Poetry Anthology, page 35
- Audio B15
- Glossary B15
- Worksheet B15.1
- Video B15.1

1 Before reading: whole class work

- Explain that the first ever nuclear bomb was dropped by the US on the Japanese city of Hiroshima at the end of World War II on August 6th, 1945, with the aim of getting Japan to surrender. It caused massive devastation, with more than 120,000 people killed instantly and many more dying of radiation sickness afterwards. More than 70% of the city of Hiroshima was flattened. Explain that the pilot of the aircraft which dropped the bomb was Paul Tibbets and the aircraft was named after his mother, Enola Gay.

- Play Video B15.1, a short news reel about the bombing of Hiroshima with commentary focusing on the role of the *Enola Gay*, the plane that dropped the bomb. Ask students how they feel watching this. What do they think about the tone of the reporting, the attitude of the pilot and the visual effect of the explosion?

Video B15.1

2 First reading: whole class work

- Listen to the audio reading of the poem, asking students to follow in their anthologies and to bear in mind the information about the bombing that they have been given.

- Ensure students have understood what is being described in each stanza in this poem, while being aware of the potentially sensitive issues (some of the imagery is very vivid). You might like to ask why the girl is scarlet and blinded. Who is 'he' at the very end of the poem?

3 Close reading: independent work

- Ask students to draw images based on five words or phrases from the poem that particularly strike them, annotating their drawings with key words and phrases from the poem. If necessary, suggest some of the following ideas: 'apricot ice', 'Marilyn's skirts', 'mermaid's tail', 'old shoe sole', 'lizard', 'ladybird'. They should be thinking about the context of these phrases within the poem – are they in fact ladybirds, for example?

- Provide students with Glossary B15 to help them understand the meaning of any unfamiliar words.

Access

Ask students to find three colours in the poem that suggest images of fire. Why might these have been used?

4 Exploring imagery: pair work

- Ask students to present their drawings from Activity 3 to a partner and discuss, in pairs, why they have depicted the phrases in the way they have. What did they think the poet was trying to convey by using these words? For example, how does 'apricot ice' help us to imagine the explosion? What are 'the eye of his belly' and 'Marilyn's skirts'?

- Take feedback as a whole class, displaying students' drawings of the phrases to develop discussion, and perhaps comparing those which depict the same phrases. Is there a theme in the imagery used by the poet?

5 Exploring interpretations: independent work

- Hand out Worksheet B15.1, asking students to annotate the poem with their answers to the questions.
- Take feedback, guiding students towards the suggested answers and encouraging them to self-assess and correct their work as necessary.

Worksheet B15.1

Extend

Point out that the key sense referred to in this poem is sight. Ask students to find the references to sight and consider why they might be included. Which are the most unusual and/or effective and why?

6 Independent writing

Ask students to answer the following question: How does Fell use words and imagery to show how the horror of Hiroshima alters the persona's point of view? Suggest that they write three paragraphs and remind them to use evidence from the poem to support their points.

7 Peer assessment

- Ask students to swap their paragraphs with a partner. Invite the students to assess how well their partner has:
  - understood Fell's use of words and images to convey her ideas about the horror of Hiroshima;
  - been able to explain, develop and support ideas, making relevant connections between the techniques used and how the ideas, themes and setting are presented.
- They should then decide which of the five bands the work falls into. You may want to refer them to Resource B17.2 (English Literature Higher Tier mark scheme), B17.3 (English Literature Foundation Tier mark scheme) or B17.4 (English mark scheme).
- Ask students to go on to comment on how the answer could have been improved, looking at the importance of supporting points with good examples.

8 Plenary

- Recap and ensure that students have:
  - understood the ways Fell has used imagery and tone to communicate ideas about the horror of nuclear war;
  - responded to the strength of the images they have encountered.
- Invite students in groups to come up with their own images to evoke the falling of a nuclear bomb and share these with the class. What kinds of image create the most powerful effect and why?
- For English Literature, find another poem in Collection B which paints vivid or colourful images, and ask students to compare the effect of these.

9 Further work

Recite the nursery rhyme lines: 'Ladybird, ladybird fly away home, your house is on fire and your children are gone'. Ask students to think about these lines and then write about the various ideas behind the last stanza of the poem.

Lesson B16
Invasion
Choman Hardi

Learning objective
To analyse how Hardi uses vocabulary and verb tense to create an ominous sense of impending conflict.

Resources
- Edexcel GCSE Poetry Anthology, page 36
- Audio B16.1
- Glossary B16
- Worksheet B16.1
- Worksheet B16.2
- Resource B16.1
- Image B16.1

1 Before reading: whole class work

- Set the context of the poem, clarifying the meaning of invasion if necessary. What feelings and ideas does the word prompt (sense of threat, conflict, etc.)?
- Display just the first stanza of the poem on the board using page 36 of the ActiveTeach and clicking on the first zoom area, which enlarges the relevant text.
- Discuss who and where 'they' and 'we' might be (the invaders/outsiders, and the invaded/the current occupiers of the land).
- Then discuss the alternative images created by 'dawn' and 'mist'. What is the general atmosphere of this opening stanza? Work towards the idea that these words often suggest peace and calm, but are clearly threatening here.

2 First reading: whole class work

- Listen to the audio reading of the poem, asking students to follow in the anthology while thinking about the previous discussion.
- Provide students with information about Choman Hardi. She was born in Iraqi Kurdistan, a distinct region of Iraq where the Kurdish people live. Her family fled to Iran when Iraq invaded Kurdistan and persecuted its people, killing thousands of Kurds between 1987 and 1989. Her family returned to Iraq after an amnesty was declared, but arrived in the UK as a refugee in 1993.
- Display Image B16.1 or travelling Kurdish refugees to help set the context for the invasion.

Image B16.1

3 Close reading: pair work

- Ask students to work in pairs and read the poem together. Provide them with Glossary B16 to help with any unfamiliar words. Pairs should find words in the poem that they associate with military conflict using Worksheet B16.1. With whom are these words associated?

Worksheet B16.1

- Ask pairs to feed back to the class, ensuring they have understood the actions taken by 'we' and 'they'. Highlight the frequent references to these pronouns as well as use of 'our'. You might also draw out the contrast between 'guns and tanks point forward' (organised offence) and 'rusty guns and boiling blood' (more disorganised, passionate desperation and anger). Ask students what tone the military words create in the poem. Draw out how a tone of despair and threat is created.

Access

Hand out Worksheet B16.2 for students to brainstorm different types of tone. Give them some scenarios to help them generate ideas, e.g. if they had to explain to their teacher that they hadn't done their homework, what tone might they use? If their friend's pet had died, what would be the tone?

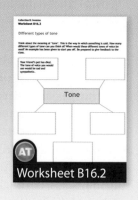
Worksheet B16.2

4   Close reading: group work

- Ask students to re-read the poem, considering what they have already learned about it and, as a group, select four phrases that they think create particularly striking images, e.g. 'death-bringing uniforms' or '[blood will] mix with our drinking water'.
- Ask them to prepare a short presentation on why they find each phrase so effective and how it evokes the feelings of the persona and the point of view of those being invaded.

5   Peer assessment

- Ask students to make their presentations, explaining their reasoning and choices to another group, and to evaluate each other's work. Invite them to assess how well the group has:
  - understood Hardi's use of language, writing and punctuation to convey her ideas about war;
  - been able to explain, develop and support ideas, making relevant connections between the techniques used and how the ideas, themes and setting are presented.
- Ask groups to decide which of the five bands the work falls into. You may want to refer them to Resource B17.2 (English Literature Higher Tier mark scheme), B17.3 (English Literature Foundation Tier mark scheme) or B17.4 (English mark scheme).
- They should then comment on how the answer could have been improved, looking at the importance of supporting points with good examples.

6   Identifying tense: independent work

- Ask students to use three colours to highlight the different tenses used in the poem (past, present, future). Recap on the key features of different tenses if necessary.
- Take brief feedback, discussing the ratio and the placing of each tense. You might want to display Resource B16.1 or use the ActiveTeach annotation tool to highlight words in different colours. Draw attention to the use of the imperative in the final stanza. Discuss the effect of the use of tense in the poem and the tone that it creates, e.g. the use of the future tense creates a sense of impending disaster and suggests that the persona has seen it all happen before and

Resource B16.1

can easily predict the future; 'freedom' is referred to as being in the past and at an end, and was 'short-lived', suggesting that they were occupied in the recent past; the last stanza barks out orders in the imperative, perhaps representing the anticipated invaders' orders.

Extend

Ask students to change the tenses used in the poem to the past tense throughout, altering the first and penultimate lines appropriately. Ask them to write about how this change of tense affects the reading of the poem.

7   Independent writing

Ask students to write two paragraphs in response to the following question: How does Hardi's use of tense convey a sense of threat and despair? Remind them to use evidence from the poem to support their points.

8   Plenary

- Recap and, drawing on the independent writing, ensure that students have:
  - understood Hardi's use of vocabulary and tense;
  - appreciated how Hardi has used these devices to convey the threat of conflict.
- Discuss with the class the different ways (including the rhythm and the use of enjambement) to build up a sense of anxiety and fear.
- For English Literature, discuss the contrast between this poem and others in Collection B which describe horrific events that are taking place or have already done so (e.g. 'August 6, 1945'). Is 'Invasion' any more or less effective because it is looking to the future rather than at the present or the past?

9   Further work

Ask students to look at the last stanza again and to write about what this suggests about the persona's attitude and how it affects our reading of the poem.

Suggested answers

Access

Possible types of tone: ironic, serious, flippant, threatening, apologetic, sympathetic, pessimistic. Give an example of each, where necessary, to help understanding.

Lesson B17
Understanding the assessment

Learning objectives
- To reinforce how poems link with the theme of the collection.
- To find links and comparisons between the poems in the collection.
- To develop the skills needed to write about poems in the assessment.

Resources
- Worksheet B17.1
- Resource B17.1
- Resource B17.2
- Resource B17.3
- Resource B17.4
- ResultsPlus interactives

1 Starter activity: whole class work

- As a class, brainstorm all of the ideas about the theme 'clashes and collisions' that are explored in the poems in this collection. Record ideas using a spider diagram.
- Ask students to come up with at least one way each poem in the collection relates to the theme. You might want to focus on particular lines or imagery from poems and discuss different responses to the same poem and reasons for these.
- It might be helpful to encourage students to sort their ideas into sub-groups.

Access

Ask students to choose one image that could be used to represent each of the poems in the collection. They could write a description of the image, draw it or find an image from a magazine or online. Each student should share their ideas with others, explaining the reasons why they have selected each image and how it links to the theme of the collection.

2 Practising writing in the exam or controlled assessment: pair work

- Divide the class into pairs. Ask pairs to draw a flow diagram showing the process of planning and writing a response to an assessed question. What will they do first in the exam or controlled assessment? What kind of things will they include in their response? How will they conclude their response?
- Hand out Resource B17.1 and ask students to compare the guidance on this sheet to their flow diagrams. Ask them to amend their diagrams accordingly and highlight areas on the Resource sheet which they feel are particularly important for them to remember.

Resource B17.1

3 Preparing for part a) of the English Literature question: whole class work

- Open a ResultsPlus interactive on the ActiveTeach which is relevant to Section B part a) of the Unit 2 English Literature exam, where students have to answer on a single poem. You may want to ensure that it is the relevant tier (either Higher or Foundation) for your students. Sample questions from other collections can often be tailored to your own needs as necessary. ResultsPlus is a unique resource designed to help students achieve their best with sample questions, graded answers and examiner tips. A sample exam question is provided alongside a sample student answer. Each answer is annotated with examiner comments to make clear why the mark has been given, and showing where and how the essay could have been improved to gain a mark in a higher band. See page 5 for guidance on using these activities.

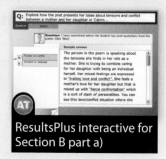
ResultsPlus interactive for Section B part a)

- Use the interactive with the class, encouraging and supporting them to explore what mark might have been given and/or how the sample answer could have been improved. You may also want to make use of the mark scheme provided in Resource B17.2 or Resource B17.3 to help students understand how their essays will be marked.

4 Comparing poems: pair work

- Explain to students who will be taking the English Literature exam that they will be required to compare and contrast the poems they have studied. They will need to think about the different ways in which the poets have approached the theme of the collection, and the ways in which they have communicated their ideas.

- Hand out Worksheet B17.1. You can find the icons to open the resources for this lesson at the bottom of the page underneath the final poem in the collection. Tell students to work in pairs and think about links between the poems in terms of a) the topic explored and the poet's ideas, and b) the use of poetic devices (such as form, language and imagery) and their effects.

Worksheet B17.1

- Take feedback as a class, exploring differences of opinion and asking students to record their thoughts. You might want to compile class spider diagrams which can be used to support students' revision later on.

5 Preparing for part b) of the English Literature question: whole class work

- Open a ResultsPlus interactive on the ActiveTeach which is relevant to Section B part b) of the Unit 2 English Literature exam, where students will be required to compare two poems.

- Use the interactive with the class, encouraging and supporting them to explore what mark might have been given and/or how the sample answer could have been improved. You may also want to make use of the

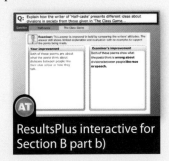

ResultsPlus interactive for Section B part b)

mark scheme provided in Resource B17.2 to help students understand how their essays will be marked.

6 Preparing for the English controlled assessment: whole class work

- Open the ResultsPlus interactive for English controlled assessment. It will help students understand how a sample response can be improved.

- Use the interactive with the class, encouraging and supporting them to explore how the sample answer could have been improved. You may also want to make use of the mark scheme provided in Resource B17.4 to help students understand how their essays will be marked.

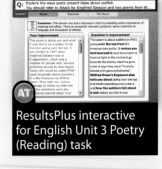

ResultsPlus interactive for English Unit 3 Poetry (Reading) task

7 Assessed question: individual work

- Ask students to think of an appropriate question for a particular poem, justifying how this would allow a student to demonstrate understanding and analysis of the poem(s).
- Ask students to swap essay questions with a partner and plan their essay in bullet points.

8 Peer assessment

Ask students to work in groups of four, share their plans with the group and assess each other's plans using the relevant mark scheme on Resource B17.2, Resource B17.3 or Resource B17.4.

Resource B17.2

Resource B17.3

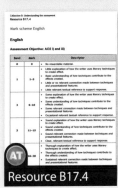

Resource B17.4

9 Further work

Ask students to plan and write an answer to one assessed question within the sample assessment material provided by Edexcel. You may like to direct students to specific questions to suit their ability.

Collection C

Somewhere, anywhere

Lesson C1
Somewhere, anywhere introduction

Learning objectives
- To consolidate students' understanding of the features of poetry and a range of poetic devices.
- To think about what issues poems with a 'somewhere, anywhere' theme might explore.
- To understand the assessment objectives for this unit.

Resources
- Glossary C1
- Worksheet C1.1
- Worksheet C1.2
- Worksheet C1.3
- Interactive C1

1 Starter activity: whole class work

- Ask the class to give examples of some devices that can be used by poets to help convey meaning. If they can, ask them to provide an example of how these devices might be used, and explain how they can be effective.
- Complete the activity in Interactive C1 as a class. The icons to open the resources for this lesson can be found on the contents page for Collection b, on page 37 of the ActiveTeach. This activity involves matching the following poetic devices with the correct definitions: alliteration, assonance, metaphor, onomatopoeia, rhyme, rhythm, personification, simile. Ask individuals to come up to the board and make what they think is the correct connection, or ask the whole class to complete the activity against the clock.

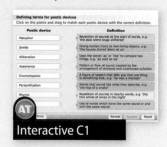

Interactive C1

- Hand out Glossary C1 for students to look at the correct definitions. Remind students that they can return to this glossary to refresh their memory at any point during their study of this collection of poems.

2 Identifying poetic devices: pair work

- Hand out Worksheet C1.1, which gives students examples of different poetic devices from the poems in the collection. They are asked to identify the poetic device used in a second set of quotations from the poems.
- Ask students to swap work with another pair and mark each other's work. Explain that if they make a mistake, each pair must explain to the other pair why they are wrong.

Worksheet C1.1

3 Looking at imagery: independent work

- Provide students with Worksheet C1.2, which gives a list of phrases from the collection that include particularly vivid imagery.
- Ask each student to choose one of these phrases and draw a picture of the item described. Tell them to think about how the words used help them to understand what the poet is trying to communicate and what the item should look like. Ask them to label the picture or write at least two sentences beneath it to explain why they have chosen to draw the image in this way, pinpointing particular words from the phrase.

Worksheet C1.2

- Ask for volunteers to share their pictures with the rest of the class. Ask students to explain why they have illustrated the phrase in this way and why they think the poet's use of imagery is effective.

4 Making inferences from shape: whole class work

- Hand out Worksheet C1.3, which indicates just the shapes of two poems: 'City Jungle' and 'London Snow'.

Worksheet C1.3

- Discuss how students know that these are poems and what they can infer from the shape of them.
- Ask pairs of students to devise a list of five to ten features that differentiate prose from poetry (this should be familiar to them from KS3 work). These might relate to line length, rhyme, rhythm, standard punctuation, grammar and stanzas.
- Ask pairs to feed back to the class and compare and contrast their ideas. Encourage them to think about how each of these aspects of poetry might help a poet convey meaning. For example, if a poem was written using the language of SMS, without any standard punctuation, what impression might this give of the poet or what message he/she is trying to communicate?

5 Exploring ideas: whole class work

- Introduce students to the theme of the collection of poems they are going to study. Ask students what they expect poems in a collection with this title will be about. Get them to focus on the significance of certain places.
- Compile a class list of the types of issues students suggest these poems might explore on the board. To prompt students you could ask them to consider books or films that they have enjoyed with a similar theme.

6 Plenary

Introduce students to the assessment objectives for this unit, according to which course they are following. Explain the skills that they will need to develop while studying these poems, in preparation for their assessment.

English

AO2:

i) Read and understand texts, selecting material appropriate to purpose, collating from different sources and making comparisons and cross-references as appropriate;

iii) Explain and evaluate how writers use linguistic, grammatical, structural and presentational features to achieve effects and engage and influence the reader.

English Literature

AO2: Explain how language, structure and form contribute to writers' presentation of ideas, themes and settings.

AO3: Make comparisons and explain links between texts, evaluating writers' different ways of expressing meaning and achieving effects.

7 Further work

Ask students to find a copy of a poem and annotate explaining what they liked or didn't like about it. Did they like the topic? Was there something particularly memorable about it? Why? They should think about language and vocabulary, any rhyme pattern, line length and form and imagery covered in the lesson. What effect did each of these have and why was it effective (or not) in their view? You might wish to guide them to use a PEEE structure. This terminology is used throughout the scheme of work for the collection and can help to guide students in their writing by ensuring they have made a **Point**, found **Evidence** for this, **Explained** the reasoning and finally **Explored** alternative interpretations and implications.

Suggested answers

Answers to worksheets are provided in the editable Word lesson plans on the ActiveTeach.

5 Exploring ideas
Suggested ideas for topics on the theme of 'somewhere, anywhere' might include the importance of home, outstanding/memorable landscapes, holiday destinations and travel. Why are these places important to us?

Somewhere, anywhere

Lesson C2
City Jungle

Pie Corbett

Learning objective
To explore how Corbett uses imagery, personification and extended metaphor to create a sense of place.

Resources
• Edexcel GCSE Poetry Anthology, page 38
• Audio C2
• Glossary C2
• Worksheet C2.1
• Worksheet C2.2
• Worksheet C2.3
• Image C2.1
• Image C2.2
• Multimedia C2

1 Before reading: independent work

Display the title of the poem on the board. Ask each student to think about the sights and the sounds they would expect to see and hear in a city and in a jungle. Ask students which sights and sounds would be found in both.

2 First reading: whole class

Listen to the reading of the poem on Audio C2 while students follow the poem in their anthologies.

• Ask them to think about the connections that are made between cities and jungles. What are their first impressions of the poem? What is the mood and tone?

3 Close reading: pair work

• Ask students to work in pairs to complete Worksheet C2.1, identifying all the nouns and verbs in the poem and explaining what kind of image is created by each group, both together and separately.

• Ask pairs to feed back to the class. Draw out the idea that the verbs make the city seem more animalistic.

Worksheet C2.1

Access

Review nouns (person, place, thing, idea) and verbs (action or state of being) with students. Ask them to brainstorm nouns they would normally associate with the jungle and verbs they would normally associate with the city.

4 Exploring imagery: independent work

• Introduce the idea of personification – that things that are not literally alive are assigned characteristics associated with a living person or animal.

• Ask students to find the examples of personification in the poem, and use the annotation tool on the ActiveTeach to highlight them. Make sure students understand how the author has used personification to connect the city and the jungle.

• Ask students to pick one example of personification in the poem and think about how the combination of the city objects and the jungle animals is effective in terms of appearance. They should be ready to feedback to the class.

5 Exploring imagery: group work

• Divide the class into two groups and ask them to compete to gain points. To receive a point, they will need to identify what kind of sound is suggested, how (e.g. through alliteration or onomatopoeia) and how it conveys atmosphere or mood. You might want to highlight these examples using the ActiveTeach annotation tools at the front of the class as you go.

Worksheet C2.2

• Then hand out Worksheet C2.2 and ask students to complete this individually.

Extend

Ask students to work in pairs to decide how the poem fits into the theme of 'somewhere, anywhere.' Encourage them to think about how imagery helps to create a sense of place and why a sense of place is important. Ask them to feed back to the class.

6 Exploring imagery: whole class work

- Explain to students what an extended metaphor is and that the continuous link between city and jungle throughout the poem is an example of one.
- Show students Images C2.1 and C2.2. Ask them to think about how cities and jungles might be similar e.g. danger or threat, size, sounds, light, etc.

Image C2.1

Image C2.2

- Ask students what vocabulary or phrases from the poem are effective in comparing the jungle and city.
- Ask students what they think is the effect of the extended metaphor. What do the jungle words portray about the city? For example, 'bare/Their yellow teeth' creates a sense of danger.
- The words 'hunched', 'cough', 'shuffle' are interesting because they relate to humans. What might these words suggest is happening to human life within the city?

7 Multimedia activity: group work

- Divide students into groups and hand out Worksheet C2.3 which briefs them on how to complete a short multimedia activity provided on the ActiveTeach. When Multimedia C2 is opened, you will be prompted to save the file somewhere on your system. The multimedia clips can then be accessed by extracting them from the zip file, and then opened in editing software for students to use and modify. The aim of the activity is to encourage students to interpret the poet's ideas, thoughts and feelings through selection and editing of the material provided. Students will require access to a software editing package and up to an hour to complete the task.

Worksheet C2.3

8 Independent writing

Ask students to write a half-page response to the following question: Explain how the poet uses personification and extended metaphor to create an unusual image of the city. Use examples from the poem.

9 Peer assessment

- Ask students to swap their answers to the independent writing task with a partner. Invite the students to mark each other's work. Students should assess how well their partner's responses: show an understanding of the use of personification and extended metaphor; use the 'PEEE' technique to show the link between form and point of view and explain what effects are created; demonstrate the ability to make relevant connections between the techniques used and the presentation of an unusual image of a city landscape.
- Students should award up to five marks, deciding which of the five bands the work falls into. Refer them to Resource C17.2 (English Literature Higher Tier mark scheme), C17.3 (English Literature Foundation Tier mark scheme) or C17.4 (English mark scheme).
- They should then comment on how the answer could be improved, looking at the importance of supporting points with good examples.

10 Plenary

- Recap and ensure that students have:
  - understood how Corbett has used imagery, personification and extended metaphor to create a sense of place;
  - responded to the sense of danger in the poet's presentation of the city landscape.
- Brainstorm the ways sights and sounds can be used to take a fresh look at familiar places and scenes, such as the countryside or railway stations.
- For English Literature, find another poem in Collection C in which extended metaphor and sights and sounds are used to create a memorable location. Give examples to support your points.

11 Further work

Design a poster aimed at a newcomer to a city, showing the atmosphere and the possible dangers they might encounter, using the ideas and images within the poem as a starting point.

Somewhere, anywhere

Lesson C3
City Blues

Mike Hayhoe

Learning objective
To evaluate how Hayhoe uses language and form to present alternative images of a city.

Resources
• Edexcel GCSE Poetry Anthology, page 39
• Audio C3
• Glossary C3
• Worksheet C3.1
• Worksheet C3.2
• Image C3.1
• Image C3.2
• Interactive C3

1 Before reading: independent work

Ask students to think about the title and what it evokes for them. What might 'blues' refer to? What experience of cities do students have? Are they positive or negative? You might then want to provide them with the first line of the poem: 'Sunday dawn in a November city'. Do their expectations of the poem change? Collate ideas to come back to at a later point.

Access

Remind students what a synonym is. Ask them to complete Interactive C3, matching words with their synonyms. Explain that use of synonyms is one of the features of this poem.

Interactive C3

2 First reading: whole class

• Listen to Audio C3, asking students to follow the reading in their anthologies.
• Ask students to feed back their feelings on the poem. What do they think is being described? Can they imagine the scene that is being depicted?
• How is the poem read? Discuss their initial responses to the unusual form and presentation of the poem. Why are words linked with lines? Students might suggest that some are synonyms, but highlight that many are not.

3 Exploring form and effect: pair work

• Ask students to work in pairs to discuss why they think the poem is presented in this way. How do the words joined by lines compare to each other? How do the different words change the meaning and mood or tone of a line?

• Encourage them to read lines aloud to each other twice, substituting a different word each time. They should concentrate on sound and the tone and mood created each time.

• Hand out Worksheet C3.1, which provides a copy of the poem with blank spaces for the alternative words. Ask students to decide, in pairs, which alternative they prefer, giving their reasons and then writing a sentence to explain the mood created.

• Students should then join with another pair to compare their versions and their effect on the reader.

Worksheet C3.1

4 Exploring ideas: independent work

• Ask students to find all references to nature.
• As a class, discuss the effect of including these references to nature in a poem about a city. Do the references seem to fit or are they out of place? Why does the author include them?

5 Exploring ideas: pair work

• Hand out Worksheet C3.2.
• In pairs, students role-play a conversation between a teacher and a student using these words and phrases.
• Each pair should perform their role-play to another pair, who should peer-assess, focusing on tone. Was the vocabulary used positively or negatively? Why?

Worksheet C3.2

• As a class, discuss whether this activity has affected their reading of the poem. Has using the vocabulary in a different way changed their picture of the city? Encourage them to link their ideas to the title of the poem.

Extend

Give students the following phrases: 'not big enough'; 'leaves into a lurch'; 'comes to the point'. Ask them to explore alternative interpretations for each phrase and the effect these have on the poem and the impression of place conveyed.

6 Exploring imagery: independent work

- Draw students' attention to the metaphorical phrases 'sets glass aflame' and 'A sheet of paper … is a swan/bird' in lines 2-5 and 11-15.
- Display Images C3.1 and C3.2. Is this how students think the poet would want us to see the city he is describing? Use these images as a starting point for a discussion on interpretation of this imagery. (e.g. 'sets glass aflame' could be seen as a beautiful image of reflecting sunlight on glass or as a more violent one connected with fire).

Image C3.1

Image C3.2

7 Independent writing

Ask students to write two paragraphs exploring the reasons why the poet might have used this unusual form. They should reference lines from the poem and discuss the alternative images of the city and sense of place.

8 Peer assessment

- Ask students to swap their answers to the independent writing above with a partner. Invite the students to mark each other's work. Students should assess how well their partner's responses:
  - show an understanding of the distinctive form employed and its effect;
  - demonstrate the ability to explain, develop and support ideas, making relevant connections between the techniques used and the theme of seeing the city in different ways.

- Students should then award up to five marks, deciding which of the five bands the work falls into. You may want to refer them to Resource C17.2 (English Literature Higher Tier mark scheme), C17.3 (English Literature Foundation Tier mark scheme) or C17.4 (English mark scheme).
- They should then comment on how the answer could have been improved, looking at the importance of supporting points with good examples.

9 Plenary

- Recap and ensure that students have:
  - understood how Hayhoe has used language and form to present different images of a city;
  - explored the effect of choosing one of the two words given in each case.
- Discuss the ways that one word can affect our view of a mood or situation. Think of and display on the board different pairs of words which can alter meaning and effect (e.g. untidy/casual; glared/gleamed; strolled/ loitered; chases/charges; helps/forces).
- For English Literature, find one other poem in Collection C which also describes a place in an unusual way. Compare them and discuss and analyse which one students think is more successful in achieving a desired effect and why. Examples should be given to back up arguments and any disagreements explored.

10 Further work

Ask students to look again at the last eight lines of the poem, from 'In the shadow/shade'. They should write a paragraph suggesting the poet's feelings about the city as portrayed in this section and in the title.

Suggested answers

4 Exploring ideas
dawn, sun, shadows, wind, trees, leaves, air, sunlight, swan, bird, shadow, shade.

Lesson C4
Postcard from a Travel Snob *Sophie Hannah*

Learning objective

To explore how Hannah uses language and irony to present two opposing attitudes towards the 'ideal' holiday.

Resources
• Edexcel GCSE Poetry Anthology, page 40
• Audio C4
• Glossary C4
• Worksheet C4.1
• Worksheet C4.2
• Video C4.1
• Video C4.2

1 Before reading: independent work

• Give students Worksheet C4.1, a postcard template. Ask them to briefly write a typical holiday postcard to an elderly relative in no more than ten sentences. Ask half the class to imagine that they are on an ideal holiday, the other half that they are having a nightmare holiday. They should think about the characteristics of the place, including facilities, activities, the company, accommodation, etc.

Worksheet C4.1

• Select some students to read out their postcards. Compose responses and relate the concept of going on holiday to the theme of 'somewhere, anywhere' – the ideal destination for one person may be another's worst nightmare.

2 First reading: whole class work

• Watch Video C4.1 of Sophie Hannah reading this poem.

• Ask students to summarise the two contrasting types of holiday destination described in the poem. Ask them to pick out words and phrases

Video C4.1

which build up an impression of each of these two different types of place. You might want to compile two separate lists at the front of the class of these words and phrases. Is there a certain type of vocabulary used for each of them? What impression of the two types of place does this vocabulary communicate? Is one portrayed in a more negative or positive light than the other? Why might this be?

3 Exploring ideas: pair work

• Draw students' attention to the phrases 'I do not wish that anyone was here' (line 1), 'perish the thought' (line 4) and 'when you're as multi-cultural as me' (line 13). Ask them to work in pairs to come up with some adjectives which describe the tone suggested by these phrases. They should also think about adjectives to describe the character of the persona in the poem.

• Ask pairs to feed back to the class. They might have adjectives such as 'superior', 'critical', 'pompous' or 'scathing'. What effect does the reversal of the stereotypical phrase in line 1 have? Do students like the persona? Does the poet like the persona? Refer them back to the title of the poem.

4 Exploring language: whole class work

• Watch Video C4.2, where Hannah talks about how she actually really enjoys the 'clichéd' package holiday and laughs at people who 'go out of their way to have an uncomfortable time'.

Video C4.2

• Discuss the concept of indirect communication. Hannah has presented the persona as a figure of ridicule and invites the reader to laugh at the persona from the outset (e.g. by including 'Snob' in the title).

• You might want to introduce the concept of irony and explain that the poet has used phrases in an ironic way in order to communicate her message.

Access

Ensure students understand the concept of indirect communication and what the tone and message of the poem is. You might want to ask them whether the poet is like the persona within the poem. You could draw their attention to the phrases 'Perish the thought' and 'When you're as multi-cultural as me'.

5 Exploring language: group work

- Hand out Worksheet C4.2, which asks students to work in groups to discuss and answer a set of questions about the poem.
- Take feedback and discuss any differences in students' responses to the poem.

Worksheet C4.2

Extend

Ask students to find out what an anthropologist does and write two paragraphs explaining how the study of human beings can be applied to the poem as a whole and how human beings view each other.

6 Exploring ideas: independent writing

Ask students to write a paragraph explaining how Hannah has used language to communicate two different attitudes to the theme of choice of holiday destination.

7 Peer assessment

- Ask students to swap their paragraphs written in answer to the independent writing activity with a partner. Invite the students to mark each other's work. Students should assess how well their partner's responses:
  - show an understanding of Hannah's use of language and how this can create tone and mood;
  - demonstrate the ability to make relevant connections between the techniques used and the presentation of the theme of alternative views on holiday destinations.

- They should then award up to five marks, deciding which of the five bands the work falls into. You may want to refer them to Resource C17.2 (English Literature Higher Tier mark scheme), C17.3 (English Literature Foundation Tier mark scheme) or C17.4 (English mark scheme).
- Finally, ask them to comment on how the answer could have been improved, looking at the importance of supporting points with good examples.

8 Plenary

- Recap and ensure that students have understood the ways in which Hannah has:
  - used irony to examine different holiday venues which some might consider 'ideal';
  - grasped the way in which contrast is used to striking effect.
- Ask students to make a chart, grid or list that they can complete/add to while studying the poems from Collection C, subdividing poems into different groups and making links between them. Show how the first poems studied might fit into this. This can then be updated at regular intervals over the course of studying poetry.
- For English Literature, choose another poem in Collection C as a group that also uses contrasts and invite students to give examples that show the effect of these contrasts.

9 Further work

Ask students to work in pairs to write a short holiday review from the point of view of a typical 'sun-and-sangria' package holidaymaker who has travelled to the holiday destination of the travel snob.

Suggested answers

3 First reading

Package holiday: *Karaoke nights, beer, drunken tourist types, seaside-town, consumer-hell, guest house, hotel, sun-and-sangria, package holiday.*

Travel snob's destination: *Peaceful, untouched by man, sleeping in a local farmer's van, where nobody speaks English, wine connoisseurs.*

Lesson C5
Sea Timeless Song

Grace Nichols

Learning objective

To understand how Nichols uses both language and inspiration from her culture to explore the universal nature of the sea.

Resources
- Edexcel GCSE Poetry Anthology, page 41
- Audio C5
- Glossary C5
- Worksheet C5.1
- Worksheet C5.2
- Image C5.1
- Image C5.2
- Image C5.3
- Image C5.4
- Video C5.1
- Video C5.2

1 Before reading: whole class work

- Brainstorm words and ideas connected with the sea. Encourage students to focus on their own experiences of, and feelings about, the sea. Draw these out by asking what the sea means to them and what memories they associate with it.
- Ask students which words work particularly well when describing the sea and what linguistic features a poet can use to help with imagery, e.g. onomatopoeia, sibilance.
- Display Images C5.1, C5.2, C5.3 and C5.4. Using Glossary C5, ensure students know what a hibiscus plant is. Explain that the images show the four nouns explored in the poem.

Image C5.1

Image C5.2

Image C5.3

Image C5.4

2 Before reading: pair work

- Hand out Worksheet C5.1, which lists words from the poem. Have students work in pairs to construct their own poem using these words. They may use each word as many

Worksheet C5.1

times as they like, but they must use each one at least once.
- Ask each pair to read out their poem to the rest of the class and discuss the different effects created.

3 First reading: whole class work

- Watch Video C5.1, available on the ActiveTeach in which Grace Nichols reads her poem.
- Ask students to identify the similarities and differences between their versions and Nichols' poem.

Video C5.1

- Focus discussion on which words Nichols has chosen to repeat. Ask them why they think the poet chose to repeat the phrase 'sea timeless'. Encourage them to think about how this links with the repetitive sound of the sea and the eternity of the tides.

4 Exploring ideas: pair work

- Hand out Worksheet C5.2, which asks students to find links and connections between the four nouns in the poem: the hurricane, hibiscus, sea and tourists.
- Take feedback, drawing out why the poet might have used those particular images and the effect they have. Discuss the temporary nature of hurricanes, flowers, and tourists and how comparing these to the sea presents a contrast and reinforces the theme that the sea is not only always there, but it is universal.

Worksheet C5.2

- Ask students how they think this theme fits in with the idea of 'somewhere, anywhere'. Ideas might include that the images are all evocative of a tropical location, and the importance and centrality of the sea for the poet.

Access

Explain that Nichols is originally from Guyana, a small country on the northern coast of South America that is part of the English-speaking Caribbean. Ask students to work in groups to discuss how the imagery in the poem would be part of Nichols' culture.

5 Exploring language: whole class work

- Check that all students understand the concept of dialect. Ask them to find examples of non-standard dialect in the poem, e.g. verbs or auxiliaries missing, non-standard verb forms.
- Discuss what effect the use of dialect has in this poem.

Extend

Students should research the oral call-and-response tradition of African Caribbean culture. Write a paragraph about the poem in the light of this tradition, referencing Nichols' use of dialect, rhythmic language and repetition.

6 Exploring meaning: Whole class work

Video C5.2

- Watch Video C5.2 in which Grace Nichols explains how she is influenced by both English and Caribbean culture in her life and writing.
- Once students have watched the poem, ask them to explain the poet's reasons for using repetition and rhythm in the poem– what does she feel it communicates? What is the significance of the sea for her and how does it join the two cultures of England and Guyana?

7 Independent writing

Ask students to write two paragraphs in response to the following question: How has Nichols used aspects of her culture to connect with a universal theme in this poem? Emphasise that they should comment on specific examples from the poem.

8 Peer assessment

- Invite students to exchange their work in response to the independent writing activity above and mark it. They should assess how well their partner's responses:
  - show an understanding of how Nichols uses language and her home culture in her poetry;
  - demonstrate the ability to make relevant connections between the techniques used and the depiction of the timeless sea.
- They should award up to five marks, deciding which of the five bands the work falls into. You may want to refer them to Resource C17.2 (English Literature Higher Tier mark scheme), C17.3 (English Literature Foundation Tier mark scheme) or C17.4 (English mark scheme).
- Ask them to comment on how the answer could have been improved, looking at the importance of supporting points with good examples.

9 Plenary

- Recap and ensure that students have:
  - understood the ways in which Nichols has used language and cultural inspiration to explore the universal nature of the sea;
  - responded to the use of rhythm and repetition.
- Discuss as a group ideas about the rhythm and power of the sea. Invite thoughts about how this creates a strong contrast with things that pass quickly: think what other symbols might have been used (e.g. butterflies, tropical storms, the blink of an eye).
- For English Literature, compare this poem with another from Collection C which also uses repetition and a strong rhythm. Give examples to show how successful the effects of these are.

10 Further work

In pairs or individually, ask students to set the poem to music, thinking about the choice of instruments or sound effects that might be appropriate.

Alternatively, they could write a letter to Grace Nichols either praising or criticising the poem and justifying their comments.

Lesson C6
My mother's kitchen *Choman Hardi*

Learning objective
To develop an understanding of how Hardi conveys her ideas about what makes a home while she is forced to move from place to place.

Resources
- Edexcel GCSE Poetry Anthology, page 42
- Audio C6
- Glossary C6
- Worksheet C6.1
- Worksheet C6.2
- Image C6.1
- Image C6.2

1 Before reading: whole class work

- Ask students what they do when they first go into a kitchen. Discuss what is distinct about a kitchen as opposed to other rooms, drawing out the experiences, expectations and purposes that are attached to it. What might they see or smell here?
- Discuss what is in their kitchen that students associate particularly with their mother or another relative. What are their earliest memories connected with their kitchen? Is there anything in their kitchen that has been inherited? What in their kitchens would they miss most if they moved away?

2 First reading: whole class work

- Listen to Audio C6 or read the poem to the class, asking students to follow it in their anthologies.
- Ask students to share their initial impressions after the first reading.
- Prompt discussion: Do they think the poet is pleased to be inheriting her mother's kitchen? How can they tell?

3 Exploring ideas: pair work

- Explain that Choman Hardi was born in Iraqi Kurdistan. Her family fled to Iran when the Iraqi government conducted a campaign of mass displacement of the Kurdish populations within northern Iraq in the 1980s. She returned to Iraq after the amnesty. In 1993 she arrived in the UK as a refugee. Display Images C6.1 and C6.2 of Kurdish refugees in temporary housing and a devastated village.

Image C6.1

Image C6.2

- Hand out Worksheet C6.1. Ask students to re-read the poem in pairs, keeping the poet's background in mind, and then to pick out at least three phrases that now seem more significant. They should then explain how each links to the poet's experiences.
- Take feedback from pairs and discuss whether students now respond differently to the poem.

Worksheet C6.1

Access

- Hand out worksheet C6.2, which asks students to identify items which the poet's mother still has that the poet will inherit, and items which have been lost.
- Students should feed back to the class, comparing answers.
- Discuss how the items still owned and those which have been lost relate to each other. How are they similar and/or different? How are they described in the poem? Why might this be?

Worksheet C6.2

4 Exploring ideas: group work

- Ask students, working in groups, to go through each stanza of the poem, thinking about the experiences from the perspective of Hardi's mother. What does each stanza say about what she must have gone through and what she must feel?
- Each group should then choose five or six words to describe her reactions to her situation.
- Ask groups to feed back to the class. Were there any words that were similar among the groups?

5 Exploring imagery: pair work

- Ask students to work in pairs to explore the implications of the last line in the poem, thinking about the symbolism of trees. Ideas they could consider include trees as a symbol of life and images of devastated trees in war zones.
- Ask students to compare the trees left behind to the transferable image of the kitchen as 'home'. What does each of these represent in the poem? How do they convey a sense of loss?
- Ask pairs to feed back to the class. Draw out the difference between movable objects of 'home' versus the static concept of trees, grapes etc. which cannot be moved. Suggest that each represents more than just a tree or a glass but a concept of 'home'.

Extend

Ask students to write a paragraph explaining what they think the poet means in the last line. Encourage them to think about the previous activities as well as the history of the poet. They should also look back at the first line of the poem. Ask them to feed back their ideas to the class. Encourage different interpretations of the line.

6 Independent writing

Ask students to use the phrases they identified in Activity 3 to write two paragraphs in response to the following question: How does the poet explore the theme of 'somewhere, anywhere' in this poem?

7 Peer assessment

- Invite students to exchange their work in response to the independent writing task and mark it. They should assess how well their partner's responses:
  - show an understanding of how Hardi uses language and structure to explore the importance of place;
  - demonstrate the ability to make relevant connections between the techniques used and the presentation of the people and places described.
- Students should then award up to five marks, deciding which of the five bands the work falls into. You may want to refer them to Resource C17.2 (English Literature Higher Tier mark scheme), C17.3 (English Literature Foundation Tier mark scheme) or C17.4 (English mark scheme).
- Then ask students to comment on how the answer could have been improved, looking at the importance of supporting points with good examples.

8 Plenary

- Recap and ensure that students have:
  - understood the ways Hardi conveys what makes a home when someone has to move frequently;
  - responded to the attention to detail, and how this is used to focus on what you can and what you cannot take away when moving from home to home.
- Ask students to update their grid/list of sub-groups within the collection, discussing why they have put this poem in a particular group.
- Collect a number of suggestions of objects of all kinds (natural, artefacts) which make a place special and which students would miss if they were without them. Discuss any common features of the list.
- For English Literature, look at two or three other poems in this collection that show affection for a place or setting. Ask students to compare how these feelings are created by use of specific examples.

9 Further work

Ask students to write a poem about something that represents 'home' to them. Encourage them to think about why they appreciate it, what it stands for to them, what it would mean to lose it. Remind them to create strong images.

Lesson C7
Cape Town morning *Ingrid de Kok*

Learning objective
To explore how de Kok uses imagery and vocabulary to convey the atmosphere of a specific place.

Resources
• Edexcel GCSE Poetry Anthology, page 43
• Audio C7
• Glossary C7
• Worksheet C7.1
• Worksheet C7.2
• Worksheet C7.3
• Video C7.1

1 Before reading: whole class work

Ask students what they know about South Africa. What do they imagine it to be like? Ask them to brainstorm some adjectives.

2 First reading: whole class work

Watch Video C7.1 of Ingrid de Kok introducing and then reading her poem. It contains some footage that links directly to the poem.

Video C7.1

3 Exploring structure: pair work

• Distribute Worksheet C7.1. Ask students to group the lines into four three-line stanzas, using association of ideas. Each line is labelled, indicating whether it is the first, second or third line of a stanza.

• Ask students to look at the poem in the anthology and compare Ingrid de Kok's version with their own version. What are the similarities and differences?

• Give students the following four nouns and ask them to identify the verbs in the poem associated with each one. Encourage them to focus on the action in the poem and the corresponding structure:
  – window panes
  – street children
  – flower sellers
  – trucks.

Worksheet C7.1

4 Looking at language: whole class work

• Remind students of the beauty, weather, poverty and violence mentioned by the poet in Video C7.1. Can they find examples of these subjects in the poem? How are they explored? What is the tone of the words used?

• Remind them of the adjectives they came up with in Activity 1. How do their initial ideas of South Africa and/or Cape Town fit with the city as described in the poem? What overall impression of Cape Town do they get from the poem at this point?

5 Analysing language: pair work

• Hand out Worksheet C7.2, which asks students to answer various questions about the poem.

• Encourage them to annotate their own copies of the poem with the answers, either as they complete the activity or following class feedback.

Worksheet C7.2

6 Exploring vocabulary: independent work

• Hand out Worksheet C7.3, which gives various words from the poem. Ask students to suggest possible pairings, giving their reasons.

• Take feedback, focusing on association of ideas, contrasts, and positive and negative connotations. Ask: What impression of Cape Town does this vocabulary give the reader?

Worksheet C7.3

Extend

Ask students to imagine that they are one of the street children in the poem and to write about waking up to this scene. What noises, sights and smells are there? How does the poem convey these? Encourage them to think about the deprivation and daily difficulties faced by such children in this type of urban landscape.

7 Exploring ideas: group work

- Organise students into four groups and ask each group to create a different tableau/freeze frame, each one representing one of the stanzas of the poem.
- Ask the groups to show their tableaux to the rest of the class.
- Discuss, comparing and contrasting the tableaux.

8 Independent writing

Ask students to respond to the following question in roughly half a page: Explain how the poet uses imagery and vocabulary to present a view of Cape Town.

9 Peer assessment

- Invite students to exchange their work in response to the independent writing task and mark it. They should assess how well their partner's responses:
  - show an understanding of how de Kok uses vocabulary and imagery;
  - demonstrate the ability to make relevant connections between the techniques used and the portrait of Cape Town she presents.
- Ask them to award up to five marks, deciding which of the five bands the work falls into. You may want to refer them to Resource C17.2 (English Literature Higher Tier mark scheme), C17.3 (English Literature Foundation Tier mark scheme) or C17.4 (English mark scheme).
- They should then comment on how the answer could have been improved, looking at the importance of supporting points with good examples.

10 Plenary

- Recap and ensure that students have:
  - understood the ways de Kok has used imagery and vocabulary to convey the atmosphere of Cape Town;
  - responded to the sights, sounds and smells of an urban landscape.
- Discuss the extremely hard life of the people she describes and how this differs from picture postcard views of South Africa they might see in publicity for tourism purposes. If you have a travel brochure or similar you can show, this might help to demonstrate the contrast.
- For English Literature, ask students to find another poem in Collection C that presents a negative or ambiguous view of a particular setting (town or country), and compare the two poems, giving examples to illustrate their points.

11 Further work

Ask students to write a short poem describing four aspects of the place where they live, showing contrasting ideas and feelings. This might include local people, attractive views, lack of amenities, etc. Encourage them to think carefully about the vocabulary they could use and the images they want to create in the mind of the reader.

Lesson C8

Our Town with the Whole of India! *Daljit Nagra*

Learning objective
To evaluate the ways in which Nagra uses language and imagery to explore Indian culture in England.

Resources
• Edexcel GCSE Poetry Anthology, pages 44–45
• Audio C8
• Glossary C8
• Worksheet C8.1
• Worksheet C8.2
• Image C8.1
• Image C8.2

1 Before reading: whole class work

• Ask students to think about their neighbourhood and list details of what they might see there. You might want to provide your own example to encourage discussion. Are there any particular festivals which are celebrated where they live? What types of activities take place where they live at different times of the year? This could be as simple as Christmas, for example.

• How do these represent their town, country or culture? What is their significance for students and what emotions do they associate with them? What are the similarities and differences between activities and what do they represent for the students? Record ideas at the front of the class.

2 First reading: whole class work

• Listen to Audio C8, asking students to follow in their anthologies. Discuss students' initial impressions of the poem. What does it make them think of? How does it make them feel?

• To what extent are the images described familiar to them? Do they see any of these things in their own home towns? What are the differences and similarities? Explain that the poem is based on the London suburb of Southall.

• Encourage them to look at the poem on the page. Draw their attention to the amount of detail in the poem and the dense layout. Ask them what the effect of this is. Draw out the idea that all of these details combine to represent the huge amount of activity that the poet sees as a key aspect of Indian culture within England within his local town.

• Refer back to the title. Point out the repeated use of 'Our' to show the poet's sense of ownership of all the action within the poem.

Access

• Display Images C8.1 and C8.2 of a pavement tandoori and jalebi sweets. Make sure students know what jalebis and the fruit and vegetables mentioned are. Refer to Glossary C8 as necessary.

• If any students know these items from first-hand experience, briefly draw out what they mean to them. Why are they mentioned in the poem?

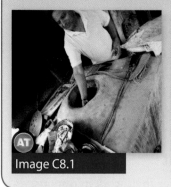
Image C8.1

Image C8.2

3 Exploring language: pair work

• Hand out Worksheet C8.1, which asks students to work in pairs and look at the first stanza to find words which are associated with traditional Indian culture. They should then find words associated with traditional British culture which link with the first set of words.

Worksheet C8.1

• Take feedback and draw out the way that names of festivals, mythological characters and words associated with food and music from Asia and the West are juxtaposed in the poem.

• Discuss the effect of this juxtaposition and comparison of words. What does this highlight about Asian culture in Britain? Are the differences between cultures as clear-cut as we think? Emphasise the diversity of British culture. What does it suggest about the atmosphere of the place?

4 Exploring ideas: group work

- Organise students into groups of three or four. Allocate five of the phrases on Worksheet C8.2 to each group. Ask them to annotate each one with ideas about the connotations of the phrase, what effect it has on the reader and/or why the poet might have chosen it. You will need to model one or two examples first. Students will need as much support as possible to complete this task, looking at the significance of the phrases within the context of the poem.

AT Worksheet C8.2

- Take feedback and compare ideas about each phrase.
- Explore how each phrase might help the reader to understand Indian culture within England and what the poet might have wanted the reader to see.

Extend

- Ask students to study the last word on each line and consider how the poet's selection and the positioning of these words help to present his ideas.
- Point out that several of these are significant, although the line breaks initially seem to be quite random, for example:
  - 'sundering' – breaking or wrenching apart – this might suggest the difficulty in maintaining one culture within another;
  - 'customised' – altered, for an occasion – perhaps used for the streets here to emphasise how the Indian and British cultures are mixing and creating a new enhanced atmosphere within the town;
  - 'Vasaikhi' – this is an important festival in many parts of India at roughly the same time as Easter.
- Ask students to select three other examples and explain their significance. Refer them to Glossary C8 where necessary.

5 Independent writing

Ask students to write three paragraphs in response to the following question: How does Nagra use language to create a vivid image of traditionally Indian culture within an English town? Suggest that they select examples of phrases from Activity 4 to help. Encourage them to think about how Nagra's poem depicts place and fits with the theme of the collection.

6 Peer assessment

- Invite students to exchange their paragraphs in response to the independent writing activity above and mark it. They should assess how well their partner's responses:
  - show an understanding of why Nagra uses imagery which is strongly linked to the senses (check examples are given and explained);
  - demonstrate the ability to make relevant connections between the techniques used and the presentation of cultural variety.
- They should award up to five marks, deciding which of the five bands the work falls into. You may want to refer them to Resource C17.2 (English Literature Higher Tier mark scheme), C17.3 (English Literature Foundation Tier mark scheme) or C17.4 (English mark scheme).
- Ask them to comment on how the answer could have been improved, looking at the importance of supporting points with good examples.

7 Plenary

- Recap and ensure that students have:
  - understood the ways in which Nagra has used language and imagery to explore aspects of traditionally Indian culture on the streets of England;
  - grasped how the poet conveys through an appeal to the senses a vibrant view of the impact of traditionally Indian culture on the English town.
- Discuss as a class which pictures stand out most strongly in their minds, and invite a list of particularly vivid town scenes familiar to them.
- For English Literature, update the chart, grid or list on connections which students have previously created. Find one or two poems in Collection C with vivid details that capture the scene in a town or city. Compare and contrast the selected poems with this one.

8 Further work

Ask students to write a detailed description of a scene in their own neighbourhood. Emphasise that they should use imagery to evoke the atmosphere. Why is the place significant for them? What kind of cultural features are present?

Somewhere, anywhere

Lesson C9
In Romney Marsh

John Davidson

Learning objective
To explore how Davidson uses form, imagery and linguistic features to convey his admiration for Romney Marsh.

Resources
• Edexcel GCSE Poetry Anthology, page 46
• Audio C9
• Glossary C9
• Worksheet C9.1
• Worksheet C9.2
• Video C9.1
• Interactive C9

1 Before reading: individual work

• Ask students to discuss their favourite landscape. Have they travelled somewhere they love? Do they have a particular area near their homes that makes them happy?

• Ask them to think of a sight, a smell and a sound associated with a particular place and come up with three adjectives to describe their overall feeling about it.

• Ask selected students to share their adjectives and sensory associations with the class.

• Explain that this poet is writing about one of his most memorable and enjoyable experiences of a specific location, Romney Marsh. Explain that this is a particularly beautiful area of salty marsh in the south-east of England. If you have internet access, it will be helpful to display a map of the location of Romney Marsh on a promontory on the south-east coast. This can be found by searching for 'Romney Marsh' on an online map database such as Google Maps.

2 First reading: whole class work

• Watch Video C9.1. Ask students to focus on the rhythm and rhyme of the poem while they listen.

• Also remind students to pay attention to the landscape of Romney Marsh shown in Video C9.1, as it will help them to understand the poem.

Video C9.1

3 Exploring form and tone: pair work

• Ask students what they noticed about the rhyme scheme and rhythm in the poem. Did they find it strong? What effect did it have on them?

• Hand out Worksheet C9.1. Ask students to work in pairs to decide where to place the removed words. Encourage them to notice the regular rhyme scheme.

• Ask pairs to feed back to the class and check their answers against the poem in the anthology.

• Discuss what effect the rhyme scheme and rhythm has on the tone of the poem. Students might feel the rhythm is similar to regular footsteps and you could refer back to the man walking in Video C9.1.

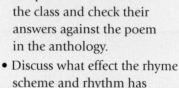
Worksheet C9.1

Access

Have students complete Interactive C9 on the ActiveTeach, matching the vocabulary words to their correct definitions.

Interactive C9.1

4 Close reading: independent work

- Ask students to use two different colours to highlight all of the different sights, and then all of the different sounds, mentioned in the poem.
- Split the class into two groups, with one team taking the visual references and the other taking the aural ones. Explain that each group should present a convincing argument for why their imagery (visual or aural) is effective.
- Individuals from each team should take turns to give a reason why they think their team's imagery is more effective. Encourage discussion between the teams. Award marks for the explanation and evaluation given by individuals, as well as teams. The team with the most points at the end wins but care should be taken to ensure that both types of imagery are seen as equally important.
- Explain that Romney Marsh is a salt marsh area bordered by the sea. Ask students what influence they think this fact has on the language of the poem. What type of visual and aural imagery and vocabulary is connected with the sea?

5 Exploring linguistic features: pair work

- Hand out Worksheet C9.2, which lists various linguistic features. Ask students to find at least one example of each feature in the poem and to write a comment about the possible effects and interpretations of each.
- Take feedback and discuss how these features communicate the poet's ideas and feelings about Romney Marsh.

AT
Worksheet C9.2

6 Independent writing

Ask students to write two to three paragraphs in response to the following question: How does Davidson use imagery and form to create a vivid picture of Romney Marsh?

7 Peer assessment

- Invite students to exchange their work in response to the independent writing activity and mark it. They should assess how well their partner's responses:
  - show an understanding of how Davidson uses imagery and form;
  - demonstrate the ability to make relevant connections between the techniques used and the vivid presentation of Romney Marsh.
- They should award up to five marks, deciding which of the five bands the work falls into. You may want to refer them to Resource C17.2 (English Literature Higher Tier mark scheme), C17.3 (English Literature Foundation Tier mark scheme) or C17.4 (English mark scheme).
- Ask them to comment on how the answer could have been improved, looking at the importance of supporting points with good examples.

8 Plenary

- Recap and ensure that students have:
  - understood the ways in which Davidson has used form, imagery and linguistic features to convey his admiration and affection for Romney Marsh;
  - responded to the sounds and sights that are evoked, and evaluated the impact of these on the reader.
- Ask the class, in groups, to give three reasons why someone might love a place such as Romney Marsh and three reasons why people might hate it. Take a vote, and briefly discuss the results of this.
- For English Literature, compare the way sights and sounds are used in this poem with any one other poem from Collection C. Which of the scenes can you imagine more clearly, and which one has made the stronger impression on you? Are these the same? If so why; if not, why not?

9 Further work

Ask students to write a paragraph about the author's attitude towards Romney Marsh. How does he convey this attitude? Encourage them to discuss rhythm and rhyme.

Somewhere, anywhere

Lesson C10
A Major Road for Romney Marsh *U.A Fanthorpe*

Learning objective
To explore how Fanthorpe uses form and language to persuade readers against the planned developments in Romney Marsh.

Resources
• Edexcel GCSE Poetry Anthology, page 47
• Audio C10.1
• Glossary C10
• Image C10.1
• Image C10.2

1 Before reading: whole class work

Image C10.1

• Show students Image C10.1 of Romney Marsh, emphasising its rural nature and isolation. Explain that the area is a sparsely populated wetland in the south-east of England, covering about 260 square km.

• As a class, discuss what the good and bad aspects of living in this area might be.

2 First reading: whole class work

• Listen to Audio C10 or read the poem to the class, asking students to follow it in their anthologies.

• Ask students what their initial thoughts about the poem are. What do they notice about it? What stands out to them? How does it match their thoughts about what might be good or bad about living there?

• How does the poem compare to their impressions of the place from reading the poem 'In Romney Marsh'? How are the style and tone different?

3 Thinking about first impressions: independent work

• Display Image C10.2, showing the deserted marshy landscape of Romney Marsh. If you have internet access, it will be helpful to display a map of the location of Romney Marsh on a promontory on the south-east coast. This can be found by searching for 'Romney Marsh' on an online map database such as GoogleMaps.

Image C10.2

• Ask students to write, in their own words, about their impression of the Marsh.

• Ask students to suggest possible reasons why the poet refers to Romney Marsh as 'a kingdom, a continent'. They might refer to isolation, individuality, independence, impression of size, etc. They might also need to refer to vocabulary in the rest of the poem to stimulate ideas (refer to Glossary C10 as necessary) or even the poem 'In Romney Marsh'.

4 Exploring language: group work

• Draw attention to the abbreviation of town names in line 18. Ask groups to identify the meanings of other abbreviated words particularly the repeated phrase 'nt fr Ing'.

• Encourage groups to discuss when they might use abbreviated forms of words (e.g. when texting). Why they might do this (e.g. it saves time in a busy world)?

• Encourage groups to discuss why they think these abbreviations are used in the poem (e.g. perhaps they represent text on road signs) and how the use of abbreviation might help to show attitudes to the countryside (e.g. harsh, ugly, busy, time-saving urban-thinking as opposed to natural rural beauty and isolation).

• Ask groups to feed back their ideas to the class.

Access

Give students the abbreviated words (sgns, syng, nt fr lng) and ask them to write them in full by adding vowels.

5 Exploring structure: pair work

• Ask students to re-read the poem aloud in pairs, with one person reading the lines on the left, the other the lines in parentheses on the right. Ask them to think about the contrasts they identify as they read.

• Ask students to discuss, in pairs, why the poet has placed the words aligned to the right in brackets.

What function do the parentheses perform? Direct them towards different perspectives on Romney Marsh.

- Ask students to decide which perspective on Romney Marsh they prefer – the traditional rural, unchanging landscape or the modern, luxurious, roadside version – and to justify this to their partner.
- Take feedback. Did the students in each pair agree?
- Ask students to discuss how the title fits with the structure of the poem.

Extend

Ask students to work in pairs to find examples of language that conveys the poet's attitudes towards Romney Marsh or the planned road. For example, they might note the alliteration of 's' in stanza two (to describe the Marsh), or the harsh 'h' alliteration in stanza three (for the planned road). Ask students to discuss how this language presents the poet's views. Ask them to feed back to the class.

6 Independent work

Ask students to write a PEEE paragraph focusing on the ways in which the poet creates two views on a single place.

7 Peer assessment

- Invite students to exchange their work in response to the activity above (6) and mark it. They should assess how well their partner's responses:
  - show an understanding of how Fanthorpe changes tone frequently within the poem through her layout and change of voice;
  - use the 'PEEE' technique to show the link between the use of the two voices and the effects created.
- They should award up to five marks, deciding which of the five bands the work falls into. You may want to refer them to Resource C17.2 (English Literature Higher Tier mark scheme), C17.3 (English Literature Foundation Tier mark scheme) or C17.4 (English mark scheme).
- Then ask them to comment on how the answer could have been improved, looking at the importance of supporting points with good examples.

8 Plenary

- Recap and ensure that students have:
  - understood the ways Fanthorpe has used language and form to persuade readers to oppose the planned major road for Romney Marsh;
  - responded to the device of parentheses and considered the effect of these, as well as to the strong use of contrast;
  - analysed closely the importance of the abbreviated words and town names to the poem's theme.
- If possible, obtain and hand out a copy of Fanthorpe's poem 'You Will Be Hearing From Us Shortly'. Ask the class to note any similarities in layout. Invite groups to compare the way each poem uses this device and the effect it has in each poem.
- Fanthorpe shows her dislike for modern development which changes country landscapes. For English Literature, compare or contrast this with another poem from Collection C which looks at modern development. How is it similar or different in terms of theme and devices used?

9 Further work

Ask students to think about the last two lines of the poem. Working in pairs, they should discuss the meaning of each line. What, specifically, does the poet mean by 'it is itself'? Ask students to write a paragraph about how Romney Marsh would change with the planned development.

Suggested answers

4 Exploring language
Abbreviated town names on line 18: Tenterden, Folkestone, Canterbury – all of them near Romney Marsh but not within it. It could be argued that a new road would speed access to these larger residential areas.

Other abbreviations: Heavy goods vehicles, water closets, articulated lorries, industrial estates, junctions, not for long.

Access
Signs, saying, not for long.

Lesson C11
Composed upon Westminster Bridge, September 3, 1802
William Wordsworth

Learning objective
To explore and evaluate how Wordsworth uses language, literary device and form to express his feelings on the view of London from Westminster Bridge.

Resources
• Edexcel GCSE Poetry Anthology, page 48
• Audio C11   • Worksheet C11.3
• Glossary C11   • Image C11.1
• Worksheet C11.1   • Image C11.2
• Worksheet C11.2   • Multimedia C11

1 Before reading: whole class work

• Ask students if they've ever seen a landscape, whether rural or urban, which has had a strong impression on them. Why was the landscape significant for them? Was it at a particular time of day, a place with memories, or a particularly beautiful view? What were their feelings?

• Provide students with some background about Wordsworth. He was an English Romantic poet, and England's Poet Laureate from 1843–1850. As a Romantic poet, his work usually emphasises strong emotion and aesthetic experiences. The Romantics focused on the beauty of nature. Here, Wordsworth turns his attention to the city and is moved to write about the view from Westminster Bridge.

2 First reading: whole class work

• Listen to Audio C11 or, if possible, watch the video of Dougray Scott reading the poem on the BBC's Poetry Season website: www.bbc.co.uk/poetryseason.

• Ask students to establish exactly what is being described in the poem and at what time of day.

3 Close reading: pair work

• Hand out Worksheet C11.1. Ask pairs to discuss and explain the meaning of one of the sentences below (refer them to Glossary C11 as necessary).
  a) Earth has not anything to show more fair
  b) Dull would he be of soul who could pass by / A sight so touching in its majesty
  c) Never did sun more beautifully steep / In his first splendour, valley, rock, or hill

Worksheet C11.1

• The last of these is particularly tricky and students may require help. Take feedback and check students' understanding of the language of the poem.

Access

Before Activity 3, ask students to discuss and decide in pairs what the following archaic words mean: doth, unto, ne'er, glideth. Encourage them to consider their context in the poem.

4 Exploring ideas: whole class work

• Display Image C11.1, explaining that it shows Westminster Bridge in 1808, only a few years after the poem was written. Also display Image C11.2, showing the same scene in modern London.

Image C11.1

Image C11.2

• Discuss which, if any, of the adjectives and poetic devices that Wordsworth used might still be used to describe London today.

5 Exploring language: pair work

• Hand out Worksheet C11.2. Ask students to list all adjectives and examples of imagery in the poem then work in pairs to fill in the table explaining the elements of personification in the poem. Recap on personification and its effect if necessary.

Worksheet C11.2

• Take feedback, focusing discussion on the effect of each example of personification.

6 Exploring ideas: group work

- Divide students into groups. Ask each group to find features of the poem that convey Wordsworth's emotions about the view of London.
- Ask groups to feed back to the class. Focus attention on: line 11; 'Dear God!' in line 13; the exclamation marks in both places and at the end of the poem; the repetition of the word 'so' throughout the poem. Ask what emotions are shown by these features.

Extend

- Define sonnet: a sonnet is a poem with 14 lines that has a regular rhyme scheme, often ending in a rhyming couple, often a love poem.
- Ask them to write about the possible reasons why Wordsworth used this form to convey his feelings about the city of London.

7 Multimedia activity: group work

Divide students into groups and hand out Worksheet C11.3 which briefs them on how to complete a short multimedia activity using the downloadable footage provided on the ActiveTeach. When Multimedia C11 is opened, you will be prompted to save the file somewhere on your system. The multimedia clips can then be accessed by extracting them from the zip file, and then opened in editing software for students to use and modify. The aim of the activity is to encourage students to interpret the poet's ideas, thoughts and feelings through selection and editing of the material provided. Students will require access to a software editing package and up to an hour to complete the task.

AT
Worksheet C11.3

8 Independent work

Ask students to write half a page describing how this poem conveys a sense of location.

9 Peer assessment

- Invite students to exchange their work in response to the activity above (8) and mark it. They should assess how well their partner's responses:

- show an understanding of how Wordsworth uses language to create a sense of place;
- demonstrate the ability to make relevant connections between the techniques used and the presentation of the London cityscape.

- Students should then award up to five marks, deciding which of the five bands the work falls into. You may want to refer them to Resource C17.2 (English Literature Higher Tier mark scheme), C17.3 (English Literature Foundation Tier mark scheme) or C17.4 (English mark scheme).
- Ask students to comment on how the answer could have been improved, looking at the importance of supporting points with good examples.

10 Plenary

- Recap and ensure that students have:
  - understood the ways in which Wordsworth has used language, literary devices and form to explore his thoughts about the view of the city from Westminster Bridge;
  - worked within the tight structure of the sonnet form to paint his pictures and thoughts swiftly and economically;
  - responded to the power of the images to give a strong sense of early morning London as a beautiful sleeping giant.
- Update the 'connections' chart, grid or list, linking this poem with others with which the students can see close connections in theme or treatment.
- For English Literature, ask students to find another poem in Collection C that also describes the beauty of a setting. Give examples that could be used to compare how these poets create an effective description of a place which draws on imagery.

11 Further work

Ask students to draw on the imagery that Wordsworth uses in this poem to produce a short piece of travel writing describing a city or other landscape that has had a big effect on them. Encourage them to think about the vocabulary and imagery that they use and what impression they want to make on the reader.

Suggested answers

6 Exploring ideas
pride in the city; awe and inspiration.

Lesson C12
London

William Blake

Learning objective
To understand of how Blake uses imagery to convey his attitude towards London.

Resources
• Edexcel GCSE Poetry Anthology, page 49
• Audio C12
• Glossary C12
• Worksheet C12.1
• Worksheet C12.2
• Image C12.1

1 Before reading: whole class work

• Show Image C12.1, an image of London from when Blake wrote his poem. Ask students to describe what they see. What do they think London life would have been like in the late eighteenth/early nineteenth centuries?

Image C12.1

2 First reading: whole class work

• Listen to Audio C12 or read the poem to the class. Draw out their initial responses to the poem. How do they think Blake feels about his surroundings? Is the general tone positive or negative?

• Show image C12.1 again and explain that if students had been alive in London in the late eighteenth/early nineteenth century, they might well have:

  – expected to live only to the age of 40.

  – had no flushing toilet; raw sewage went into open gutters and drained into the Thames, giving off a constant stench.

  – had no shoes, very few clothes and no running water or electricity.

  – had many brothers and sisters, some of whom might well have died in infancy because disease was very common.

  – been working from the age of five, perhaps in a factory.

  – not been able to read or write.

• Explain that this poem is Blake's expression of his reaction to the poverty he saw in London at that time.

3 Exploring language: pair work

• If possible, watch the video of DJ Nihal talking about Blake's poem on the BBC Poetry Season website at www.bbc.co.uk/poetryseason. He mentions the way in which The Verve's song 'History' paraphrased the first verse of this poem.

• Draw students' attention to the lines 'And mark in every face I meet / Marks of weakness, marks of woe.' Ask them to think about why these lines might stand out for a reader (e.g. alliteration, rhythm and balance).

• Ask students to complete Worksheet C12.1, finding examples of repetition and alliteration and discussing their effect.

• Ask pairs to feed back to the class to initiate a group discussion on the effect of literary devices in the poem. Encourage students to discuss how the devices affect the tone.

Worksheet C12.1

Access

Hand out Worksheet C12.2. Ask students to identify which apostrophes indicate old-fashioned usage and which are there to form possessive words. Feed back to the whole class and clarify the meaning of the archaic words where necessary using Glossary C12. Discuss grammatical points, including possessive apostrophes, and vocabulary as necessary.

Worksheet C12.2

4 Exploring ideas: group work

- Divide students into four groups and allocate each group one of the following characters/lines: chimney-sweeper (lines 9–10); soldier (lines 11–12); harlot (last stanza), and infant (last stanza). Ask them to think about the meaning of these lines based on the information they know already and to work out what Blake is describing.
- Take feedback on each character and clarify the meaning of the lines as a class. Point out that young boys had to climb up inside black chimneys to clean them. Why might a church be 'appalled' at this? 'Palace walls' might prompt discussion on Blake's views on how England was governed (only a small proportion of men had a vote). Encourage students to draw on their knowledge of the high infant mortality rate and high incidence of disease in understanding the final stanza and the last line.

Extend

Ask students to write a response to the following prompt: Drawing on evidence from within the poem, explore the possible interpretations of the phrase 'The mind-forg'd manacles'.

5 Exploring ideas: group work

Divide students into groups, asking them to create a tableau of a London street, including characters representing the misery of life in London as described by Blake in his poem.

6 Peer assessment

- Invite students to assess the work done in groups for the activity above, creating a tableau of a London street. They should assess how well each group:
  - shows an understanding of how Blake's vivid language can enable a detailed scene to be created;
  - demonstrates connections between Blake's descriptions and the presentation of the different scenes.
- They should then consider what evidence, if any, the tableau gives of meeting the Assessment Criteria. You may want to refer them to Resource C17.2 (English Literature Higher Tier mark scheme), C17.3 (English Literature Foundation Tier mark scheme) or C17.4 (English mark scheme).
- Ask students to comment on how the tableaux could have been improved, looking at the importance of basing the visual re-creation on close examples from the text.

7 Independent writing

Ask students to write a response to the question: How does Blake convey his despair about London's poverty in this poem?

8 Plenary

- Recap and ensure that students have:
  - understood the ways in which Blake has used imagery to convey his attitudes to London life and people;
  - appreciated the striking yet negative picture of London presented.
- Discuss with the class how poetry can be used for social comment, just as can novels (cf. Dickens); you might want to read a vivid extract from a Dickens novel and invite responses showing the similarity of moral purpose.
- For English Literature, compare 'London' with another poem in Collection C where the poet is making a comment on society and making use of the importance of physical setting to understand the society depicted.

9 Further work

Ask students to write one or two further stanzas for Blake's poem describing poverty in contemporary London. They could use extracts from the novel *Stone Cold* by Robert Swindells as inspiration.

Lesson C13
London Snow

Robert Bridges

Learning objective
To explore how Bridges uses language and form to convey the way in which snowfall transforms the appearance and atmosphere of a familiar place.

Resources
• Edexcel GCSE Poetry Anthology, page 50
• Audio C13
• Glossary C13
• Worksheet C13.1
• Worksheet C13.2
• Worksheet C13.3
• Worksheet C13.4
• Worksheet C13.5

1 Before reading: whole class work

• Ask students to think about the last time it snowed where they live or images on news reports. How did the landscape change? What were their own, and other people's, reactions to the snow? Did anything unusual happen?

• Explain that the poem is the poet's description of how both the London landscape and the people in it are affected by snow.

2 First reading: whole class work

• Listen to Audio C13 or read the poem to the class, asking students to follow it in their anthologies.

• Discuss the feelings, such as excitement and wonder, that are explored in the poem. Ask students to pick out words or phrases that support their ideas.

3 Exploring sounds: group work

• Explain that the sound, rhythm and rhyme in this poem are important. Read the first four (or nine) lines aloud to provide guidance on how they should make the most of the sounds, rhyme and rhythm.

• Split the class into groups and allocate several lines to each group. Each group should discuss any significant sounds within their allocated lines, e.g. onomatopoeia, alliteration, rhyme. Give them a few minutes to familiarise themselves with the sound/ feeling of their reading.

• Each group should read their allocated lines. Discuss why they read their lines as they did, what contributed to the sound/emotion of the poem, and why the poet might have used particular words.

4 Exploring language: pair work

• Working in pairs, ask students to look closely at the first nine lines of the poem and identify the seven adverbs as well as the participles.

• Ask the pairs to discuss what image of the snow is created by these words and their abundance.

Access

• Recap on adverbs, and the different function of adjectives, and model some examples to check understanding.

• Ask students to complete Worksheet C13.1.

• Why did the poet choose to use these words?

Worksheet C13.1

5 Exploring images: independent work

• Hand out Worksheet C13.2 and ask students to create a storyboard to show four key images, selecting a word or phrase from the poem to accompany each.

• Select students to present their storyboards.

• Draw out their initial impressions of how the poet uses language to create a description in discussion.

Worksheet C13.2

6 Exploring language: pair work

• Hand out Worksheet C13.3 which asks pairs to find and sort examples of images in the poem that appeal to the different senses.

• Students should then look at the context of each example and discuss how it contributes to the atmosphere of London which Bridges is creating.

Worksheet C13.3

7 Clarifying meaning: independent work

- Hand out Worksheet C13.4, which asks students to write a modern version of five lines to show their understanding. Glossary C13 will help with vocabulary.
- Share the modern versions of each line, discussing any differences in interpretation as a class.
- Ask students to think about the last two lines and write down how they reflect the attitudes and feelings that Bridges explores in the rest of the poem. Ask them to feed back to the class, sharing their answers.

AT
Worksheet C13.4

Extend

Ask students to think about how the poet uses poetic devices such as alliteration, assonance and onomatopoeia to convey the atmosphere in London after the snow has fallen . Draw their attention to interesting phrases such as 'uncompacted lightness' (line 11) and 'sorrow slumber' (line 36) as a starting point.

8 Exploring ideas: group work

- Ask students to work in groups to complete Worksheet C13.5, filling in the table to explore the rhyme pattern and its effect within the poem.
- Take feedback, leading a discussion on the specific examples of words and the overall effect of rhyme in the poem.

AT
Worksheet C13.5

9 Independent writing

- Model writing one paragraph exploring how Bridges uses language to create a sense of awe and wonder e.g. 'The poet creates a sense of awe and wonder by the contrast between "large white flakes" and "city brown" emphasising the difference made by the snow. The silence is evoked by a series of words such as "hushing" and "muffling", giving the impression of the enforced transformation of a bustling industrial city.'
- Ask students to write their own paragraph.

10 Peer assessment

- Invite students to exchange their work in response to the independent writing and mark it. They should assess how well their partner's responses:
  - show an understanding of why Bridges uses so much imagery connected with snow to build up an impression of place;
  - demonstrate the ability to make relevant connections between the techniques used and the presentation of a London scene transformed by snow.
- They should award up to five marks, deciding which of the five bands the work falls into. You may want to refer them to Resource C17.2 (English Literature Higher Tier mark scheme), C17.3 (English Literature Foundation Tier mark scheme) or C17.4 (English mark scheme).
- Finally, ask them to comment on how the answer could have been improved, looking at the importance of supporting points with good examples.

11 Plenary

- Recap and ensure that students have:
  - understood the ways Bridges has used language and form to convey how a familiar place is transformed by the fall of snow;
  - appreciated the beauty of the snow and the scenes it creates.
- Pool suggestions from the class about words and phrases which appeal to the senses and create the vivid scene, first from the poem and then more generally: How does this make them feel about the effectiveness of Bridges' description of the scene?
- For English Literature, choose two or three poems from Collection C and look at how the beauty of a scene and setting is created, giving examples.

12 Further work

Students should write two paragraphs in response to the following questions: What view of London is created by the poem? How does the presentation of place compare with other poems that students have studied in this collection?

Suggested answers

4 Exploring language
Image of snow created: *quietness, almost sneaky, slow, ongoing, abundant, layer on layer.*

Lesson C14
Assynt Mountains

Mandy Haggith

Learning objective

To explore how Haggith uses extended metaphor to create a picture of a distinctive landscape.

Resources

- Edexcel GCSE Poetry Anthology, page 51
- Audio C14
- Glossary C14
- Worksheet C14.1
- Worksheet C14.2
- Image C14.1
- Video C14.1
- Video C14.2

1 Before reading: whole class work

- As a class, ask students to think of any mountains they know of and to suggest words that describe them.
- Ask them to think about what they look like at different times of day, in different weathers and what emotions they might associate with a mountainous landscape.
- Compile ideas on a whiteboard at the front of the class.

2 First reading: whole class work

- Now watch Video C14.1 of Haggith reading the poem, available on the ActiveTeach.
- Ask students to compare the language and imagery in the poem with the words and phrases they thought of in Activity 1. Refer them to Glossary C14 as necessary. Draw their attention to the phrase 'row of crones', 'rugs on knees' and 'ancient…gums' and explain that the imagery we normally connect with old age is not present. Instead, clarify that the poet uses words associated with old women in order to stimulate the imagination and create an image of exactly what the rocks look like.

Video C14.1

3 Exploring language: independent work

- Hand out Worksheet C14.1, which asks students to explain what the key phrases from the poem represent in terms of the mountain.

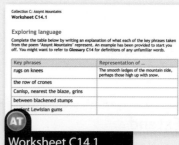
Worksheet C14.1

For example, 'rugs on knees' might represent smooth ledges in the mountainside. Refer students to Glossary C14 as necessary.

Access

Support students in identifying the meaning of any words they are unsure of and in selecting strategies to work out the meanings, including the use of dictionaries/glossaries and/or discussion.

4 Exploring ideas: pair work

- Display Image C14.1 of Canisp, explaining that it is a mountain in the far north of Scotland, in the parish of Assynt. Then explain that Canisp is one of the Lewisians (see Glossary C14).
- Ask students to work in pairs to compare the features of the mountain in Image C14.1 to the images they produced as a result of the language in the poem. Do they think that the imagery in the poem is effective? They should justify their answers.

Image C14.1

5 Exploring language: pair work

- Hand out Worksheet C14.2, which asks students to consider various questions about the poem.

Worksheet C14.2

- Take feedback and encourage students to annotate their anthologies with notes on the answers to these questions.

6 Understanding imagery: whole class work

- Watch Video C14.2 as a class, in which Mandy Haggith explains her reasons for writing the poem and the things which have inspired her. After watching, discuss whether students' understanding or opinions on the poem have changed.

Video C14.2

Extend

Ask students to write a response to the following questions: How does the poet use language and imagery to convey emotion in this poem? What emotional connection does the poet have with this particular place?

7 Independent writing

Ask students to write a response to the following question: How does the poet use a metaphor to describe a mountain range? Encourage them to use words and phrases from the poem to support their answers.

8 Peer assessment

- Invite students to exchange their work in response to the independent writing activity and mark it. They should assess how well their partner's responses:
  - show an understanding of Haggith's use of the old women/mountains metaphor;
  - demonstrate the ability to make relevant connections between the techniques used and the poet's feelings about the landscape.
- They should then award up to five marks, deciding which of the five bands the work falls into. You may want to refer them to Resource C17.2 (English Literature Higher Tier mark scheme), C17.3 (English Literature Foundation Tier mark scheme) or C17.4 (English mark scheme).
- Ask them to comment on how the answer could have been improved, looking at the importance of supporting points with good examples.

9 Plenary

- Recap and ensure that students have:
  - understood the ways Haggith has used metaphorical language to present an unusual way of looking at mountains;
  - considered how the poem shows the poet's affinity with this ancient landscape.
- Ask the class if they prefer places which seem very old, like these mountains or an ancient city, or much younger (such as a swift-running river, or a modern city). Do they all feel the same way? If so, why? If not, why not?
- For English Literature, ask them to update their chart, grid or list of connections, and discuss whether other poems in Collection C are similar in the way the writer thinks about the place described. What connections can they see and how should these be reflected on the chart?

10 Further work

Ask students to imagine the conversation that might take place between the 'crones', and write a short script. Ask them to keep in mind why images of old ladies might help to convey the nature of a mountain range.

Suggested answers

1 Before reading
Mountains: *climb, crag, high, summit, peak, range, snow.*

Somewhere, anywhere

Lesson C15
Orkney / This Life

Andrew Greig

Learning objective
To explore how Greig uses language and imagery to link Orkney with love, life and death.

Resources
- Edexcel GCSE Poetry Anthology, pages 52–53
- Audio C15
- Glossary C15
- Worksheet C15.1
- Resource C15.1
- Image C15.1
- Image C15.2

1 Before reading: whole class work

- Display Images C15.1 and 15.2 of Orkney. Explain that the Orkneys are a group of islands off the north-east coast of Scotland and that the poet Andrew Greig is a resident of Orkney.

- Display Resource C15.1, sharing with students what the poet says about what inspired him to write 'Orkney / This Life'.

Image C15.1

Resource C15.1

Image C15.2

2 First reading: whole class work

- Either listen to Audio C15 or read the poem to students, asking them to follow it in the anthology. Remind them that the poem was written to explore the reasons why the poet loves living in Orkney.

- Ask students to read the poem again independently and think about the themes he mentions – Orkney itself, love, life and death.

- Take feedback from the students. Did they find evidence of Orkney, love, life and death? Were they linked together?

- Draw students' attention to the repeated phrase '(It is) the way...' Ask them what function this phrase plays in the poem.

- Discuss any initial ideas they have about why the poem is split into three stanzas.

Access

Remind students that the poet wrote this poem as a reflection of why the islands are so important to him. Ask them to work in pairs to create a list of all the reasons he gives. Help by encouraging them to look for the 'it is' statements.

3 Exploring language: pair work

- Hand out Worksheet C15.1. Ask pairs to decide on possible meaning for each of the five phrases and the effects of each phrase on the reader. Ensure they understand the vocabulary in the poem, referring them to Glossary C15.

Worksheet C15.1

- Take feedback, ensuring that reasonable discussion time is given to a wide range of interpretations. This task is challenging so provide students with as much support as necessary.

- Emphasise that the island has an effect on every aspect of the poet's life. Prompt students to find any further examples of words or phrases that show this. Discuss them as a class.

4 Exploring themes: pair work

- Remind students that the theme 'somewhere, anywhere' often involves not just a location but the way the poet feels about that location, or what it represents to them.

- Ask students, working in pairs, to come up with some ideas about how this poem fits into the theme of 'somewhere, anywhere'. Encourage them to look at the sense of place as well as the place's meaning and what it represents. What other poems in the collection does it remind students of?

- Ask pairs to feed back to the class. Encourage discussion about how the theme is portrayed in this poem.

5 Independent writing

- Draw students' attention to the last line of the poem. Why do they think that the rhythm of the engine sounds like the words 'this life' to the poet? How has he explored this idea elsewhere in the poem?
- Ask them to write a paragraph exploring how the poet has shown the connection between Orkney, in its natural setting, and his own life (relationship, community, outlook). Emphasise that they should comment on the poet's use of language, giving specific examples.

6 Peer assessment

- Invite students to exchange their paragraphs in response to the independent writing activity and mark it. They should assess how well their partner's responses:
  - show an understanding of how Greig's language connects himself closely to the place and community;
  - use the 'PEEE' technique to show the link between the language and the place.
- They should award up to five marks, deciding which of the five bands the work falls into. You may want to refer them to Resource C17.2 (English Literature Higher Tier mark scheme), C17.3 (English Literature Foundation Tier mark scheme) or C17.4 (English mark scheme).
- They should then comment on how the answer could have been improved, looking at the importance of supporting points with good examples.

Extend

Point out examples of enjambement, e.g. in lines 3–4 and lines 8–10. Ask students what the effect of this technique is. Why do they think the poet has used it? How does it link to the meaning of the lines?

7 Plenary

- Recap and ensure that students have:
  - understood the ways in which Greig has used language and imagery to link Orkney with love, life and death;
  - appreciated how Greig's strong feelings about the place are brought out by the powerful descriptions of it;
  - responded to the poem's structure and the use of repetition.
- If you are able, you might want to play the song 'Somewhere' from West Side Story and discuss its theme of finding an ideal place, away from life's troubles. Can they see links with the way writers often seem to wish to escape from cities to a 'rural idyll' (Arcadia)?
- Ask students to update the 'connections' chart, grid or list, linking this poem with others with which the students can see close connections in theme or treatment.
- For English Literature, find another poem in Collection C that uses metaphor, and ask students to compare the use of this device in the two poems, making use of relevant quotations in support of the points made.

8 Further work

- Ask students to imagine that they are residents in Orkney and to write a short note to a friend explaining why it is so appealing to live in. Remind them of the quotation from the poet on Resource C15.1 which might help them with initial ideas.
- Ask them to imagine that they are tourists visiting Orkney for the first time. They should write to a friend explaining what they *dislike* about the place. In each case they should draw on ideas in the poem and think about the two different perspectives.

Suggested answers

2 First reading

The first stanza is about the physical characteristics of the islands, the second is about love and the third is more focused on life and perhaps death.

Extend

Lines 3–4 incline the reader to visualise the horizon and the relationship between sea and sky; lines 8–10 emphasise the duration of the gale and the solitariness of the 'single bird'.

Lesson C16
The Stone Hare

Gillian Clarke

Learning objective
To evaluate how Clarke uses language and form to explore the relationship between a beautiful object and the earth.

Resources
• Edexcel GCSE Poetry Anthology, page 54
• Audio C16
• Glossary C16
• Worksheet C16.1
• Worksheet C16.2
• Image C16.1

1 Before reading: whole class work

• If possible, show students some examples of fossils or display Image C16.1.

Image C16.1

• Ask if they know what material fossils are made of. The answer will most likely be stone. Ask what they were before they were stone. Draw out that they were sea-based animals that became stone through a process called calcification and that many forms of stone, such as limestone, are made through this hardening of sea animals and other ocean material.

2 First reading: whole class work

• Listen to Audio C16, or read the poem to the class. Ask students to follow it in their anthologies.
• Remind students of the title of the poem and ensure they know that the object which is the focus of the poem is a stone statue of a hare. Why do they think that in a poem with this title there are references to a 'reef', 'coral' and 'the warm Palaeozoic seas'? Refer back to the discussion in Activity 1.

3 Close reading: pair work

• Ask students to work in pairs to discuss and check their understanding of the vocabulary in the poem, referring to Glossary C16 as necessary. Instruct each pair to go through the poem and explain what each line means. Ask the pairs to feed back to the class.

• Hand out Worksheet C16.1. Ask students to look at lines 6–12 and work in pairs to identify the phrases which describe the stages in the process of creating the stone hare. They should insert these into the flow diagram on their worksheet, illustrating the stages if they wish to.

Worksheet C16.1

• Ask pairs to swap their lists with another pair and discuss any different responses.
• Take feedback. Ask: Why does the poet see the creation of the hare as the same thing as 'the story of the earth'? What are the meaning and significance of the phrase 'its eye a planet' on line 12?

4 Exploring language and form: whole class work

• Ask students to look at the last word on each line, circling examples of rhyme and underlining examples of assonance in their anthologies.
• Display the poem using the ActiveTeach and annotate the loose rhyme pattern (abba, cddc, effe, gg). Explain that some of the rhymes rely on assonance rather than true rhyme. Discuss the effect of the pattern, noting the true rhyme in the final two lines.
• Lead students towards recognition of the sonnet form (they may need to count the lines as a final clue). Recap on the traditional aspects of a sonnet, including the theme of love and/or admiration.
• Ask students why they think the poet used the sonnet form for this poem. Prompt them to look particularly at the last two lines (the rhyming couplet), which are often important in a sonnet.

Access

Recap on rhyme and assonance. Hand out Worksheet C16.2, which asks students to identify pairs of words and whether they are examples of rhyme or assonance.

Worksheet C16.2

5 Extend

Ask students to discuss how this poem fits in with the theme of 'somewhere, anywhere'. What sense of place does it convey? Ask students to write a paragraph comparing this poem with Wordsworth's sonnet about London. How are they similar/different in terms of subject matter and devices used? Remind them to use examples from the poems in their responses.

6 Independent writing

Ask students to write a paragraph exploring why the poet might have chosen the sonnet form for this poem. You might want to think about the importance of the process of making the hare and the poet's admiration of this.

7 Peer assessment

- Invite students to exchange their work in response to the independent writing activity and mark it. They should assess how well their partner's responses:
  - show an understanding of how Clarke uses the sonnet form;
  - demonstrate the ability to make relevant connections between the techniques used in writing a sonnet and the presentation of the themes of continuity and change.
- Ask students to award up to five marks, deciding which of the five bands the work falls into. You may want to refer them to Resource C17.2 (English Literature Higher Tier mark scheme), C17.3 (English Literature Foundation Tier mark scheme) or C17.4 (English mark scheme).
- They should then comment on how the answer could have been improved, looking at the importance of supporting points with good examples.

8 Plenary

- Recap and ensure that students have:
  - understood the ways in which Clarke has used form, structure and language to link a single man-made object with the timeless rocks;
  - appreciated the importance of living things changing to stone and the near-reversal of this process through skill (metamorphosis);
  - considered the use of the sonnet form to provide a strong structure for the poem's solid themes.
- Invite the class to come up with some ideas of metamorphosis in nature (e.g. tadpoles or caterpillars), science (change from one state of matter to another e.g. water to steam) or art (e.g. a lump of clay into a fine pot). Why does this theme fascinate us?
- For English Literature, find another poem in Collection C that uses the sonnet form, and ask students how the poet's use of this form contributes to the effect of the poem on the reader.

9 Further work

Ask students to research the hare. Why does this make a good symbol for what the poet is trying to say? Instruct them to look into the hare as a symbol of new life and then relate their findings to lines 12–14. Encourage them to consider the connections between the hare's eye, a planet, moonlight, the sea, etc.

Suggested answers

4 Exploring language and form
A traditional form links with idea of history/the story of the earth; it reflects the admiration and awe that the poet feels for the stone hare, having been created through this long process; the use of assonance as well as rhyme reflects the metamorphosis of life/the stone in that the poem form continues to evolve; the rhyming couplet makes the very direct link of bone to stone.

Lesson C17
Understanding the assessment

Learning objectives
- To reinforce how poems link with the theme of the collection.
- To find links and comparisons between the poems in the collection.
- To develop the skills needed to write about poems in the assessment.

Resources
- Worksheet C17.1
- Resource C17.1
- Resource C17.2
- Resource C17.3
- Resource C17.4
- ResultsPlus interactives

1 Starter activity: whole class work

- As a class, brainstorm all of the ideas about the theme 'somewhere, anywhere' that are explored in the poems in this collection. Record ideas using a spider diagram.
- Ask students to come up with at least one way each poem in the collection relates to the theme. You might want to focus on particular lines or imagery from poems and discuss different responses to the same poem and reasons for these.
- It might be helpful to encourage students to sort their ideas into sub-groups.

Access

Ask students to choose one image that could be used to represent each of the poems in the collection. They could write a description of the image, draw it or find an image from a magazine or online. Each student should share their ideas with others, explaining the reasons why they have selected each image and how it links to the theme of the collection.

2 Practising writing in the exam or controlled assessment: pair work

- Divide the class into pairs. Ask pairs to draw a flow diagram showing the process of planning and writing a response to an assessed question. What will they do first in the exam or controlled assessment? What kind of things will they include in their response? How will they conclude their response?
- Hand out Resource C17.1 and ask students to compare the guidance on this sheet to their flow diagrams. Ask them to amend their diagrams accordingly and highlight areas on the Resource sheet which they feel are particularly important for them to remember.

Resource C17.1

3 Preparing for part a) of the English Literature question: whole class work

- Open a ResultsPlus interactive on the ActiveTeach which is relevant to Section B part a) of the Unit 2 English Literature exam, where students have to answer on a single poem. You

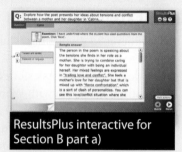

ResultsPlus interactive for Section B part a)

may want to ensure that it is the relevant tier (either Higher or Foundation) for your students. Sample questions from other collections can often be tailored to your own needs as necessary. ResultsPlus is a unique resource designed to help students achieve their best with sample questions, graded answers and examiner tips. A sample exam question is provided alongside a sample student answer. Each answer is annotated with examiner comments to make clear why the mark has been given, and showing where and how the essay could have been improved to gain a mark in a higher band. See page 5 for guidance on using these activities.
- Use the interactive with the class, encouraging and supporting them to explore what mark might have been given and/or how the sample answer could have been improved. You may also want to make use of the mark scheme provided in Resource C17.2 or Resource C17.3 to help students understand how their essays will be marked.

4 Comparing poems: pair work

- Explain to students who will be taking the English Literature exam that they will be required to compare and contrast the poems they have studied. They will need to think about the different ways in which the poets have approached the theme of the collection, and the ways in which they have communicated their ideas.

- Hand out Worksheet C17.1. You can find the icons to open the resources for this lesson at the bottom of the page underneath the final poem in the collection. Tell students to work in pairs and think about links between the poems in terms of a) the topic explored and the poet's ideas, and b) the use of poetic devices (such as form, language and imagery) and their effects.

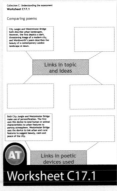

Worksheet C17.1

- Take feedback as a class, exploring differences of opinion and asking students to record their thoughts. You might want to compile class spider diagrams which can be used to support students' revision later on.

5 Preparing for part b) of the English Literature question: whole class work

- Open a ResultsPlus interactive on the ActiveTeach which is relevant to Section B part b) of the Unit 2 English Literature exam, where students will be required to compare two poems.

- Use the interactive with the class, encouraging and supporting them to explore what mark might have been given and/or how the sample answer could have been improved.

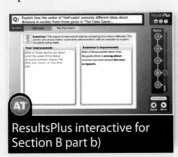

ResultsPlus interactive for Section B part b)

You may also want to make use of the mark scheme provided in Resource C17.2 to help students understand how their essays will be marked.

6 Preparing for the English controlled assessment: whole class work

- Open the ResultsPlus interactive for English controlled assessment. It will help students understand how a sample response can be improved.

- Use the interactive with the class, encouraging and supporting them to explore how the sample answer could have been improved. You may also want to make use of the mark scheme provided in Resource C17.4 to help students understand how their essays will be marked.

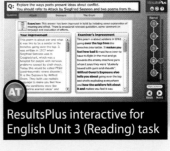

ResultsPlus interactive for English Unit 3 (Reading) task

7 Assessed question: individual work

- Ask students to think of an appropriate question for a particular poem, justifying how this would allow a student to demonstrate understanding and analysis of the poem(s).
- Ask students to swap essay questions with a partner and plan their essay in bullet points.

8 Peer assessment

Ask students to work in groups of four, share their plans with the group and assess each other's plans using the relevant mark scheme on Resource C17.2, Resource C17.3 or Resource C17.4.

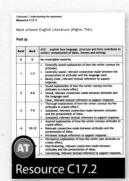

Resource C17.2

Resource C17.3

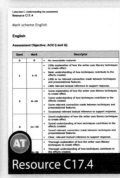

Resource C17.4

9 Further work

Ask students to plan and write an answer to one assessed question within the sample assessment material provided by Edexcel. You may like to direct students to specific questions to suit their ability.

Collection D

Lesson D1
Taking a *stand* introduction

Learning objectives
- To consolidate students' understanding of the features of poetry and a range of poetic devices.
- To think about what issues poems with a 'taking a stand' theme might explore.
- To understand the assessment objectives for this unit.

Resources
- Glossary D1
- Worksheet D1.1
- Worksheet D1.2
- Worksheet D1.3
- Interactive D1

1 Starter activity: whole class work

- Ask the class to give examples of some devices that can be used by poets to help convey meaning. If they can, ask them to provide an example of how these devices might be used, and explain how they can be effective.

- Complete the activity in Interactive D1 as a class. The icons to open the resources for this lesson can be found on the contents page for Collection D, on page 55 of the ActiveTeach.

Interactive D1

This activity involve matching the following poetic devices with the correct definitions: alliteration, assonance, metaphor, onomatopoeia, rhyme, rhythm, personification, simile. Ask individuals to come up to the board and make what they think is the correct connection, or ask the whole class to complete the activity against the clock.

- Hand out Glossary D1 for students to look at the correct definitions. Remind students that they can return to this glossary to refresh their memory at any point during their study of this collection of poems.

2 Identifying poetic devices: pair work

- Hand out Worksheet D1.1, which gives students examples of different poetic devices from the poems in the collection. They are asked to identify the poetic device used in a second set of quotations from the poems.

- Ask students to swap work with another pair and mark each other's work. Explain that if they make a mistake, each pair must explain to the other pair why they are wrong.

Worksheet D1.1

3 Looking at imagery: independent work

- Provide students with Worksheet D1.2, which gives a list of phrases from the collection that include particularly vivid imagery.

Worksheet D1.2

- Ask each student to choose one of these phrases and draw a picture of the item described. Tell them to think about how the words used help them to understand what the poet is trying to communicate and what the item should look like. Ask them to label the picture or write at least two sentences beneath it to explain why they have chosen to draw the image in this way, pinpointing particular words from the phrase.

- Ask for volunteers to share their pictures with the rest of the class. Ask students to explain why they have illustrated the phrase in this way and why they think the poet's use of imagery is effective.

4 Making inferences from shape: whole class work

- Hand out Worksheet D1.3, which indicates just the shapes of two poems: 'The world is a beautiful place' and 'Remember'.

- Discuss how students know that these are poems and what they can infer from the shape of them.

Worksheet D1.3

- Ask pairs of students to devise a list of five to ten features that differentiate prose from poetry (this should be familiar to them from KS3 work). These might relate to line length, rhyme, rhythm, standard punctuation, grammar and stanzas.

- Ask pairs to feed back to the class and compare and contrast their ideas. Encourage them to think about how each of these aspects of poetry might help a poet convey meaning. For example, if a poem was written using the language of SMS, without any standard punctuation, what impression might this give of the poet or what message he/she is trying to communicate?

5 Exploring ideas: whole class work

- Introduce students to the theme of the collection of poems they are going to study. Ask students what they expect poems in a collection with this title will be about.

- Compile a class list of the types of issues students suggest these poems might explore. To prompt students you could ask them to consider books or films that they have enjoyed with a similar theme.

6 Plenary

Introduce students to the assessment objectives for this unit, according to which course they are following. Explain the skills that they will need to develop while studying these poems, in preparation for their assessment.

English

AO2:

i) Read and understand texts, selecting material appropriate to purpose, collating from different sources and making comparisons and cross-references as appropriate;

iii) Explain and evaluate how writers use linguistic, grammatical, structural and presentational features to achieve effects and engage and influence the reader.

English Literature

AO2: Explain how language, structure and form contribute to writers' presentation of ideas, themes and settings.

AO3: Make comparisons and explain links between texts, evaluating writers' different ways of expressing meaning and achieving effects.

7 Further work

Ask students to find a copy of a poem and annotate it, explaining what they liked or didn't like about it. Did they like the topic? Was there something particularly memorable about it? Why? They should think about language and vocabulary, any rhyme pattern, line length and form and imagery covered in the lesson. What effect did each of these have and why was it effective (or not) in their view? You might wish to guide them to use a PEEE structure. This terminology is used throughout the scheme of work for the collection and can help to guide students in their writing by ensuring they have made a **Point**, found **Evidence** for this, **Explained** the reasoning and finally **Explored** alternative interpretations and implications.

Suggested answers

Answers to worksheets are provided in the editable Word lesson plans on the ActiveTeach.

5 Exploring ideas

Suggested ideas for topics on the theme of 'taking a stand' might include protest, anger, fear, fighting and differing opinions.

Lesson D2
On the Life of Man Sir Walter Raleigh

Learning objective
To understand how Raleigh uses linguistic features, including extended metaphor, to communicate his view of life.

Resources
• Edexcel GCSE Poetry Anthology, page 56
• Audio D2
• Glossary D2
• Worksheet D2.1
• Worksheet D2.2
• Worksheet D2.3
• Worksheet D2.4
• Image D2.1

1 Before reading: whole class work

Brainstorm ideas that students might want to include if they were writing a poem entitled 'Life'. Write students' ideas on the board or display them at the front of the class so that they can be referred to later in the lesson.

2 First reading: pair work

• Play the Audio D3 or read the poem to the class.

• Hand out Worksheet D2.1, which asks students to fill in the missing words in a copy of the poem, using context and rhyme to help them decide which word goes where.

Worksheet D2.1

• Take feedback and help students to recognise the rhyming couplets in the poem. Discuss how rhyme is used by the poet to closely connect the ideas in the poem. Ensure that students note the partial rhyme in the first two lines.

Access

Prepare students for their work on Worksheet D2.1 by handing out Worksheet D2.2, which asks them to find out and record the meanings of some of the words from the poem. Afterwards, ask them to compare their definitions to those in the glossary.

Worksheet D2.2

3 Exploring ideas: whole class work

• Give students some background information about Sir Walter Raleigh, provided in Glossary D2, and display Image D2.1 of him.

Image D2.1

• Sir Walter Raleigh was born in 1552. At different times in his life he was an expeditionary, a renowned poet and a Member of Parliament. In 1581 he became a favourite of Queen Elizabeth I and was knighted in 1585. In 1591 he secretly married Elizabeth Throckmorton, one of the Queen's ladies-in-waiting, without requesting the Queen's permission, for which he and his wife were sent to the Tower of London. After his release, they retired to his estate at Sherborne, Dorset. After Queen Elizabeth died in 1603, Raleigh was again imprisoned in the Tower, this time for allegedly being involved in the Main Plot against King James I. Although he was released, he was beheaded at Whitehall on 29 October 1618.

• Ask students if they know any other information about Sir Walter Raleigh. Explore with students what impact these contextual factors might have had on the writing of this poem.

4 Close reading: independent work

- Ask students to highlight the twelve words in the poem that are associated with theatre.
- Hand out Worksheet D2.3, which asks students to match the explanations provided to words and phrases in the poem, to help students understand aspects of the poem more clearly.
- Next, ask students to identify how the explanations divide into pairs, according to the links that Raleigh makes in the poem.
- Take class feedback. Ensure that students understand how Raleigh is comparing life to the stage in this poem.
- Introduce the idea that this is an extended metaphor.

Worksheet D2.3

5 Exploring metaphor: whole class work

- Explain to students what is meant by an extended metaphor.
- Model how an extended metaphor can be created by asking students to generate words connected with plants (e.g. bud, stem, seed, flower, blossom, etc.) and then using them to create a description of a child growing.
- Discuss how the term 'extended metaphor' applies to this poem. You might want to refer back to the ideas about 'life' that were brainstormed in Activity 1 and see if Raleigh covers these in his poem. Discuss how the points are made more effectively through the comparison with theatre.

Extend

Hand out Worksheet D2.4, which encourages students to find links between Raleigh's and Shakespeare's ideas, in addition to rewriting Shakespeare's words in modern English.

Worksheet D2.4

6 Independent writing

Ask students to answer the following question: How does Raleigh use an extended metaphor to reflect his attitude towards life?

7 Peer assessment

- Ask students to swap their answers to the independent writing question with a partner. Invite the students to mark each other's work. Students should assess how well their partner's responses:
  - show an understanding of Raleigh's use of the extended metaphor;
  - demonstrate the ability to explain, develop and support ideas, making relevant connections between the techniques used and how the ideas, themes and setting are presented.
- They should award up to five marks, deciding which of the five bands the work falls into. You may want to refer them to Resource D17.2 (English Literature Higher Tier mark scheme), D17.3 (English Literature Foundation Tier mark scheme) or D17.4 (English mark scheme).
- Ask them to comment on how the answer could have been improved, looking at the importance of supporting points with good examples.

8 Plenary

- Recap and ensure that students have:
  - understood the ways Raleigh has used linguistic devices to achieve his effects;
  - responded to the language in the poem.
- Invite students to suggest a modern version of this metaphor, such as a sporting occasion or concert/'gig', finding images for birth, stages of life and death.
- For English Literature, find another poem in Collection D that uses extended metaphor, and ask students to compare the use of this device in the two poems.

9 Further work

Ask students to think about how this poem might fit with the collection's theme of 'taking a stand'. What is Raleigh's overall view of life? Is it positive or negative? In what sense might he be 'taking a stand'? They should write a paragraph, picking out examples of language that support their argument.

Suggested answers

4 Close reading

play, passion, mirth, music, tiring-houses, dressed, comedy, spectator, act, curtains, play, playing, jest.

Lesson D3
I Shall Paint my Nails Red *Carole Satyamurti*

Learning objective
To develop an understanding of how Satyamurti uses form and imagery to convey a sense of a specific mood.

Resources
• Edexcel GCSE Poetry Anthology, page 56
• Audio D3
• Glossary D3
• Worksheet D3.1
• Image D3.1
• Image D3.2
• Image D3.3

1 Before reading: whole class work

• Brainstorm possible connotations of the word 'red'. You may want to display Images D3.1, D3.2 and D3.3 to stimulate discussion.

• Collate all the ideas generated on the board so that they can be referred to later on in the lesson. Possible answers include love, danger, alert, emergency, blood, passion, brightness, rage, source of help.

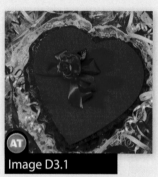
Image D3.1

Image D3.2

Image D3.3

2 Before reading: pair work

• Hand out Worksheet D3.1. Explain that each line is a reason for the poet deciding to paint her nails red. Draw students' attention to the repetition of the first word in each line. Students should cut up the jumbled lines of the poem into separate strips and arrange the reasons into their order of importance.

Worksheet D3.1

• Take feedback, encouraging students to discuss and justify their decisions.

3 Before reading: independent work

Ask students to reflect on how they have ordered the lines. Does this order make a good poem or would they rearrange them in any way? Encourage students to experiment with alternative orders and be prepared to explain the choices they have made.

4 First reading: whole class work

• Listen to the audio recording of the poem. After they listen, students should compare Satyamurti's poem to their own ordering of the lines.

• Ask students which version they think is better and why. Why has the author chosen this order for the lines in the poem? Ask the class to think about the first and last lines in particular.

5 Close reading: pair work

• As a class, read the first line. How does this line link with the word 'red' in the title? The words 'colour' and 'public service' might suggest a bus which, in some locations, is red.

• Ask students to work in pairs to look closely at the rest of the poem to find further links with 'red', and annotate the poem accordingly. You could provide them with Glossary D3 to help them understand any challenging words.

• Take feedback and discuss the connections that students have identified.

Access

Ask students to write a character profile of the persona in the poem. Give students the following opening: 'The persona in the poem seems to be a busy woman because she is pleased to save time on her appearance when she says "Because it is quicker than dyeing my hair."' Ask them to add further points to the character profile, ensuring they find evidence for these in the lines of the poem.

6 Close reading: whole class work

- Look closely at the title. Discuss occasions when someone might use the phrase 'I shall'. For example, when we are promising others, promising ourselves, defending ourselves. Discuss whether 'I shall' shows assertiveness or insecurity. Discuss what might prompt such a vocal assertiveness.
- Ask the class to consider how this title links with the theme of taking a stand.

Extend

Encourage students to go beyond the surface meaning of each idea in the poem. They should think about how the idea of red suggests rebellion and the idea of 'taking a stand'. Ask students to identify whether the ten lines can be grouped in any way, for example, practical, ambitious, self-pleasing.

7 Exploring ideas: independent work

- Ask students to draw around both their hands on a plain sheet of paper. Draw their attention to the fact that there are ten lines in the poem and ten nails to paint.
- Ask students to write the word 'Because' in the centre of each hand and then, in each finger/ thumb, to write an explanation in their own words of the ten lines in the poem. You could give them a possible explanation of the first line to start them off – for this line they could write 'Because I can cheer up other people'.

8 Peer assessment

- Ask students to swap their responses to the independent work with a partner. Students should assess how well their partners' explanations of the lines in the poem show an understanding of Satyamurti's ten reasons. They should particularly look out for analysis of the vocabulary and imagery used by Satyamurti.
- Ask them to decide which of the five bands the work falls into. You may want to refer them to Resource D17.2 (English Literature Higher Tier mark scheme), D17.3 (English Literature Foundation Tier mark scheme) or D17.4 (English mark scheme).
- They should then comment on how the answer could have been improved, looking at the importance of supporting points with good examples.

9 Plenary

- Recap and ensure that students have:
  - understood the way Satyamurti has used the ten-line structure and linguistic devices to convey her mood and feelings;
  - responded to the images they have encountered.
- Suggest the title for a poem, such as 'I shall change my hairstyle'. Quickly create on the board a ten-line poem, taking reasons from different members of the class. Invite them to say how they think this works, compared with Satyamurti's version. Why is her choice of vocabulary and images so effective? How does the poem link with the theme of 'taking a stand'?
- For English Literature, compare this poem with Raleigh's poem 'On the Life of Man' and think about the ways in which the two poets manage to express their thoughts and images economically in a ten-line structure.

10 Further work

Students should write their own version of the poem, taking a stand against issues that are important to them. They should use the same structure but change the title to another colour or an item of clothing, for example, 'I Shall Wear a Red T-Shirt'.

Suggested answers

5 Close reading

hands – red hands suggest 'women's work'; woman – femininity; survivor – blood; traffic jams – red stop light/ strawberry jam; lover – passion; dyeing – colour; the more able may suggest moratorium – temporary ban i.e. stop.

7 Exploring ideas

- *make people smile/brighten lives/look after other people.*
- *creative/vain/women's work.*
- *vain/seen as inferior/enjoys femininity.*
- *strength and resilience.*
- *vain/busy life.*
- *wants to annoy her daughter/wants to be recognised as more than just a mother.*
- *wants to be seen as an individual/lover gives a hint of mystery/breaking out of the mould.*
- *busy/not wanting to or being able to spend too much time on appearance/having the time to.*
- *a pause in her busy life/time for herself.*
- *can be changed, not for ever/she may not be ready to accept the person she is inside.*

TAKING A STAND

Learning objective

To explore the ways in which Hardi uses allusion and language to show how the widows of Anfal coped with their situation.

Resources
- Edexcel GCSE Poetry Anthology, page 57
- Audio D4
- Glossary D4
- Worksheet D4.1
- Worksheet D4.2
- Worksheet D4.3
- Image D4.1

Lesson D4
The Penelopes of my homeland *Choman Hardi*

1 Before reading: whole class work

Tell students the story of Penelope and Odysseus and display the image of Penelope and her suitors, Image D4.1.

Image D4.1

Penelope was the wife of Odysseus. During his long absence fighting in the Trojan War, she remained faithful to him, even though she received proposals of marriage from more than a hundred suitors. Instead of giving up hope that Odysseus would return home and remarrying, Penelope devised ploys to put off the suitors. She told them she would not choose a new husband until she had finished weaving a shroud for her father-in-law. For three years she wove the shroud during the day and pulled it apart at night, weeping for Odysseus, not knowing if he were alive and hoping for his return. Odysseus finally returned twenty years later. Penelope is renowned in mythology for her loyalty and virtue.

2 First reading: whole class work

- Ask students to read the poet's dedication. Give students information about Hardi and the Kurdish War, pointing out that she is a Kurdish immigrant who had to leave because of the turmoil in the country. Explain the al-Anfal campaign to the students: in the late 1980s the Iraqi government conducted a campaign of mass displacement and disappearance of an estimated 182,000 Kurds in Northern Iraq, mostly men. Up to 100,000 women were left widowed by the disaster.

- Listen to the audio recording of the poem or read the poem to the class, asking students to follow along in their anthologies and think about the references to widowhood.

3 Close reading: group work

- Split the students into three groups and hand out Worksheet D4.1. Assign each group two stanzas of the poem and have them decide how the women felt and what they did while their husbands were away. Ask them to find language in the poem to support their answers.

Worksheet D4.1

- Take feedback on the examples that students have identified, annotating the poem using the annotation tool in the ActiveTeach.

- In their groups, students should discuss how someone waiting for the return of a loved one might respond to their situation. Answers might include: disappointment, resilience, optimism, hopelessness, defeat.

Access

Ask students to complete Worksheet D4.3, highlighting all the examples of alliteration and repetition in the poem in two different colours. They should then write down an effect of each of these examples.

Worksheet D4.3

4 Close reading: group/pair work

- Remind students what allusion is, and explain that Hardi uses the allusion to Penelope to explore the experience of the Anfal widows.

- Have students work in groups or pairs to discuss how the widows in the poem relate to the story of Penelope and Odysseus. Ask them to make a list of similarities and differences between Penelope and the widows on Worksheet D4.2 and be prepared to feed back to the class, referring to the text to support their answers.

Worksheet D4.2

- Take feedback from the groups/pairs to facilitate a class discussion on how Hardi uses allusion to make a statement about the situation of these women. Be sure to emphasise that the widows were waiting for their husbands without any information of their wellbeing, but unlike Penelope, their husbands will never return. Refer to both obvious connections, such as names, and to ideas, such as 'holding on to hopes'.

Extend

The poet seems to distance herself from most of the events in the poem but she does repeat the phrase 'my homeland'. Ask students why they think she does this. Ask them to consider the effect of the poet's use of the first person here.

5 Independent writing

Ask students to write a PEEE paragraph, exploring the poet's use of allusion and language to convey emotion. Take feedback as a whole class.

6 Peer assessment

- Ask students to swap their answers to the independent writing question with a partner. Invite the students to mark each other's work. Students should assess how well their partners' responses show an understanding of Hardi's presentation of the lives of the widows.

- They should then award up to five marks, deciding which of the five bands the work falls into. You may want to refer them to Resource D17.2 (English Literature Higher Tier mark scheme), D17.3 (English Literature Foundation Tier mark scheme) or D17.4 (English mark scheme).

- Ask them to comment on how the answer could have been improved, looking at the importance of supporting points with good examples.

7 Plenary

- Recap and ensure that students have:
  - understood the way Hardi has used allusion and language to create effects;
  - responded to the situations and descriptions of people's lives they have encountered.

- In pairs, find three examples of lines (or parts of lines) that they found particularly striking. Pool ideas, using the board.

- For English Literature, compare the ways in which Hardi and one other poet in Collection D present attitudes to death. Give examples from the texts to support the points made.

8 Further work

Ask students to identify the words in the poem which suggest resilience and optimism. Discuss how the poet uses the contrast between these and the negative images to convey her feelings about the stand taken by the 'Penelopes' (i.e. widows).

Lesson D5
A Consumer's Report *Peter Porter*

Learning objective
To evaluate how Porter uses language and extended metaphor to comment on life.

Resources
- Edexcel GCSE Poetry Anthology, page 58
- Audio D5
- Glossary D5
- Worksheet D5.1
- Worksheet D5.2
- Worksheet D5.3

1 Before reading: whole class work

- Ask students to think about the last product review they read or even wrote. Ask students: What product was it for, e.g. shampoo, a computer game? What kind of information did it contain?
- Choose one type of product, such as trainers. Ask students: What do people look for in this product? How do they balance cost against function, looks, brand image, etc.? Why might people not want to wear supermarket trainers? How satisfied do we expect to be with a product: 100%? 50%? How do we make an overall decision about whether to buy, e.g. balance advantages and disadvantages, cost, reliability, friends' recommendations?

2 First reading: whole class work

- Give students Worksheet D5.1. This shows the poem written as a prose passage with the name of the product removed.
- Ask them to discuss what product the text could refer to. Brainstorm ideas about what this product could be. Lead students towards the conclusion that it is 'Life'.

Worksheet D5.1

- Listen to the audio recording and discuss the poem now that students know what the subject is. Remind students of the definition of a metaphor. Explain that this poem, in which life is presented as a consumer product, is an example of extended metaphor. By drawing comparisons between life and a consumer product, the poet is able to make some interesting statements about life.

3 Close reading: pair work

- Hand out Worksheet D5.2, asking students to work in pairs to identify the words and phrases in the poem that answer the product questionnaire and to explain what these responses suggest about life.
- Ask students to decide whether the overall view of life in the poem is negative or positive and feed back to the class.

Worksheet D5.2

Access

Hand out Worksheet D5.3 as an alternative to Worksheet D5.2. This worksheet encourages students to look more closely at the poem by writing down what is suggested by selected phrases within the poem, and helps them to deduce whether the overall impression of life given is negative or positive.

Worksheet D5.3

4 Peer assessment

- Students should assess each other's ideas, focusing on whether they have identified the poet's main ideas.
- Invite them to award up to five marks, deciding which of the five bands the work falls into. You may want to refer them to Resource D17.2 (English Literature Higher Tier mark scheme), D17.3 (English Literature Foundation Tier mark scheme) or D17.4 (English mark scheme).
- Ask them to comment on how the answers could have been improved, looking at the importance of drawing on appropriate examples from the poem.

5 Close reading: whole class work

- Take feedback on parts 1 and 2 of Worksheet D5.2 and/or Worksheet D5.3.
- Draw students' attention to the line 'So finally, I'd buy it.' Ask students what aspects of the 'product', life, would persuade them to buy it. Ask students: Is the overall view of life from this poem positive or negative? (This is the final question on both worksheets.)

6 Exploring form: pair work

- Ask students to work in pairs to structure the prose passage on Worksheet D5.1 into a poem.
- Ask students to compare the structure of the poem in their anthologies with their own versions, commenting on any features of the form which they find particularly surprising or effective. Discuss the reasons for students' choices of line breaks, for example, or punctuation and words they feel are significant.

Extend

Ask students to consider how the poet uses humour and cliché to convey his attitude towards life. Explain the meaning of 'cliché' as necessary.

7 Looking at meaning: whole class work

Ask students to look at the final three lines of the poem. Ask: What is the tone of the poet in these three lines? What is the poet trying to say about our attitude to life? How is he 'taking a stand' with this poem?

8 Plenary

- Recap and ensure that students have:
  - understood the ways Porter has used language and extended metaphor to comment on life;
  - responded to the strength of the images they have encountered.
- Pool ideas of making the product 'life' more attractive to buy, by creating some more positive images.
- Ask students to make a chart, grid or list that they can complete or add to while studying the poems from Collection D, subdividing poems into different groups and making links between them. Show how the first poems studied might fit into this. This can then be updated at regular intervals.
- For English Literature, compare the use of a first-person speaker in this poem with a first-person speaker in another poem in Collection D. Give evidence to support your views.

9 Further work

Ask students to write a consumer's report on the 'competitive product' mentioned in the final line of the poem. You might wish to suggest ideas for what this product might be, e.g. death, afterlife, parallel universe. You might want to give students a list of the key information they should provide on the product, e.g. price, appearance, popularity. Ask them to think about what overall impression of their 'product' they want to communicate (positive/negative).

Lesson D6
Pessimism for Beginners *Sophie Hannah*

Learning objective
To explore how Hannah uses exaggeration and ridicule to humorous effect in looking at our everyday attitude to life.

Resources
- Edexcel GCSE Poetry Anthology, page 60
- Audio D6
- Glossary D6
- Worksheet D6.1
- Worksheet D6.2
- Video D6.1
- Video D6.2
- Interactive D6

1 Before reading: whole class work

- Brainstorm what ideas and images might be suggested by the words 'pessimism' and 'optimism'. List students' suggestions on the board so that they can be referred to later in the lesson.
- Establish that these two ideas contrast and that pessimism is normally thought of as negative.
- Discuss the title 'Pessimism for Beginners'. Compare this to the titles of handbooks, such as 'Guitar for Beginners', and ask students to identify whether there is anything strange about this title. Students should recognise that it is unusual to provide guidance on how to be pessimistic as it's such a negative and abstract concept.

Access

Ensure students understand the concept of pessimism and the characteristics of a pessimistic person. To help students engage with this, set up the scenario of waiting for the results of a job interview or a call from someone they like. Discuss the fact that a pessimistic person would believe that they will never get the job or receive the call. Explain that the poem they are going to read is encouraging this pessimistic frame of mind because if you take this standpoint you will never be disappointed.

2 Before reading: group work

Use Interactive D6, available on the ActiveTeach, to help students match words from the poem with the correct definitions.

Interactive D6

3 First reading: whole class work

Watch Video D6.1 of Sophie Hannah reading this poem. Discuss students' initial reactions. Ask students: What is the tone of the poem? Do you think the poem is negative or positive?

Video D6.1

4 Close reading: whole class work

- Ask students to read the poem again in pairs and high-light the ten words that appear most negative to them.
- Next ask pairs to highlight, in another colour, the ten words that seem most positive to them.
- Ask students to look at the positioning of the negative and positive words in the poem. Can they see a pattern?

5 Close reading: whole class work

- Discuss the idea that the focus of the poem moves from negative to positive, focusing on the message in the last two lines. Ensure that students understand the wording and logic of the conclusion.
- Summarise the message of the poem – that if you believe the worst you may be pleasantly surprised.
- Discuss how this poem presents 'advice for life'. Hand out Worksheet D6.1 and have students work in pairs to determine how the different phrases fit with the message of the poem, and ask them whether they agree or not.
- Ask students whether they think the approach of being pessimistic is a good one. Is the persona serious in telling the reader we should follow this approach in life?

Worksheet D6.1

6 Exploring imagery: pair work

- Hand out Worksheet D6.2, which asks students to annotate the underlined phrases to explain why they are effective.
- Discuss why these eight phrases have been selected, drawing out that they are all examples of exaggeration used to ridicule a point of view. Help students to understand that they are not meant to be taken literally.

Worksheet D6.2

- Ask pairs to share their annotations with the class. Discuss how Hannah has used exaggeration to create humour. You might want to look at how the tongue-in-cheek approach reflects and pokes fun at our insecurities and worries in life.

7 Exploring content: whole class work

Show students Video D6.2, an interview with Hannah, who talks about the style of her poetry and her own favourite poets. You may want to concentrate on the first section where she discusses the rhythm and rhyme of her poetry.

Video D6.2

Extend

Ask students to comment on how the humour in the poem helps us to interpret the poet's message. Students should think about the poet's use of rhyme, alliteration and juxtaposition of words.

8 Independent writing

Ask students to write a paragraph, starting as follows: 'The poet uses exaggeration in this poem in order to …' Support them in understanding the tongue-in-cheek tone of the poem. Is Hannah serious in suggesting that we should be pessimistic in order to be pleasantly surprised? Help them to find evidence for their points within the poem.

9 Peer assessment

- Ask students to swap their paragraphs with a partner. Invite them to mark each other's work, awarding up to five marks, deciding which of the five bands the work falls into. You may want to refer them to Resource D17.2 (English Literature Higher Tier mark scheme), D17.3 (English Literature Foundation Tier mark scheme) or D17.4 (English mark scheme).
- Then ask them to comment on how the answer could have been improved, looking at the importance of supporting points with good examples.

10 Plenary

- Recap and ensure that students have:
  - understood the ways Hannah has used exaggeration and ridicule to communicate her message;
  - analysed the effect of the images they have encountered.
- Invite students to find pairs of statements that reflect the difference between the attitudes of a 'half-full' and 'half-empty' glass (give an example such as 'At least it isn't snowing' and 'Typical – rain again'). Invite thoughts on which type of person each student thinks he/she is and why.
- For English Literature, find another poem in Collection D that uses humorous or exaggerated effects to convey attitudes to life, and ask students to compare the two poems.

11 Further work

Ask students to write an email advising a friend on the best ways to be optimistic in approach to life. They should use exaggerated images to reinforce a positive message. In preparation, you might wish to refer back to the ideas about optimism in Activity 1 and brainstorm ideas and images that express a positive attitude to life.

Suggested answers

4 Close reading

Negative words: *waiting, missing, cursing, hissing, vile, illegal, leave, vomit, loathe, Hitler.*

Positive words: *young, friend, parent, lover, stalwart, irresistible, appealing, better, hopes, joy.*

Lesson D7
Solitude

Ellie Wheeler Wilcox

Learning objective
To understand how Wilcox explores reasons for solitude in life through form, language and rhyme.

Resources
• Edexcel GCSE Poetry Anthology, page 61
• Audio D7
• Glossary D7
• Worksheet D7.1
• Worksheet D7.2

1 Before reading: whole class work

• Brainstorm ideas associated with the concept of solitude, especially the types of emotions people might feel when alone. Then ask what types of feelings students have when they're not alone (i.e. when they're with others).

• Hand out Worksheet D7.1 and ask students to construct an acrostic poem using the word 'Solitude'. Ask them to think about their feelings both when they are alone and when they are with others. Remind them how an acrostic verse is constructed as necessary (the first letters of each line form a word when put together).

Worksheet D7.1

• Share the poems that students have written. Draw out any similarities in students' poems including attitudes, feelings, relevance and implications for the way we live.

2 First reading: pair work

• Listen to the audio recording of 'Solitude' and have students follow along in their anthologies.

• Ask students to work in pairs to identify feelings in the poem connected with solitude and those connected with company.

• Start a discussion about the poem by taking feedback from the pairs. Ask students what they think the poem says about solitude. Draw out the idea that people like to celebrate with you but often shy away from your times of trouble or need.

• Ask students if they think that the poet regards solitude as negative or positive. Is the poet sending us a message about the attitude we should have in life?

Access

Hand out Worksheet D7.2 and ask students to work in pairs to identify the negative and positive words in the poem which contrast. After listing these words, have the pairs discuss what these images show. Ask the pairs to feed back to the class.

Worksheet D7.2

3 Close reading: whole class work

• Re-read the poem, this time focusing on the strong rhythm. Identify the rhythm (two lines of three beats, one of four, and a final line of three). Ask students if this reminds them of other poems they have read or heard. You could suggest that it is reminiscent of nursery rhymes addressing young children, for example 'Hickory, Dickory Dock'. Ask students what effect this might have on the reader.

• Ask students to identify the rhyming pattern in the poem (end rhyme in second and fourth lines), perhaps by asking two students to read alternate lines. Annotate the rhyme pattern using the annotation tool on the ActiveTeach. Ask students to mark the words which rhyme in their anthologies.

• Discuss what effect this rhyme scheme has – you may decide it helps to bring out the contrast between shared joy and positivity and solitary grief and negativity.

4 Looking at literary devices: group work

- Ask students to find five examples of alliteration and five examples of internal rhyme and to think about what effects these have. Ask: How do these examples help reinforce what the poet is trying to communicate?
- Ask students to share their responses and mark examples on the board or highlight them using the annotation tool on the ActiveTeach. Discuss the effect of the internal rhyme and alliteration. Both contribute to the sense of rhythm and the idea of imparting advice for life. Reading sections aloud may help students to understand the effect.

5 Independent writing

Students should write two paragraphs about how the poet explores the reasons for solitude through use of negative and positive images.

6 Self/Peer assessment

- Ask students to swap their paragraphs with a partner. Invite the students to mark each other's work. They should compare their responses, deciding which strengths each has, in understanding the images presented.
- Ask them to award up to five marks, deciding which of the five bands the work falls into. You may want to refer them to Resource D17.2 (English Literature Higher Tier mark scheme), D17.3 (English Literature Foundation Tier mark scheme) or D17.4 (English mark scheme).
- They should then comment on how their partner's answer could have been improved, looking at the importance of supporting points with good examples.

7 Plenary

- Recap and ensure that students have
  - understood the ways Wilcox has developed her views about 'solitude';
  - responded to the various effects used to show either a negative or a positive view of life.
- Invite students to make suggestions in two columns on the board (or on paper) for the advantages and drawbacks of being alone.
- For English Literature, find another poem in Collection D which relies strongly on contrasting attitudes or emotions, and ask students to compare the use of contrast and its effect in the two poems.

8 Further work

- Ask students to research the background of the poet and find out about the New Thought Movement.
- Ask students to re-read the poem in the light of this information and write a paragraph explaining the impact of Wilcox's beliefs on the poem.

Extend

Ask students to work in pairs to discuss the following questions: Why did Wilcox write this poem? How does it link with the theme of the collection? Do you agree with the poet's message? Students should write a paragraph in response to each question, including references to the text in their answers.

Suggested answers

4 Looking at literary devices
Alliteration: *sing/sigh; grieve/go; not/need; feast/fast; long/lordly.*

Internal rhyme: *bound/sound; measure/pleasure; glad/sad; give/live; one/on.*

Lesson D8
No Problem

Benjamin Zephaniah

Learning objective
To explore how Zephaniah uses language to communicate that we should challenge preconceptions.

Resources
- Edexcel GCSE Poetry Anthology, page 62
- Audio D8
- Glossary D8
- Worksheet D8.1
- Image D8.1
- Image D8.2

1 Before reading: whole class work

- Ask students whether they've ever been stereotyped. If so, in what way and why? How did it make them feel?
- Explain that this is a poem in which the persona feels he has been stereotyped by other people.

Access

Show Image D8.1. Ask students about this person, for example, what music taste this person might have or what he might do in his spare time. Now show them Image D8.2 and ask similar questions. Discuss their responses and ask students on what they based their judgements. Work towards the idea that these perceptions are based around stereotypes, concepts of what is seen as 'typical'.

Image D8.1

Image D8.2

2 First reading: whole class work

- Listen to the audio recording of the poem, asking students to follow in the anthology.
- Discuss students' first impressions of the poem. Ask students: What is the overall tone of the poem? What is the stereotype people have used in their initial judgements of the persona?

3 Exploring perspective: independent work

- Hand out Worksheet D8.1. Ask students to complete the table by identifying the things which Zephaniah says people think about him, as well as the things people don't see or notice.

Worksheet D8.1

- Take feedback on the previous activity, leading to discussion on racial stereotyping. Ask students to consider the reasons for Zephaniah's objection to being 'branded athletic' and his assertion that he can 'do more dan dance'.

4 Close reading: pair work

- Ask students what they understand by the words 'accent' and 'dialect'. Establish that the poet has tried to convey a specific dialect in this poem.
- Ask students to work in pairs to rewrite the poem using Standard English, including full stops. Refer them to the glossary if they need help with understanding any of the vocabulary.
- Ask students what accent is represented, first focusing on how it is conveyed and, particularly, on the use of 'd' for 'th' in the words 'de', 'dey', 'dan' and 'wid', for example.
- In their pairs, ask students to think of three reasons why Zephaniah has used this accent instead of using Standard English. Does it change how we think of the persona? Does accent contribute to our judgement of people? Ask pairs to share their responses and compare ideas as a class.

5 Looking at message: group work

- Divide the class into small groups. Draw students' attention to the first line. Ask students: Where else is this line used? Are there any similar lines? What is the effect of this repetition? What is the problem?
- Discuss students' ideas on the effect of the repetition and what the poet identifies as the problem, encouraging them to give evidence. Link back to the opening activity, and establish that it is stereotyping and prejudice which Zephaniah objects to.
- Ask students why they think he has chosen this title.
- How does the poem link to the theme of 'taking a stand'?

Extend

Ask students to think about Zephaniah's use of imagery and/or symbolism. Why, for example, does he refer to Timbuktu? What does it represent? You might also like to draw their attention to 'pigeon hole' and 'chips on me shoulders' and 'Mother country'.

6 Independent writing

Ask students to use ideas from the discussion and their own work so far to write three or four paragraphs to answer the question: How does Zephaniah use language and form to put forward his point of view?

7 Peer assessment

- Ask students to swap their paragraphs with a partner and invite them to mark each other's work, looking at the understanding shown of Zephaniah's use of language and form to convey his themes.
- Invite students to award up to five marks, deciding which of the five bands the work falls into. You may want to refer them to Resource D17.2 (English Literature Higher Tier mark scheme), D17.3 (English Literature Foundation Tier mark scheme) or D17.4 (English mark scheme).
- They should then comment on how the answer could have been improved, looking at the importance of supporting points with good examples.

8 Plenary

- Recap and ensure that students have:
  - understood the ways Zephaniah has communicated his defiant attitudes to stereotypes;
  - responded to the effects of the use of dialect.
- Invite students to come up with a strong statement saying why individuals should not be classed under stereotypes. Some stereotyping statements might be given, e.g. 'All blondes are dumb'; 'people who wear glasses are always swots/nerds/geeks'; 'people who live in big houses are all snobs'.
- Update the 'connections' chart, grid or list, linking this poem with others with which the students can see close connections in theme or treatment.
- For English Literature, find another poem in Collection D in which there is a strong sense of defiance, and ask students to compare the way attitudes are conveyed in the two poems.

9 Further work

Ask students to write a short poem explaining why teenagers are 'no problem'. They might like to include non-Standard English to convey their point of view, either representing an accent or dialect, or perhaps a means of communicating such as SMS.

Lesson D9

Those bastards in their mansions *Simon Armitage*

Learning objective
To evaluate how Armitage uses rhythm, rhyme, assonance and allusion to portray a hostile attitude towards others.

Resources
• Edexcel Poetry Anthology, page 63
• Audio D9
• Glossary D9
• Worksheet D9.1
• Worksheet D9.2
• Worksheet D9.3
• Video D9.1
• Video D9.2

1 Before reading: pair work

• Hand out Worksheet D9.1, which asks students to match the words from the poem in pairs and categorise each pair as an example of rhyme or assonance.

• Take feedback, sharing the Suggested answers available on the ActiveTeach with students.

Worksheet D9.1

2 First reading: whole class work

Read the poem to the class or listen to Audio D9 together, following in the anthology. Ask students to think about the words that rhyme within the poem (these might be full or partial rhyme). Where are they placed in the poem and why? What effect does this have on the rhythm and rhythm of the poem? Draw out that the effect is quite staccato, suggesting very strong feelings, perhaps even violence. What effect does this have on the reader?

Access

Give students a definition of assonance: a similarity in sound between internal letters in neighbouring words. Clarify the difference between assonance and rhyme. Read off each of the following pairs of words and ask the class to identify whether they are examples of assonance or rhyme: sting/bring; fall/shawl; feel/steer; door/floor; billow/pillow; fire/light.

3 Looking at tone: whole class work

• Watch Video D9.1 of Simon Armitage reading this poem. As they follow in their anthologies, ask students to think about the tone of voice and how they would describe Armitage's attitude.

Video D9.1

• Ask students when they think the poem might be set. Discuss ideas as a class and ask students to identify words that might give them clues. Refer students to the glossary as necessary.

• What issues are brought out by the poem? What are the poet's attitudes? How and why is he 'taking a stand'?

4 Close reading: pair work

• Hand out Worksheet D9.2. Ask students to re-read the poem and annotate it with their answers to the questions.

• Feed back and discuss answers as a class.

Worksheet D9.2

Extend

Ask students to write about the moral standpoint of the persona, with specific reference to the first and last lines.

5 Exploring meaning: whole class work

Show students Video D9.2 of Simon Armitage explaining the use of the myth of Prometheus within the poem. After watching, discuss students' understanding of the poem in the light of this. You might want to draw their attention to the references in line 6

Video D9.2

and 12 in particular. How does the use of the myth help shed light on the resentment and class frictions the poet seems to feel? How does it help us understand how the poem explores the theme of 'taking a stand'? How might our view of the poet change when we understand his use of this learned myth?

6 Independent writing

Ask students to write a PEEE paragraph exploring the persona's view of people with wealth and privilege. They should support their points with examples from the poem throughout.

7 Peer assessment

- Ask students to swap their writing with a partner, and compare views on the moral standpoint which they feel has been expressed. Has their partner explored the ways in which this is communicated?
- Invite the students to mark each other's work, awarding up to five marks, deciding which of the five bands the work falls into. You may want to refer them to Resource D17.2 (English Literature Higher Tier mark scheme), D17.3 (English Literature Foundation Tier mark scheme) or D17.4 (English mark scheme).
- Ask them to comment on how the answer could have been improved, looking at the importance of supporting points with good examples.

8 Plenary

- Recap and ensure that students have:
  - understood the ways Armitage has used a variety of effects to portray strong attitudes towards privilege;
  - responded to the strength of the linguistic devices they have encountered.
- Invite students in pairs to think of as many examples as they can of words and phrases using sound effects (assonance, alliteration, onomatopoeia) to present a vivid picture of a book, television or film character of their choice. You might want to provide an example such as James Bond: 'silky smooth, suave, sophisticated' or Ron Weasley: 'weak, weedy and whiny'. Write down a range of suggestions and vote for the most effective.
- For English Literature, find another poem in Collection D that uses violent or military imagery, and ask students to compare the use of this device in the two poems.

9 Further work

Ask students to research the legend of Prometheus and fill in the blanks on Worksheet D9.3. Students should write an explanation of how this myth links to the poem and the idea of 'taking a stand'.

Worksheet D9.3

Suggested answers

3 Looking at tone

Time setting: *one of class war, rebellion of the poor, revolution.*

Clues: *mansions, stocking feet, threadbare britches, burning torches, shackles, lords and ladies, palaces and castles.*

Lesson D10
Living Space

Imtiaz Dharker

Learning objective
To understand how Dharker uses a specific image to explore the precarious and unpredictable nature of life.

Resources
- Edexcel GCSE Poetry Anthology, page 64
- Audio D10
- Glossary D10
- Worksheet D10.1
- Image D10.1
- Image D10.2
- Image D10.3
- Video D10.1
- Video D10.2

1 Before reading: whole class work

Image D10.1

- Discuss the phrase 'living space', displaying images D10.1, D10.2 and/ or D10.3 of contrasting living spaces. Ask students: What ideas does this phrase make you think of? What is your own living space like? What effect does your living space have on your life?
- Ask students to write their own individual definition of the phrase 'living space'.

Image D10.2

Image D10.3

2 First reading: whole class work

- Watch Video D10.1 and ask students to follow in their anthologies as they listen to the poem.
- Discuss what the space described in each stanza reminds them of and what they think of it.

LIVING SPACE
by Imtiaz Dharker

Video D10.1

- Ask students to think about Dharker's idea of a living space, picking out words which not only have physical implications but also suggest something about 'living'.

- Watch Video D10.2 which is an interview with Dharker about the poem. Ask students if listening to the interview helped them with their understanding of the poem. If so, how?

Video D10.2

3 Close reading: pair work

- Draw attention to the word 'lines' in line 2.
- Ask students to find six words in the poem that could describe a line and eight words or phrases that relate to a building.
- Encourage students to find a way of explaining the link between the two lists of words.
- Take feedback, leading to the question: Is this poem just about a building?
- Discuss ideas about what the poem is about, guiding students to understand that Dharker is using an extended metaphor.

Access

Define metaphor: describing an object or person by saying they are something else, e.g. she is an angel, the house was a pig-sty. Ask students to come up with their own examples and share them with the class. Give them the metaphor 'life is an egg' and explain that this is the metaphor in the poem. Get initial reactions. Why might the poet have chosen this metaphor?

4 Exploring ideas: whole class work

- Write 'living space' on the board and recap on the earlier discussion about the title. On one side of the board, write a definition students agree with (e.g. house, bedroom, home) and on the other write: 'the space between birth and death (life)'.

- Discuss this new interpretation of the title and how it affects the reading of the poem.

5 Exploring ideas: pair work

- Ask students to highlight seven words or phrases in the poem that imply a sense of risk and danger, keeping in mind the idea that the poem is a metaphor for life.
- Ask students to describe Dharker's views on life and living, guiding them to the idea that life is a challenge and includes danger, excitement, difficulty and the unknown or unexpected. Ask students to comment on how this fits with the theme of the collection, 'taking a stand'.

6 Exploring language: whole class work

- Hand out Worksheet D10.1, which shows key words from the third stanza. Check students' understanding of each of the words (eggs, fragile, universe, light, faith) in context.
- Groups are asked to discuss possible links between the words.

Worksheet D10.1

Extend

Ask students to explain why they think the poet has used line breaks at these particular points: line 1–2, line 2–3, line 3–4, line 9–10, line 14–15, line 16–17, line 21–22. Ask students: How does this use of enjambement help to convey the poet's ideas?

7 Independent writing

Ask students to use the words on Worksheet D10.1 to write an explanation of what Dharker is saying about life in the third stanza. How does the image of life within the poem link to the theme of 'taking a stand'?

8 Peer assessment

- Ask students to swap their work with a partner and comment on each other's response, noting one point they agree with and one they feel could be more fully explained.

- Invite the students to mark each other's work, awarding up to five marks, deciding which of the five bands the work falls into. You may want to refer them to Resource D17.2 (English Literature Higher Tier mark scheme), D17.3 (English Literature Foundation Tier mark scheme) or D17.4 (English mark scheme).
- They should then comment on how the answer could have been improved, looking at the importance of supporting points with good examples.

9 Plenary

- Recap and ensure that students have:
  - understood the ways Dharker has used an image to explore the nature of life;
  - responded to the language used to develop this image.
- Invite students to think of a metaphor for an exciting event they have attended and extend this as far as possible with different ideas. Examples might include thinking of a varied holiday as a patchwork quilt, or a 'gig' or concert as a walk through a forest or art gallery. Discuss how easy or difficult this was and whether it helped them express their feelings about the event.
- For English Literature, find another poem in Collection D that uses a developed image or motif, and ask students to compare the use of this device in the two poems.

10 Further work

Ask students to write about an experience in their life that they found challenging. Ask them to pay attention to the language they use to describe this experience.

Suggested answers

3 Close reading

Lines: *straight, flat, parallel, vertical, curves, slanted.*

Building: *beams, supports, nails, seams, structure, frame, living space, walls.*

Link: *The different lines suggest the shapes involved in building; the second list contains materials and elements of construction.*

5 Exploring ideas

balance crookedly, thrust of, clutch at, leans dangerously, squeezed, dared, hung out.

Lesson D11
The archbishop chairs the first session *Ingrid de Kok*

Learning objective
To evaluate how de Kok uses form and language to explore the emotion and significance behind the Truth and Reconciliation Commission in South Africa.

Resources
- Edexcel GCSE Poetry Anthology, page 65
- Audio D11
- Glossary D11
- Worksheet D11.1
- Image D11.1
- Image D11.2
- Video D11.1
- Video D11.2
- Interactive D11

1 Before reading: whole class work

- Ask students what they think the purpose of a 'Truth and Reconciliation Commission' might be. What ideas do the words 'truth' and 'reconciliation' suggest?
- Display the images of segregation during apartheid and of Archbishop Desmond Tutu.

Image D11.1

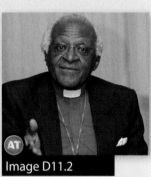
Image D11.2

- Explain that after the abolition of apartheid in South Africa, the Truth and Reconciliation Commission, a court-like body, was assembled. Victims of gross human rights violations were invited to give statements about their experiences, and some were chosen for public hearings. People known to be involved in violence could also give testimony and request amnesty from both civil and criminal prosecution. Archbishop Desmond Tutu was the chairman of the Commission.
- You might want to show students Video D11.2 of the interview with the poet, where she discusses the significance of the Commission. Ask students how this process might link to the theme of 'taking a stand'.

Video D11.2

2 First reading: whole class work

- Watch Video D11.1 of Ingrid de Kok reading this poem, asking students to bear in mind what they have already learned as they listen. Please note that as this is an older reading of the poem, de Kok reads line 20 as 'PhDs' and not 'doctorates'.

Video D11.1

- Discuss their first impressions, particularly about why the Archbishop might 'weep'. Use the glossary to clarify the meaning of any unfamiliar words.

Access

Use Interactive D11, available on the ActiveTeach, to have students match the words listed to the correct definitions.

Interactive D11

3 Looking at form: group work

- Divide students into groups and ask them to find all the full stops in the poem. How many sentences are there in total? Are there any examples of enjambement (where sense carries over onto the next line without any punctuation mark)? How do each of the sentences end? Help them to identify that three out of six of them end in the same way, with the word 'wept'.
- Ask them to feedback and suggest reasons for the poet's use of such long sentences and abundant use of commas. Lead a discussion on what effect the length of each of the stanzas has on the reader. What tone and mood does each stanza create? You might want to compare the first two short sentences with stanzas two and three, and then

look at stanzas four and five. It could be argued that shorter sentences have more impact and hit us hard with the tragedy that precipitates the Archbishop's weeping, whereas the longer sentences with commas overwhelm the reader with the action and emotions involved, e.g. in the third stanza, although the poet dismisses these, saying 'It doesn't matter…

4 Close reading: pair work

- Hand out Worksheet D11.1. Ask students to work in pairs to note down three things they like about the poem, three things they find challenging and three questions they would like to ask the poet about. They could select examples of word choices, imagery, structural aspects or ideas, for example.
- Organise the pairs into groups of four so they can compare their ideas and questions. Encourage them to discuss the reasons for their choices and to try to answer each other's questions, identifying any that cannot be answered.
- Take feedback, making sure that any unanswered questions are addressed in further discussion.

Worksheet D11.1

Extend

Ask students to consider the last line: 'That's how it began'. Why is it separated from the rest of the poem? What effect does this separation have? What tone do the words create? How does it compare to the first line? How does the line reflect back on the rest of the poem? What might it suggest about the poet's attitude to the events described?

5 Independent writing

- Ask students to choose words and phrases in the poem that convey emotion and use them to write a paragraph to explain how de Kok creates a sense of drama about the Commission. Prompt students with any of the following examples as necessary: 'wept', 'grey head', 'weeping', 'misted glasses', 'sobbing shoulders', 'sorrows', 'lionizes', 'romanticizes', 'mystifies'. Remind them to think about why de Kok chose those particular words and phrases, and how they contribute to the drama.

6 Peer assessment

- Ask students to swap their paragraphs with a partner. Invite the students to mark each other's work, awarding up to five marks, deciding which of the five bands the work falls into. You may want to refer them to Resource D17.2 (English Literature Higher Tier mark scheme), D17.3 (English Literature Foundation Tier mark scheme) or D17.4 (English mark scheme).
- Invite comment on how the answer could have been improved, looking at the importance of supporting points with good examples.

7 Plenary

- Recap and ensure that students have
  - understood the ways in which de Kok has used form and language to explore the session of the Truth and Reconciliation Commission in South Africa;
  - responded to the complex language and pictures they have encountered.
- Invite students to think of occasions when they have seen public figures (e.g. sportspeople or 'celebrities') crying. Discuss: has crying become 'devalued'? When is it an appropriate response to a situation? In what type of situation does the sight of someone crying have a real emotional effect on them?
- For English Literature, find another poem in Collection D that deals with recent historical events, and ask students to compare why these are important to the writers of the two poems.

8 Further work

Ask students to write the opening of a news report on the first day of the Truth and Reconciliation Commission based on the poem. They could research additional background information if they wish.

Lesson D12

The world is a beautiful place *Lawrence Ferlinghetti*

Learning objective

To explore how Ferlinghetti has used form and tone to convey views on human nature and life.

Resources

- Edexcel GCSE Poetry Anthology, page 66
- Audio D12
- Glossary D12
- Worksheet D12.1
- Image D12.1
- Image D12.2
- Image D12.3
- Image D12.4

1 Before reading: whole class work

Ask students to think about the title of this poem. Would they agree with this statement? Ask them to give reasons for their opinion.

2 First reading: whole class work

- Listen to the audio recording of the poem and ask students to follow it in their anthologies.
- Ask students what their initial thoughts on the tone of the poem are. If they have trouble with this, draw their attention to the repeated lines at the start of the first three stanzas, particularly '…if you don't mind…' and the ideas which follow each time. Ask students to compare their own thoughts on the title (from Activity 1) with the tone of the poem.

3 Exploring meaning: group work

- Remind students of the structure with the title repeated as the first line of each stanza.
- Allocate each group a stanza. Ask each group to work together to come up with a summary of the ideas explored within their stanza after these initial lines. Ask students to consider what points the poet is making about life, or what aspects of life he is drawing to the reader's attention. Ask students: Are the points largely negative or positive? Encourage them to refer to the glossary where necessary.
- Ask groups to give feedback to the class. You might want to draw their attention to lines 9–11 for the first stanza, line 14 for the second stanza, lines 23–24 for the third, and lines 58–59 for the final stanza. The last stanza might need most attention, particularly the last line. You might like to look at phrases such as 'Name Brand society' (implies designer labels, foreign sweat shops, importance of the right clothes) and 'smiling/mortician'. Encourage students to evaluate how the meaning of their stanza is communicated through language, form and tone.

4 Looking at meaning: pair work

- In pairs, students should discuss to what extent the poem's message is summarised in the phrase 'Beauty is in the eye of the beholder'. Show students the paired images which show contrasting views on the world (Images D12.1 and D12.2 – a rabbit and a fur coat; Images D12.3 and D12.4 – a stunning mountain and a destructive volcano). Discuss whether this accurately reflects what the poet is saying. Ask students to provide evidence for their arguments.

Image D12.1

Image D12.2

Image D12.3

Image D12.4

Access

Hand out Worksheet D12.1. Ask students to select eight words or phrases from the poem that link with the idea of a beautiful place and eight which do not. Have students write an analysis of why and how the poet has used each of these. Ask students to share and discuss their ideas. Support students as necessary.

Worksheet D12.1

5 Looking at meaning: whole class work

- As a class, re-read the last stanza, paying particular attention to the last lines. Ask students to suggest why the poet has chosen particular imagery in this last stanza, for example, 'smelling flowers' and 'making babies'. As a class, compare students' ideas, encouraging debate.
- Move on to the final lines. Ensure that students know the meaning of the word 'mortician'. Ask students to suggest reasons why the poet has chosen the adjective 'smiling' to describe the noun 'mortician'. Ideas might include the idea that everything is superficially cheerful, even death. Or perhaps the poet is emphasising that although you can enjoy the good things in life, death will still happily snatch you away in the end.

6 Looking at form: pair work

- In pairs, students should come up with ideas about why the poet might have chosen the zig zag arrangement of lines in this poem.
- Have pairs share their ideas with the class and take turns at using the annotation tool on the ActiveTeach to demonstrate their points. Students may suggest that the form supports the tone – the initial first line of each stanza is then undermined by the following, separated lines and the zig zag effect reflects contrasting opinions or perspectives. The phrase 'if you don't mind' is also given emphasis by the chosen line division as is the addition of 'Oh' to emphasise meaning at the start of line 20 and 'Yes' at lines 40 and 60.

Extend

Ask students to discuss how Ferlinghetti is 'taking a stand' in this poem. Ideas might include that he is rejecting the cliché that 'the world is a beautiful place' by highlighting all the negative things about the world and reminding the reader of the presence of death.

7 Independent writing

Ask students to write a paragraph on how the poet has used form and tone in the poem to convey his message that the world isn't always a beautiful place. Encourage them to support their answer with evidence from the poem and put forward different interpretations where possible.

8 Peer assessment

- Ask students to swap their paragraphs with a partner and mark each other's work, looking in particular at the relationship between form and tone and the messages conveyed.
- Students should award up to five marks and decide which of the five bands the work falls into. You may want to refer them to Resource D17.2 (English Literature Higher Tier mark scheme), D17.3 (English Literature Foundation Tier mark scheme) or D17.4 (English mark scheme).
- Finally, students should comment on how the answer could have been improved, looking at the importance of supporting points with good examples.

9 Plenary

- Recap and ensure that students have:
  - understood the ways Ferlinghetti has used form and tone to convey views on life;
  - responded to the strength of the contrasting images they have encountered.
- Invite students in pairs to underline their three favourite lines from the poem. Using the board, compare responses and ask for evaluation.
- For English Literature, compare the effect of the use of short lines in this poem and one other from Collection D. Give examples to support your points.

10 Further work

Explain that Ferlinghetti was one of the most political of the 'Beat' poets, a group who became famous in the 1950s for their rejection of mainstream American values. He later became poet laureate of San Francisco. In his role, he gave many speeches. Ask students to find out more about Ferlinghetti and then write a version of this poem as a speech to residents of San Francisco, thinking carefully about the points Ferlinghetti raises.

Lesson D13
Zero Hour

Matthew Sweeney

Learning objective
To explore how Sweeney shows us a possible image of the future through the use of tone and language.

Resources
• Edexcel GCSE Poetry Anthology, page 68
• Audio D13
• Glossary D13
• Image D13.1
• Worksheet D13.1
• Worksheet D13.2
• Multimedia D13

1 Before reading: whole class work

Discuss what students think the future might be like. What are their hopes and fears? What issues might endanger the future as they would like to see it? Ask students to suggest how their children's lives might differ from their own. Ask them if they feel we have to 'take a stand' against anything currently in order to ensure a better future.

2 First reading: whole class work

Listen to the audio recording of the poem, asking students to think about Sweeney's vision of the future as they listen.

3 Close reading: whole class work

• Draw students attention to the words 'as I write' in line 19 and explain that the poem is a narrative description of current events.

• Open a discussion of the poem by asking students to explain what they think has happened in the poem and what life must be like for the narrator. Ask them: How does he feel? What is he scared of? What will happen to him?

• Discuss how students' visions of the future compare with the future as presented in the poem, noting the similarities and differences, and leading to the idea that the poem's view is very negative and fearful.

Image D13.1

• You may want to display Image D13.1 of a city to stimulate discussion.

Access

Ask students to re-read the first stanza in pairs and find words that suggest the end of something. Refer them to Glossary D13 as necessary. Remind them to be prepared to justify their choices.

4 Exploring language: independent work

• Hand out Worksheet D13.1, which asks students to explain the implication of each phrase from the poem in their own words.

• Take feedback, with students assessing their own work.

• Discuss the overall tone of the poem and how this is achieved through the poet's choice of vocabulary and the details mentioned. Encourage discussion and debate on what the tone is, asking students to support their ideas with lines from the text.

Worksheet D13.1

Extend

Draw attention to the rhetorical questions in the last stanza. Ask students to write about why the author has used these rhetorical questions and what effect they have.

5 Multimedia activity: group work

Divide students into groups and hand out Worksheet D13.2 which briefs them on how to complete a short multimedia activity using the downloadable footage provided on the ActiveTeach. When Multimedia D13 is opened, you will be prompted to save the file somewhere on your system. The multimedia clips can then be accessed by extracting them from the zip file, and then opened in editing software for students to use and modify. The aim of the activity is to encourage students to interpret the poet's ideas, thoughts and feelings through selection and editing of the material provided. Students will require access to a software editing package and up to an hour to complete the task.

Worksheet D13.2

6 Independent writing

Using the line 'To be in possession of a bicycle/is to risk your life' as a stimulus, students should write the script for a TV news bulletin about the situation, including detail from the poem. Prompt students to choose words, phrases and details that convey a negative, fearful or matter-of-fact tone and perspective.

7 Peer assessment

- Have students present their TV news bulletins to the class. Encourage peer assessment based on the effectiveness of the tone conveyed and the detail included.
- Invite the students to mark each other's work, awarding up to five marks. Students should decide which of the five bands the work falls into. You may want to refer them to Resource D17.2 (English Literature Higher Tier mark scheme), D17.3 (English Literature Foundation Tier mark scheme) or D17.4 (English mark scheme).
- Students should then comment on how the work could have been improved, providing specific examples.

8 Plenary

- Recap and ensure that students have:
  - understood the ways Sweeney has shown a vision of the future through the use of tone and language;
  - responded to the strength of fears and uncertainties expressed.
- Invite students to work in pairs to produce one 'rhetorical' question which they feel sums up a nightmare vision of the future (e.g. 'How shall we drive to work when all the petrol is used up?' or 'How long before the shelves are empty in the supermarkets?')
- For English Literature, find another poem in Collection D that looks to the future, and ask students to compare the reflections in the two poems.

9 Further work

Ask students to convert and develop their bulletins into news articles about the situation. Remind them to make sure the same tone is sustained.

Suggested answers

Access

stop, stranded, immobilised, abandoned, closed-off

Lesson D14
One World Down the Drain *Simon Rae*

Learning objective
To explore how Rae uses humour, rhythm and rhyme to communicate his message that we must take an active stand against global warming.

Resources
- Edexcel GCSE Poetry Anthology, page 69
- Audio D14
- Glossary D14
- Worksheet D14.1
- Image D14.1
- Image D14.2
- Image D14.3
- Image D14.4

1 Before reading: whole class work

- Tell students the title of the poem: 'One World Down the Drain'. You might suggest that 'one' implies that there is another and 'down the drain' suggests flushing something away without much thought to its value. Ask them to guess what the poem will be about.
- Display the information on One World Week provided underneath the title of the poem by zooming in using the ActiveTeach. Discuss possible interpretations of the final sentence as well as the implication of the inclusion of the date, for example that time is racing on and not much has changed.
- Draw out students' views on global warming. Display Images D14.1 and D14.2 showing two different effects of global warming to stimulate discussion. Ask students if they think global warming is an issue and whether they do anything to reduce its effects or take a stand against it. Then show Images D14.3 and D14.4 and discuss whether they think these are effective.

Image D14.1

Image D14.2

Image D14.3

Image D14.4

2 First reading: whole class work

- Ask students to list the range of different responses that people have to the issue of global warming, e.g.:
  - There's nothing I can do about it.
  - It won't make a difference in my lifetime.
  - It's just another scare story whipped up by the media.
  - We are responsible for the planet.
  - We owe a duty of care to our children and grandchildren.
  - We would improve our lives by stopping global warming.
- Listen to the audio recording of the poem and ask students to follow in their anthologies. Ask them to keep in mind the previous discussion on global warming.
- Ask students: What do you think the poet's opinion on global warming is, based on this first reading? What is the tone of the poem? Any points where this is particularly noticeable?

3 Close reading: pair work

- Hand out Worksheet D14.1. Ask students to work in pairs to list all the effects predicted in the poem and all the phrases that seem to be excuses or imply a lack of concern.
- Refer them to Glossary D14 as necessary to help with any unfamiliar vocabulary.

Worksheet D14.1

4 Exploring meaning: whole class work

- Take feedback on the previous activity. Ask students how they would describe the overall tone of the poem.
- Encourage students to find evidence of humour in the poem, e.g. 'The Maldives take a dive', 'Pity', 'Ciao', 'our acid greenhouse party', 'bad luck Kiribati', 'global warming/'s habit-forming'.

- As a class, explore the effect of the humour in the poem on the reader. What is the poet's serious message? How does this link to the idea of 'taking a stand'? How effective is it in making us sit up and think about global warming?

Foundation Tier mark scheme) or D17.4 (English mark scheme);

– comment on how the answer could have been improved, looking at the importance of supporting points with good examples.

Extend

- Draw students' attention to lines 8, 14 and 20-23 in particular. Ask them what the tone of these lines is. Does the poet really think it's simply 'bad luck' for Kiribati? Does he think another conference will solve the problem?
- Aim to draw out that the poet is being ironic in these lines (using language of the opposite meaning) in order to ridicule what he thinks is a misguided point of view. You might want to introduce the fact that this is called satire and explain that it is one of the key ways in which the poet communicates his message. Students will need a lot of guidance in understanding this concept, and you may wish to refer them to Glossary D1 to support them.
- Ask students to find other examples of satire and to analyse their effect on the reader.

5 Exploring rhyme: pair work

- Ask students to highlight all of the examples of rhyme, including internal rhyme, in the poem.
- In pairs, students should discuss the effect this has on the sound and tone of the poem, and what the author is trying to communicate.

6 Independent writing

Ask students to write two PEEE paragraphs explaining how Rae uses humour, rhythm and rhyme to convey a serious point of view.

7 Peer assessment

Ask students to swap their paragraphs with a partner. Invite the students to mark each other's work. They should:

- see how well the 'PEEE' technique has been used to show the link between form and point of view;
- award up to five marks, deciding which of the five bands the work falls into. You may want to refer them to Resource D17.2 (English Literature Higher Tier mark scheme), D17.3 (English Literature

8 Plenary

- Recap and ensure that students have:
  - understood the ways Rae has used a variety of effects (humour, rhythm and rhyme) to communicate his message about global warming;
  - thought about the tone adopted to deal with a serious theme.
- Invite students to come up with a number of reasons why we should live for future generations and not just for our own times, and with suggestions of how we could do this in a better way than we now do.
- Review and update the chart/grid being created for cross-references between the poems.
- For English Literature, find another poem in Collection D that uses irony or other forms of humour to convey a message, and ask students to compare the use of this device in the two poems.

9 Further work

Ask students to respond to the following:

The poet says 'the future has no vote'. Defend your generation's attitude towards global warming.

Do you agree with the poem's message, that we are not doing enough to tackle the problem? Think about what kind of tone you will adopt in your writing. How will it compare to the tone of the poem?

Suggested answers

5 Exploring rhyme

The rhyme creates a light-hearted sound similar to a song, an effect enhanced by the regular rhythm. These factors give the poem a cheerful and frivolous tone.

Lesson D15

Do not go gentle into that good night *Dylan Thomas*

Learning objective

To explore how Thomas has communicated his thoughts on old age and death through his use of language and form.

Resources
- Edexcel GCSE Poetry Anthology, page 70
- Audio D15
- Glossary D15
- Worksheet D15.1
- Worksheet D15.2
- Worksheet D15.3

1 Before reading: whole class

- Explain to the class that this is a poem written by Dylan Thomas to his dying elderly father, having watched him get weak and frail. Ask students what emotions the poet might be feeling at this time.

- How might it link with the theme of 'taking a stand'? How might it link with other poems you have read within the collection so far?

2 First reading: pair work

- Hand out Worksheet D15.1. Explain to students that villanelles are 19th-century poems that have 19 lines with a strict rhyme pattern in which two rhyming lines are repeated as a refrain at regular intervals through the poem.

  Worksheet D15.1

- Ask pairs to place the refrain lines into the missing lines of the poem where they think they best fit and also to decide on the stanza breaks.

- Take feedback as a class and look at the poem as a whole, perhaps using the ActiveTeach at the front of the class and listening to Audio D15. Ask students: What is the poet's overall message? What effect does the repetition of two specific lines and the stanza arrangement have within the poem? What is the effect of the rhyming scheme? Students should look particularly at the last words of each line.

3 Close reading: independent work

- Ensure students understand that the poet's message is to fight against death.

- Hand out Worksheet D15.2. Ask students to select phrases in the poem which represent death and then those that imply fighting against death. They should then think about how effective these words are.

  Worksheet D15.2

- Ask students to share their ideas with the class. Encourage them to think about the image of death (dark) and the attitude towards it (violent struggle) portrayed by the vocabulary. Ask students how this compares with the treatment of death in other poems they have studied. You might want to compare this with 'Remember' where death is simply a 'silent land' and readers are urged to accept death and 'forget and smile' when a loved one dies.

4 Exploring ideas: pair work

- Highlight the fact that the poet emphasises his argument by looking at four different types of men and the reasons why they would all want to fight against death.
- Hand out Worksheet D15.3. Ask students to re-read the poem and match each of the types of men (wise, good, wild and grave) to one of the explanations given.

Worksheet D15.3

- Ask pairs to then look at the final stanza. How do the previous four stanza lead up to this one? Working together, they should write a paragraph about how the poet has used language, direct address, use of example and repetition here to strengthen his argument and why this is effective.

Extend

- Ensure that students understand what an oxymoron is, giving examples if necessary, e.g. the silence was deafening, an open secret, organised chaos.
- Ask students to find and highlight examples of oxymorons and think about why the poet might have included them. What is the effect of these oxymorons?
- Share responses as a class, using the ActiveTeach annotation tool as necessary.

5 Peer assessment

- Discuss the final stanza as a class. Students should swap work with another pair and assess their paragraphs on the basis of this discussion, writing a comment beside the work.
- Invite the students to mark each other's work, awarding up to five marks, deciding which of the five bands the work falls into. You may want to refer them to Resource D17.2 (English Literature Higher Tier mark scheme), D17.3 (English Literature Foundation Tier mark scheme) or D17.4 (English mark scheme).
- They should then comment on how the answer could have been improved, looking at the importance of supporting points with good examples.

6 Plenary

- Recap and ensure that students have:
  - understood the ways Thomas has used language and form to give strong personal views about how to approach old age and death;
  - responded to the theme of preparing for someone's expected death.
- Invite students in groups to compare their own attitudes to death with those expressed by Thomas. Pool responses, using the board to group them under headings such as fear, uncertainty, optimism and indifference. Why the differences?
- For English Literature, find another poem in Collection D that uses repeated lines or phrases, and ask students to compare the use of this device in the two poems.

7 Further work

Ask students to answer the following questions: What is Thomas's attitude towards death? How does he convey his attitude in this poem? Remind them to think about the use of refrain and the choice of vocabulary to communicate a message. What is the overall tone of the poem? How does it link with the theme of the collection?

Suggested answers

Extend

Blind sight, fierce tears: *To express the constant battle between life and death.*

Lesson D16
Remember

Christina Rossetti

Learning objective
To understand how Rossetti uses form and repetition to explore attitudes towards coping with death and loss.

Resources
- Edexcel GCSE Poetry Anthology, page 71
- Audio D16
- Glossary D16
- Worksheet D16.1
- Worksheet D16.2
- Worksheet D16.3

1 Before reading: independent work

- Give students the phrase 'the silent land'. Ask them to write a paragraph describing the place they visualise from this phrase. Encourage them to include simile, metaphor and any other imagery in their description.
- Share some of their paragraphs and discuss how each student interprets 'the silent land'. Interpretations might range from the purely geographic to the idea of death, perhaps with religious connotations. Approach the subject of bereavement and grief carefully through these interpretations. Explain that this poem is about the poet's thoughts on how she wants others to deal with their grief when she dies.

2 First reading: pair work

- Hand out Worksheet D16.1, which presents the poem as a prose passage. Ask students, perhaps by reading the poem aloud, to decide on line breaks to structure the passage as a poem.
- During feedback, discuss the choices students made and the reasons for their decisions. You might want to display the poem using the ActiveTeach at the front of the class. Encourage recognition of the rhyme pattern as the principal factor, although rhythm should be mentioned as well.

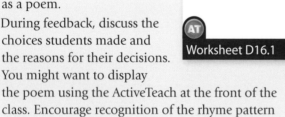

Worksheet D16.1

3 Close reading: whole class work

- Listen to the audio recording of the poem, asking students to pay particular attention to the meaning as well as the rhyme. Refer them to the glossary as necessary. You could display Glossary D16, on the ActiveTeach at the front of the class or print it out for students.
- Ask students to highlight the end-of-line rhymes in different colours to identify the pattern.
- Discuss the effects of the rhyming pattern, for example the juxtaposition of the words 'away' and 'stay' (opposites) and 'grieve' and 'leave' (consequence). You might also explore the effect of the repetition of 'remember', and the juxtaposition of the words 'smile' and 'sad' at the end of the poem.

4 Exploring meaning: pair work

- Recap on students' ideas about 'the silent land' from Activity 1. Ask them to remember these ideas as they explore the meaning of the poem in more depth.
- Hand out Worksheet D16.2. Ask students to work in pairs to discuss and answer the questions about the meaning of the poem.
- Take feedback, concentrating on the ideas raised by Question 5. Ask students: How does the poem fit within the theme of 'taking a stand'? Students may suggest that the twist at the end of the poem is unusual – people normally want to be remembered after death, but the poet/persona here is more concerned that his/her loved ones take a stand against traditional grieving, be strong in dealing with their loss, and are happy instead.

Worksheet D16.2

Access

Before undertaking Activity 4, ask students to re-read the poem, making sure they understand the language. Advise them to use the glossary and dictionaries to help, and tell them to think about who this poem might be addressed to.

5 Independent writing

- Ask students to write a PEEE paragraph in response to the following question: How does Rossetti explore the possible attitudes to loss and grief through her use of form and language?
- Remind them to think about the rhyme, rhythm, repetition and juxtaposition of words, as well as imagery, and to justify their points with brief, relevant and integrated quotations from the poem.

6 Peer assessment

- Ask students to assess each other's work, looking for inclusion of evidence and exploration of theme. Have all the different parts of PEEE been covered clearly?
- Invite the students to mark each other's work, awarding up to five marks, deciding which of the five bands the work falls into. You may want to refer them to Resource D17.2 (English Literature Higher Tier mark scheme), D17.3 (English Literature Foundation Tier mark scheme) or D17.4 (English mark scheme).
- Ask them to comment on how the answer could have been improved, looking at the importance of supporting points with good examples.

Extend

Hand out Worksheet D16.3, which provides a copy of Shakespeare's 'Sonnet 73' ('That time of year …'). Students are asked to:

- list the similarities and differences between the sonnet and 'Remember';
- think about why Rossetti uses this form to write about death and how this compares to Shakespeare's use of the sonnet.

Worksheet D16.3

7 Plenary

- Recap and ensure that students have:
  - understood the ways Rossetti explores attitudes towards death and loss through form and language;
  - responded to the effect of repetition on the tone and mood of the poem.
- Invite students to think about the idea of 'grief'. Why do psychologists say that it is important to grieve, while Rossetti asks her lover not to grieve?
- Finish updating the 'connections' chart, grid or list, linking this poem with others with which the students can see close connections in theme or treatment.
- For English Literature, find another poem in Collection D (e.g. 'The archbishop chairs the first session') in which 'remembering' is important, and ask students to compare the use of this device in the two poems.

8 Further work

Ask students to explain the differences and similarities between 'Remember' and 'On the Life of Man', looking in particular at the use of imagery. Alternatively, they might want to compare the attitudes towards death in this poem and 'Do not go gentle into that good night'.

Lesson D17
Understanding the assessment

Learning objectives
- To reinforce how poems link with the theme of the collection.
- To find links and comparisons between the poems in the collection.
- To develop the skills needed to write about poems in the assessment.

Resources
- Worksheet D17.1
- Resource D17.1
- Resource D17.2
- Resource D17.3
- Resource D17.4
- ResultsPlus interactives

1 Starter activity: whole class work

- As a class, brainstorm all of the ideas about the theme 'taking a stand' that are explored in the poems in this collection. Record ideas using a spider diagram.
- Ask students to come up with at least one way each poem in the collection relates to the theme. You might want to focus on particular lines or imagery from poems and discuss different responses to the same poem and reasons for these.
- It might be helpful to encourage students to sort their ideas into sub-groups.

Access

Ask students to choose one image that could be used to represent each of the poems in the collection. They could write a description of the image, draw it or find an image from a magazine or online. Each student should share their ideas with others, explaining the reasons why they have selected each image and how it links to the theme of the collection.

2 Practising writing in the exam or controlled assessment: pair work

- Divide the class into pairs. Ask pairs to draw a flow diagram showing the process of planning and writing a response to an assessed question. What will they do first in the exam or controlled assessment? What kind of things will they include in their response? How will they conclude their response?

- Hand out Resource D17.1 and ask students to compare the guidance on this sheet to their flow diagrams. Ask them to amend their diagrams accordingly and highlight areas on the Resource sheet which they feel are particularly important for them to remember.

3 Preparing for part a) of the English Literature question: whole class work

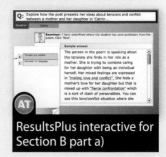

ResultsPlus interactive for Section B part a)

- Open a ResultsPlus interactive on the ActiveTeach which is relevant to Section B part a) of the Unit 2 English Literature exam, where students have to answer on a single poem. You may want to ensure that it is the relevant tier (either Higher or Foundation) for your students. Sample questions from other collections can often be tailored to your own needs as necessary. ResultsPlus is a unique resource designed to help students achieve their best with sample questions, graded answers and examiner tips. A sample exam question is provided alongside a sample student answer. Each answer is annotated with examiner comments to make clear why the mark has been given, and showing where and how the essay could have been improved to gain a mark in a higher band. See page 5 for guidance on using these activities.
- Use the interactive with the class, encouraging and supporting them to explore what mark might have been given and/or how the sample answer could have been improved. You may also want to make use of the mark scheme provided in Resource D17.2 or Resource D17.3 to help students understand how their essays will be marked.

4 Comparing poems: pair work

- Explain to students who will be taking the English Literature exam that they will be required to compare and contrast the poems they have studied. They will need to think about the different ways in which the poets have approached the theme of the collection, and the ways in which they have communicated their ideas.

- Hand out Worksheet D17.1. Tell students to work in pairs and think about links between the poems in terms of a) the topic explored and the poet's ideas, and b) the use of poetic devices (such as form, language and imagery) and their effects.

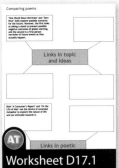
Worksheet D17.1

- Take feedback as a class, exploring differences of opinion and asking students to record their thoughts. You might want to compile class spider diagrams which can be used to support students' revision later on.

5 Preparing for part b) of the English Literature question: whole class work

- Open a ResultsPlus interactive on the ActiveTeach which is relevant to Section B part b) of the Unit 2 English Literature exam, where students will be required to compare two poems.

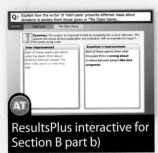
ResultsPlus interactive for Section B part b)

- Use the interactive with the class, encouraging and supporting them to explore what mark might have been given and/or how the sample answer could have been improved. You may also want to make use of the mark scheme provided in Resource D17.2 or Resource D17.3 to help students understand how their essays will be marked.

6 Preparing for the English controlled assessment: whole class work

- Open the ResultsPlus interactive for English controlled assessment. It will help students understand how a sample response can be improved.

- Use the interactive with the class, encouraging and supporting them to explore how the sample answer could have been improved. You may also want to make use of the mark scheme provided in Resource D17.2 to help students understand how their essays will be marked.

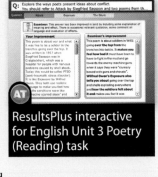
ResultsPlus interactive for English Unit 3 Poetry (Reading) task

7 Assessed question: individual work

- Ask students to think of an appropriate question for a particular poem, justifying how this would allow a student to demonstrate understanding and analysis of the poem(s).
- Ask students to swap essay questions with a partner and plan their essay in bullet points.

8 Peer assessment

Ask students to work in groups of four, share their plans with the group and assess each other's plans using the relevant mark scheme on Resource D17.2, Resource D17.3 or Resource D17.4.

Resource D17.2

Resource D17.3

Resource D17.4

9 Further work

Ask students to plan and write an answer to one assessed question within the sample assessment material provided by Edexcel. You may like to direct students to specific questions to suit their ability.

Unseen poetry

Unseen poetry

Lesson 1
Making sense of the poem

Learning objective
To learn how to gain an informed overview of the theme and subject matter of a poem.

Resources
• 'Nettles' by Vernon Scannell
• 'Do not go gentle into that good night' by Dylan Thomas
• Worksheet 1.1
• Worksheet 1.2
• Sticky notes

1 Starter activity

• Give students the title of the poem: 'Nettles'. In pairs, ask students to discuss any occasions on which they have encountered nettles. They should then make a list of five words that they associate with nettles.

• Each pair should share their ideas with another pair.

2 Whole class discussion

Ask the class what they are expecting to find in a poem with this title. Students might come up with the idea of the countryside or think of pain; they might find the title uninteresting or intriguing.

3 First reading

• Show students the first line of the poem: 'My son aged three fell in the nettle bed'. You might want to use page 14 of the ActiveTeach for this, zooming in on the first section.

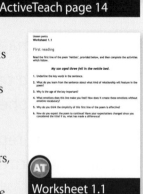

ActiveTeach page 14

Worksheet 1.1

• In pairs, students should discuss the questions on Worksheet 1.1 based on this first line. All worksheets and resources for Unseen poetry, along with the lesson plans containing worksheet suggested answers, can be found within the Teacher Guide section of the ActiveTeach when the Unseen poetry button is selected.

• Working with their partner, students should read through the rest of the poem in their anthologies and underline any words that convey the idea of war. They should think about how these words are used and why they are effective.

• Ask pairs to feedback on why they think the use of these words is effective. What emotions do students associate with war? Pairs should share their ideas with another pair in the class.

4 Whole class discussion

• Explain the term 'lexical field' to the class. Ask students how they think identifying a lexical field can help them to understand a poem they have not seen before. Establish that identifying words that have a thematic link can give them important clues about the meaning and theme of an unseen poem.

• Point out that the words about war in this poem make up a lexical field related to war. Ask the class how the number of words about war in this poem helps them to understand the poet's views or the theme of the poem.

• In pairs, students should identify any words or other aspects of the poem that they do not understand. Encourage students to work together to overcome these difficulties and then to consider what the importance of these are to the poem.

Access

• Give students the titles of several different poems and ask them to guess what the poems will be about. Then complete a similar task looking at the first lines of a range of poems.

• Show students two or three lines from a couple of different poems and ask them to identify the different lexical fields in each example. Ask what conclusions they can draw about meaning from these lexical fields.

5 Close reading

- Check that students understand the concepts of theme and writer's voice.

- In pairs, students should discuss the questions on Worksheet 1.2, then share their responses in groups of four. These questions ask students to consider how emotions are expressed in the poem and to comment on the theme and writer's voice.

- Encourage students to comment on the connotations of specific words and images in the poem, focusing on how the poet's choice of words reflects his feelings about the subject.

Worksheet 1.2

6 Independent work

- Ask students to focus on the last line of the poem ('My son would often feel sharp wounds again') and write a paragraph discussing:
  - what this line means in terms of the storyline of the poem;
  - how this line can be interpreted to give a wider or deeper meaning to the poem.

- In their responses, students should discuss the connotations of the word 'wounds' and may identify different kinds of wounds the son might experience as he grows older, e.g. physical, emotional, mental. They could consider how taking a risk or rising to a challenge can inflict wounds. No-one can be protected indefinitely from these life experiences, although temporary relief can be given.

7 Peer assessment

- In groups of three, students should read each other's responses, commenting on how successfully each student has presented his/her interpretation of the poem.

- Ask the groups to produce a joint response to the question in the light of their discussion about the strengths and weaknesses of their individual responses.

8 Plenary

Ask each student to write on a sticky note one top tip for how to understand the meaning of a previously unseen poem, based on what they have learned in this lesson. Stick all of the sticky notes on walls or boards around the room and invite students to view them. If possible, retain these notes for display in subsequent lessons.

Extend

- Students should annotate a copy of 'Do not go gentle into that good night' by Dylan Thomas on page 70 of the Poetry Anthology, identifying any words or phrases that make up a lexical field of anger. What is the effect of these?

ActiveTeach page 70

- Students should then write a comment on the effectiveness of the repeated line, 'Rage, rage against the dying of the light'.

Unseen poetry

Lesson 2
Non-standard forms

Learning objective
To learn how language choices, especially the use of non-standard forms, create tone and contribute to the poet's presentation of theme, ideas and setting.

Resources
• 'Green Beret' by Ho Thien (provided on Worksheet 2.2)
• 'Our Town with the Whole of India!' by Daljit Nagra
• Worksheet 2.1
• Worksheet 2.2
• Worksheet 2.3
• Sticky notes from last lesson (on display)

1 Starter activity

• Check that students understand the difference between standard and non-standard forms of language by asking them to complete the card sort activity from Worksheet 2.1.

• Ask pairs to list the ways in which a standard form differs from a non-standard form.

• Ask students to share their ideas with the class and add points suggested by other pairs to their own lists.

Worksheet 2.1

2 Whole class discussion

Ask students: How might the use of non-standard forms of language affect the tone of a poem? Students' suggestions should include humour, levels of formality, shock, anger and empathy. Students should be encouraged to realise that the use of dialect, slang or swear words on a poem can have a variety of different effects. It can create humour, add authenticity, provide an element of informality or be used to shock the reader out of a sense of complacency.

3 First reading

• Hand out Worksheet 2.2 and ask pairs of students to read 'Green Beret' by Ho Thien which is provided on this worksheet. Ask them to underline any dialogue and non-standard forms of language, including Americanisms.

Worksheet 2.2

• With their partner, students should discuss the questions on Worksheet 2.2 about the use of speech and non-standard forms in this poem. Students should be encouraged to evaluate the effectiveness of the use of non-standard forms of language in all cases.

• Take feedback from students and as a class discuss the following question: What difference does the use of non-standard forms make to this poem?

4 Close reading

• In pairs, students should underline five words or phrases that help create the tone of the poem.

Worksheet 2.3

• Hand out Worksheet 2.3. In pairs, students should then discuss the questions on Worksheet 2.3, which ask students to consider how the phrases they have selected, in addition to some specific examples, help to create the tone of the poem.

Access

Remind students of the meaning of tone by asking them to join up with a pair and say the word 'yes' to each other in as many different ways as they can. They should note down what type of situation each of these might be used in, and start to explore the ways in which tone of voice influences meaning.

5 Whole class discussion

- As a class, discuss the following question: How does a poet's choice of language help the presentation of theme?
- Students should be encouraged to come to the conclusion that the correct choice of language is vital to creating the right tone and therefore the delivery of the theme. Looking at non-standard forms of language gives a good indication of which words or feelings the poet wishes to emphasise, and what his/her attitude is to the subject being explored. For example, in 'Green Beret' the clipped words of the American soldier emphasise that he is an alien presence and that his attitude is harsh and unfeeling.

6 Independent response

Individually, students should underline all the words in the poem that are connected with fear. They should then write two sentences that explain how the use of this lexical field helps the poet to present the theme.

7 Peer assessment

In groups of three, students should read through the sentences they have each produced. Each group should decide which pair of sentences offer the best explanation and why.

8 Plenary

Ask students to work in pairs and role-play two friends meeting for coffee. One is anxious to find out how to decipher the meaning of an unseen poem, the other is giving advice on the basis of this lesson and the previous one.

Extend

Ask students to read 'Our Town with the Whole of India!' which is on page 44 of the ActiveTeach and student Poetry Anthology. They should highlight the non-standard forms used in the poem, and feed

ActiveTeach page 44

back to the class. You may want to collate ideas using the ActiveTeach highlighting tool. Three examples of the use of a non-standard form should then be chosen and, for each one, students should write a comment on how this example helps to establish a dialogue with the reader.

Unseen poetry

Lesson 3
Writing about imagery

Learning objective
To be able to explain how use of imagery helps a poet to present theme and ideas.

Resources
• 'City Jungle' by Pie Corbett
• 'Exposure' by Wilfred Owen
• Worksheet 3.1
• A3 plain paper

1 Starter activity

• Give the class the title 'City Jungle'. In groups of four, students should produce a freeze-frame improvisation of what the title conjures in their minds.

• Invite each group to present their freeze-frame to either another group or the whole class, who should interpret what they see.

2 Whole class discussion

• Ask the class: What techniques does a poet use to bring 'pictures' or images into a poem?

• Encourage students to volunteer ideas. They should suggest the use of similes, metaphor and personification. Check that all students understand what these techniques are.

Access

• Give students a range of phrases from poems within the anthology which include particularly vivid imagery. For example:

  And the hapless Soldier's sigh
  Runs in blood down Palace walls

  ...The tight
  red rope of love which we both
  fought over...

  Street children sleep, shaven mummies in sacks

• Ask students to decide which are the key words in each phrase that give clues to the tone and theme of the poem. What does the imagery used suggest about the soldiers, love and the street children in each case? If they can identify the literary device used then this is beneficial, but the focus should be on looking at the effect of the words used and the overall atmosphere created.

3 First reading

• Read the poem 'City Jungle' to the class or use Audio C2 from the ActiveTeach, asking them to follow on page 38 of the student Poetry Anthology.

ActiveTeach page 38

• Divide the class into pairs. Allocate each pair one of the images from the poem, ensuring that, as far as possible, all images are covered by at least one pair. Each pair should draw a sketch of their allocated image on A3 paper and label it, explaining why they have chosen to draw the image in this way.

• Display the images at the front of the classroom and discuss how the imagery in the poem has helped students to 'see' the things being described. Why has the poet chosen these specific examples of images?

• In pairs, students should decide which is the main technique used in this poem (metaphor) and discuss how the images help to create the tone and setting of the poem. Encourage students to explore the connotations of the images: they suggest harshness and fear and have a predatory feel. They should explore how the feelings created by the images colour their view of the city. Students should be encouraged, as part of their discussions, to understand the concept and importance of context. They should be able to test their hypotheses in the light of the meaning of the whole poem, and learn to reject what does not fit.

4 Close reading

- Ask students to work in pairs to underline the words in the poem that suggest threat or danger, and discuss effectiveness.

- They should then discuss the questions on Worksheet 3.1, which ask students to consider the effect of the imagery used in the poem.

AT
Worksheet 3.1

- Discuss with the class how looking closely at imagery can help them to work out the meaning of a previously unseen poem. Students should be reminded to keep the title of the poem in mind and try to explore its deeper meanings as the discussions unfold. What comment is being made about urban life? Is the threat real or imaginary? Is the poet really concerned about potential danger, or playing with a clever concept?

5 Independent response

Ask students to use the PEEE technique to write a comment on the effectiveness of the poet's use of imagery in the final stanza, from 'The motorway's' to the end of the poem. They should explain what things are being compared and why this choice of image is suitable in the context of the whole poem.

6 Peer assessment

Ask students to work in groups of three and read each other's comments. They should give each other feedback, considering the following questions.

– Are the comparisons clear?

– Has the PEEE technique been used effectively?

– Is there a clear and plausible comment on why the choice of image is suitable in context?

7 Plenary

Without looking at any notes, students should list the strategies they would use to help them understand an unseen poem.

Extend

Read 'Exposure' by Wilfred Owen on page 24 of the ActiveTeach and Poetry Anthology. Using three different colours, students should highlight similes, metaphors and use of personification.

AT
ActiveTeach page 24

They should then write a short comment explaining the effectiveness of the use of three separate images in the poem.

Unseen poetry

Lesson 4
The use of sound to create tone and atmosphere

Learning objective
To be able to explain how a poet uses alliteration and onomatopoeia to create an appropriate tone and atmosphere for the theme.

Resources
- 'City Jungle' by Pie Corbett
- 'Exposure' by Wilfred Owen
- '04/01/07' by Ian McMillan
- 'London' by William Blake
- 'The Class Game' by Mary Casey
- Worksheet 4.1
- Worksheet 4.2
- Resource 4.1 – Edexcel mark scheme (HT)
- Resource 4.2 – Edexcel mark scheme (FT)

1 Starter activity

- Check that students understand the meaning of the terms 'alliteration' and 'onomatopoeia'.
- Write the phrase 'The gutter gargles' on the whiteboard or display it using page 38 of the ActiveTeach. Tell the class that this line is taken from 'City Jungle' and can have at least three literary labels attached to it. Ask them to identify what these are (personification, alliteration and onomatopoeia).

- In pairs, students should look at 'City Jungle' and the second and third stanzas of 'Exposure' on page 24 of the ActiveTeach and Poetry Anthology. Ask them to highlight at least three more examples of onomatopoeia and alliteration, then discuss how effective these techniques are in these poems.

ActiveTeach page 38

ActiveTeach page 24

2 Paired work

- Read '04/01/07' with the class or listen to Audio A16 on page 18 of the ActiveTeach.
- Students should work in pairs to highlight examples of onomatopoeia in the poem.

ActiveTeach page 18

- Next, pairs should discuss the questions on Worksheet 4.1. Students should comment on the way in which the poet uses onomatopoeia to present the idea of the real world continuing despite the raw emotions of bereavement. They should note that the 'ordinary world' is associated with everyday sounds such as the delivery of milk.

Worksheet 4.1

- Take feedback and discuss how the use of onomatopoeia and sounds in this poem helps to create a sense of place. Ask students why they think the creation of a sense of place is important in this poem. For example, the reader can associate with the sounds, which lends immediacy to the painful experience explored in the poem. This also highlights the fact that bereavement heightens some senses and makes people want to cling to the familiar in the face of loss.

3 Independent response

Students should write a paragraph exploring the effect of the use of onomatopoeia in '04/01/07'. Remind students of the importance of using quotations to support their points.

Access

Some students will benefit from working together to produce a writing frame to help them to organise their responses. At this stage it would be helpful to look at the structure of individual sentences to see how quotations can be effectively incorporated.

Extend

Students should read 'London' by William Blake on page 49 of the student Poetry Anthology and then answer the following question:

Explore how Blake uses language to present a negative picture of London.

They should look out for lexical fields of decay, sickness and sadness and comment on the effect of these.

ActiveTeach page 49

5 Plenary

Students should choose one target for improvement they think is particularly helpful (not necessarily the one on their own work) and write it on a sheet of paper. Display the targets and discuss them with the whole class. The display can be re-used in future lessons.

6 Further work

- Students should read 'The Class Game' by Mary Casey on page 28 of the Poetry Anthology and create a table of non-standard forms and the equivalent standard form using Worksheet 4.2.

ActiveTeach page 28

- Next, students should write a paragraph commenting on the tone created by the use of non-standard forms in this poem. Students should consider connotations, the element of shock, crudeness and defiance, as well as how non-standard forms help to present the theme of prejudice. They should be able to describe and comment on the writer's voice in this poem.

Worksheet 4.2

4 Peer assessment

- In groups of three, students should mark each other's work using the sample Edexcel mark scheme (either Resource 4.1 or 4.2, depending on Tier).

- Students should identify good points by underlining them and in the margin identify areas that could be improved. Encourage students to try to decide which band each piece of work falls into. It may be helpful to model marking a piece of work first. Alternatively you could break down the mark scheme and ask students to look for evidence of one skill at a time.

- Students should write one target for improvement at the end of each piece of writing.

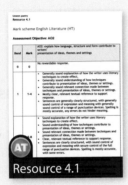

Resource 4.1

Resource 4.2

Unseen poetry

Lesson 5
Rhyme, rhythm, repetition, structure and form

Learning objective
To be able to explain how a poet uses rhyme, rhythm, repetition, structure and form to present theme and ideas.

Resources
- 'The Penelopes of my homeland' by Choman Hardi
- 'Sonnet 116' by William Shakespeare
- 'Your Dad Did What?' by Sophie Hannah
- Worksheet 5.1
- Worksheet 5.2
- Worksheet 5.3
- Resource 5.1 – Glossary of terms for poetry

1 Starter activity

Worksheet 5.1

- Divide the class into pairs and hand out Worksheet 5.1, which contains the first ten lines of 'The Penelopes of my homeland'. In pairs, students should sort these into the correct order, either by numbering them or by cutting them out and moving them into place.

- With their partner, students should discuss how they decided on the order for the lines. They should then answer the question: How important was rhythm and the pattern of repetition in deciding on the order of the lines?

2 First reading

ActiveTeach page 57

- In pairs, students should read the full version of 'The Penelopes of my homeland' on page 57 of their Anthologies and annotate the poem to identify stressed and unstressed syllables, the rhythmic pattern and repetition.

- Based on the activities they have just completed, ask students to suggest some tips for tackling unseen poems that deal with unfamiliar material. For example, if you have never read the story of Penelope and Odysseus, how can you make sense of the theme? Encourage students to focus on what they do know, and return to the idea of identifying main lexical fields to understand meaning. Point out that students should never make wild guesses that are not rooted in textual evidence; they should capitalise on what they know.

Access

You could encourage students to think about rhythm by getting them to clap the stressed and unstressed syllables in their names and other polysyllabic words. Students could then go on to mark the stressed and unstressed syllables of 'The Penelopes of my homeland'.

3 Whole class discussion

Worksheet 5.2

- Discuss how effectively the poet uses lack of rhyme, rhythm, and repetition to underpin the theme of loss and lack of fulfilment in 'The Penelopes of my homeland'. You might want to consider:
  - the feelings evoked by the lack of a regular rhythm and stanza form
  - why the poet has begun lines with lower case letters
  - the significance of the level of formality created by the lack of a rhyme scheme
  - the use of repetition to underpin the sense of futility.

- In pairs, students should complete Worksheet 5.2, which focuses on the effect of the rhyme, rhythm and repetition in this poem, and be prepared to feed back to the rest of the class.

Access

Focus on enabling students to spot the changes in rhythmic patterns rather than stressing jargon. When they have spotted a change, ask them to explain why the poet has chosen to do this. You could help them to produce a list of possible reasons – emphasis, marking a pause, underlining a sense of shock, marking a significant passage of time, offering a personal interjection.

Extend

- In pairs, students should read 'Sonnet 116' on page 4 of the Anthology and annotate it to identify the following features:
  - the rhyme scheme
  - the rhythmic pattern.

  They should consider how the form contributes to the development of ideas. What is the effect of the final rhyming couplet?

- In pairs, students should complete Worksheet 5.3, which focuses on the effect of the rhyme, rhythm and repetition in this poem. You could provide students with Resource 5.1 which includes key terms related to rhythm and poetic form if appropriate, so that they can use these where needed.

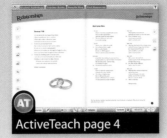

ActiveTeach page 4

Worksheet 5.3   Resource 5.1

5 Independent response

Ask students to write a paragraph focusing on the use of rhythm and rhyme in 'The Penelopes of my homeland' or 'Sonnet 116'. They should explore the impact on the reader of either a regular rhyme and rhythm (Shakespeare is making a definitive, measured, formal statement that cannot be questioned) or an irregular rhyme and rhythm (Hardi is suggesting uncertainty and presents an imperfect world as she invites the reader to empathise with the plight of the widows).

6 Peer assessment

In groups of three, students should read through each other's work, discussing the validity of the different interpretations. They should draw each other's attention to any points that need clarification or where textual evidence needs to be provided.

7 Plenary

On a sticky note, each student should write down one way in which a poet might use rhyme, rhythm or repetition to reinforce the theme. Display the sticky notes in class and encourage students to read each other's comments.

8 Further work

Read 'Your Dad Did What?' by Sophie Hannah on page 27 of the Poetry Anthology. Students should annotate the poem to identify the rhyme scheme, stressed and unstressed syllables

ActiveTeach page 27

and use of repetition. They should then write two or three sentences explaining how the poet has used language to present her ideas about loss.

Lesson 6
Form, structure and voice

Learning objective
To be able to explain how use of personal pronouns, enjambement and the ordering of lines into stanzas helps to create voice.

Resources
• 'Nettles' by Vernon Scannell
• 'City Jungle' by Pie Corbett
• 'The Stone Hare' by Gillian Clarke
• 'Valentine' by Carol Ann Duffy
• 'The Drum' by John Scott
• Worksheet 6.1
• Worksheet 6.2
• Worksheet 6.3

1 Starter activity

• Ask pairs of students to read 'Nettles' on page 14 of the ActiveTeach and Anthology and underline all the personal pronouns and determiners. Ask students: What do the words you have underlined tell you about the poet's feelings towards his son?

ActiveTeach page 14

• Next, students should underline any use of enjambement (a line that runs on to the next without any form of punctuation) and any full stops that appear in the middle of a line. Ask students what effect this has on the level of formality of the poem.

• Remind students of the definitions of key words to describe poetic devices (using their glossary as appropriate). Remind students that feature-spotting in itself will not gain them marks in their assessment; terminology is simply an aid to writing effectively about poetry.

2 First reading

• In pairs, students should look closely at 'City Jungle' on page 38 and 'The Stone Hare' on page 54 of the Anthology.

ActiveTeach page 38

ActiveTeach page 54

• Using Worksheet 6.1, they should compare the formality, pace, tone and voice in these two poems.

• Next, students should discuss with their partner the questions in the second half of the worksheet, which focus on the effect of the use of these features in creating the tone.

Worksheet A6.1

Extend

Hand out Worksheet 6.2. This gives students a list of literary devices and features. For each of them, students write a definition and then go on to list one way each can be used to help a poet to express ideas and themes effectively. They should find an example of the use of each technique in a poem from the Anthology.

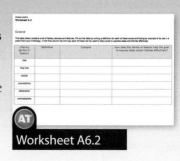
Worksheet A6.2

3 Whole class discussion

Discuss what techniques poets can use to create an informal or a formal atmosphere. Discuss why the creation of an appropriate atmosphere is important to the effective presentation of the poet's ideas.

4 Close reading

- Read 'Valentine' by Carol Ann Duffy on page 2 of the Anthology or listen to Audio A2.

Worksheet 6.3

- In pairs, students should complete Worksheet 6.3 by annotating the poem to identify examples of metaphor, simile, repetition, personal pronouns, emotive vocabulary and any words that form a lexical field. They are then asked to explore the effect of the use of these techniques in creating tone and setting and the presentation of ideas in the poem.

5 Independent response

- Give students the following task. An additional lesson may be required to complete it:

  You have been asked to give a two-minute talk on 'Valentine' to a group of students preparing for a GCSE Literature exam. Write your talk, commenting on the techniques Duffy uses to encourage the reader to consider the reality of being in love.

- In their talks students should include brief examples and analytical comments. Although the talk is an independent response, students would benefit from preparatory guidelines. Remind students that it is techniques you are looking for – imagery, structure, lexical fields, repetition, sound and their effects. Be strict about the time limit.

6 Peer assessment

In groups of three, students should take it in turns to deliver their talks to each other. After each talk, they should ask each other questions and make observations about the points that were made. You could ask one person to present their talk to the whole class and model the sort of questions that might be asked, which could include points of clarification, more details about why an image is particularly effective, points of accuracy, details about rhyme and rhythm. All questions should point towards the effectiveness of the language and imagery chosen.

7 Plenary

Without referring to any notes, students should write down as many key poetic terms as they can in one minute. They should then share lists in pairs and create a combined list. By the side of each term, students should write a brief definition. They could check their answers using their glossary of terms.

8 Further work

Students should read aloud 'The Drum' by John Scott on page 31 twice, first reading it as it stands, then substituting 'The drum has a discordant sound' for the first line of each stanza and omitting 'to me' on line 11. They

ActiveTeach page 31

should answer the question: What is the effect of removing the personal element from the poem? Students should also reflect on the effect that would be created if 'we' were used instead of 'I'.

Unseen poetry

Lesson 7
Tackling the unseen poetry question

Learning objective
To learn how to write a successful response to the unseen poetry examination question.

Resources
- 'From the motorway' by Anne Stevenson (provided on Worksheet 7.1)
- 'Dress Sense' by David Kitchen (provided on Worksheet 7.2)
- Worksheet 7.1 – Edexcel sample exam question (HT)
- Worksheet 7.2 – Edexcel sample exam question (FT)
- Resource 7.1 - Edexcel mark scheme – (HT)
- Resource 7.2 - Edexcel mark scheme – (FT)

1 Starter activity

Divide the class into teams and hold a quiz on the meaning of key poetic terms and their importance in helping a poet to present themes and ideas. Glossary 1 from Collections A, B, C, and D contain many poetic terms that you may want to use.

2 First reading

- Give students a copy of Worksheet 7.1 (if Higher Tier) or Worksheet 7.2 (if Foundation Tier), which contains a sample question and a range of questions that guide students to explore the poem.

- Ensure that students understand what they will need to focus on in their response to the question. In particular, check that Foundation candidates are clear about what the bullet points ask them to do – they will need to write about what is happening, how the poet uses voice and how the poem is organised.

Worksheet 7.1

Worksheet 7.2

3 Assessment criteria

- Give students a copy of the mark scheme provided on Resource 7.1 (if Higher Tier) or Resource 7.2 (if Foundation Tier).

- In pairs, students should read through the mark scheme for unseen poetry. They should make a note of any points they don't understand.

- Ask students which aspects they found confusing. Discuss these issues with the class, ensuring students understand the mark scheme.

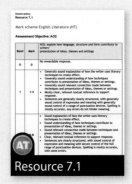
Resource 7.1

Resource 7.2

4 Independent response

- Ask students to write a plan for their response to the question. This could take the form of a list, pyramid plan, tree diagram or any other form the student finds helpful. It may be helpful to discuss the amount of detail you are expecting in the plan.
- The plan should:
  - give a clear indication of all the key areas of the essay;
  - show the order in which the information will appear in the essay;
  - include selected relevant quotations to support and develop each point;
  - include comments on language, structure and form.
- In their planning they may also want to think about how to structure their response into paragraphs. Make sure that they understand exactly what is required of them – the mark scheme should make it clear.

5 Peer assessment

- Ask students to work in small groups and discuss their plans. They should use the mark scheme to identify areas that have not been sufficiently covered in the plans. To do this they could colour-code the various aspects of the mark scheme, then colour-code the plans.
- In the same groups, students should work together to suggest ways in which each plan could be adapted to obtain a higher mark. When amendments are made they should include specific points from the poems. Students should then choose the best plan from their group.

6 Plenary

Students should share the best plans from each group. If possible, allow time for questions between each presentation.

7 Further work

Individually, students should write a response to the exam question. They should spend no longer than 35 minutes on their response. This would need to be completed for homework or in an extra lesson.

Access

Some students may benefit from compiling a writing frame to help them to structure their written response effectively. You could also provide a list of connectives and other words and phrases appropriate for this type of formal writing.

Unseen poetry

Lesson 8
Marking the unseen poetry question

Learning objective
To understand how the examination answer will be assessed.

Resources
- Resource 8.1 – Edexcel mark scheme (HT)
- Resource 8.2 – Edexcel mark scheme (FT)
- Resource 8.3 – Sample answer 1 (HT)
- Resource 8.4 – Sample answer 2 (HT)
- Resource 8.5 – Sample answer 3 (HT)
- Resource 8.6 – Sample answer 1 (FT)
- Resource 8.7 – Sample answer 2 (FT)
- Resource 8.8 – Sample answer 3 (FT)
- Edexcel sample exam paper (HT)
- Edexcel sample exam paper (FT)
- ResultsPlus interactive
- Students' essays

1 Starter activity

- In pairs, ask students to read through the Edexcel sample exam paper available in the Sample Assessment Material (you should provide them with either Higher Tier [p. 181] or Foundation Tier [p. 215], as appropriate).
- Draw their attention to the layout and the fact that the question is the one which they answered in the previous lesson and/or for homework.
- Hand out the relevant mark scheme, Resource 8.1 for Higher Tier or Resource 8.2 for Foundation Tier (also provided in Lesson 7). Remind them of the key aspects of an answer that will be assessed.

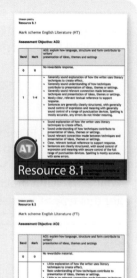

Resource 8.1

Resource 8.2

2 Marking sample answers

- Students should then mark the sample answers provided on Resources 8.1 to 8.3 (Higher Tier) or Resources 8.4 to 8.6 (Foundation Tier). Before students do this, check that they understand that they are looking for points that will gain marks and comments that are irrelevant – they should annotate both positive and negative features of the scripts.

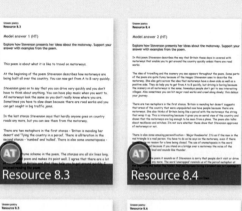

Resource 8.3

Resource 8.4

Resource 8.5

Resource 8.6

Resource 8.7

Resource 8.8

- In pairs, students should read through the relevant sample answers and give each one a mark using the mark scheme criteria. They should annotate each answer to give a brief written explanation of how they arrived at the mark. They could colour code the mark scheme and their marking as they did with the plans in the previous lesson.

- Pairs should share their marking with another pair and arrive at a consensus. If there is a disagreement there should be discussion, with group members providing evidence for the points they make.

- Each group of four should present its findings to the whole class and a whole class consensus should be agreed. Take steps to promote discussion, for example by taking a controversial stance. Students will learn most from having to argue their point of view.

3 Peer assessment

In groups of three, students discuss and mark their own essays using the mark scheme criteria and decide on a mark for each piece of work.

4 Independent response

Students read through their own essays and make pencil amendments. At the end of the essay they should list ways in which their work could be improved. Students can then hand in their essays for teacher marking.

5 Plenary

- In pairs, students discuss the strategies they have found most valuable for answering unseen poetry questions.

- As a class, discuss what students have learned and gauge how confident they now feel about tackling this section of the paper. Provide an opportunity for students to ask questions to clarify anything about which they are unsure.

- At this point, you might also want to make use of the ResultsPlus interactives for Unseen poetry provided on the ActiveTeach. These engage students in marking model answers and/or clearly identifying how model answers can be improved. There is one for each of the two tiers, Higher and Foundation.

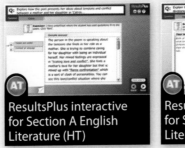

ResultsPlus interactive for Section A English Literature (HT)

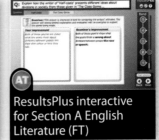

ResultsPlus interactive for Section A English Literature (FT)

Extend

Ask students to produce a leaflet for Year 11 students on how to do well on the unseen poetry element of the examination. The leaflet should include details of the exam, the assessment criteria, strategies for exploring an unseen poem and students' own top tips for success.